Travelling Abroad with Children

Travelling Abroad with Children

The Complete Guide

Samantha Gore-Lyons

ARROW

First published by Arrow in 2003

1 3 5 7 9 10 8 6 4 2

First published in the United Kingdom in 2000 by
Virgin Publishing Ltd as *Are We Nearly There?*

This fully revised and updated edition
first published in the United Kingdom in 2003 by
Arrow, 20 Vauxhall Bridge Road, London, SW1V 2SA

Random House Australia (Pty) Limited
20 Alfred Street, Milsons Point, Sydney,
New South Wales 2061, Australia

Random House New Zealand Limited
18 Poland Road, Glenfield,
Auckland 10, New Zealand

Random House (Pty) Limited
Endulini, 5A Jubilee Road, Parktown 2193,
South Africa

The Random House Group Limited Reg. No. 954009

www.randomhouse.co.uk

A CIP catalogue record for this book is available
from the British Library

Papers used by Random House are natural, recyclable products
made from wood grown in sustainable forests. The manufacturing
processes conform to the environmental regulations of the country
of origin

Design and Make up by Roger Walker

Typeset in Minion and Formata

Printed and bound in the United Kingdom by
Bookmarque Ltd, Croydon, Surrey

ISBN 0 09 944525 5

To my accompanying adventurer
and perfect travelling companion,
my little man, Paris James, and
our determined little explorer,
Luca.

Contents

PART TWO
Preparation

PART THREE
While You Are Away

Author's Note

The information contained within this book is correct at the time of going to print. Malaria prophylaxis changes constantly and epidemics break out in virtually every country of the world from time to time. Travel clinics will be able to advise you of current risks that develop.

Advice is not intended to be a substitute for skilled medical care if good care is available.

List of Figures

Acknowledgements

With grateful thanks to my father, Dr Peter Gore, for his help and support of the facts.

Many thanks to the National Meteorological Library and Archive for their assistance, and for taking the time and trouble to provide me with information about world weather conditions.

Pasteur Merieux MSD for their objective advice and supply of vital literature and information.

The Liverpool School of Tropical Medicine for the use of their library.

The Malaria Reference Library for the up-to-date information on malaria diagnosis and UK incidence.

With appreciation to my encouraging editor and friend, Anna Cherrett.

Introduction

The first time I travelled abroad with my eldest son he was a stow-away. We had visited five countries together before I even knew he existed. After an overnight coach journey from Manchester to London, I jumped on a train bound for Moscow, on impulse and alone, unaware that I was pregnant. During the five-day trip I was arrested, molested and deported with smugglers. I arrived in Warsaw in the middle of the night where, unable to find a hotel, I slept on a waiting room floor in Warsaw Central station alongside forty tramps before catching the next available homeward-bound train to safety. It was another six weeks after returning home that I discovered that I had been seven weeks pregnant at the time of my adventure. My baby had been with me the whole time.

When I was a child I dreamed of journeying to the four corners of the world. Travel was more than a passion – it was imperative for my future contentment and, before my first baby arrived, it was an essential part of my life. After leaving university I had enjoyed ten years of independent and relaxing roving. I spent every spare penny I had on foreign soil. By the time I became pregnant I had visited over one third of the countries of the world. My hunger for travel should have been satisfied, but I couldn't be happy thinking that I wouldn't be able to travel again until my baby reached whatever age my friends and family deemed appropriate.

When I decided to book a holiday abroad soon after the birth of my baby son, whom I named Paris James, many of my friends and family advised me to wait until he was out of nappies. Others declared that I should wait until he was five or six before taking him travelling. Even a GP I asked was cautious about sanctioning my trip. 'There is no point in risking tragedy by going abroad. Have a holiday in England,' he told me.

I was a very experienced traveller and couldn't imagine why travelling with a child should be so different from travelling as a couple. I knew it would be a challenge for me, but judged that as long as I picked my destination carefully, my son would be in no greater danger in many countries of the world than he would be at home.

I returned to work just a few weeks after the birth and became increasingly exhausted. I needed some sunshine and a break. My mum offered to look after the baby at home while my husband and I took a week's holiday, but it wasn't a break from my son I needed, it was escape from the telephone, the washing machine and a full-time job.

I decided that a family trip abroad would be a tonic for us all. It would be the first time I had all day to relax and enjoy my baby since leaving the hospital with him when he was five days old.

I returned to my doctor. He advised me to choose a clean destination with good medical facilities. He also urged me to wait until my son had received the routine childhood immunisations. This advice I took. I booked a holiday in Tobago, an island in the Caribbean, departing when my baby would be five months old.

Despite a bout of mild heat-stroke, this was one of our more relaxing and uneventful holidays. Our son was powerless and, although he could roll around, he was relatively immobile and easy to keep out of danger.

This trip gave us the confidence to travel the world.

Suddenly I found that I had to learn how to travel all over again. My baby demanded more luggage, more expensive accommodation and a lot more preparation. But he also brought fresh, increased pleasure to a walk on the beach, stroking a sting-ray, feeding a giant tortoise or picking mangoes straight from the tree.

Travelling with a child is never easy, but what about parenting ever is? These little packages of our own genes enslave us to their will. We suffer sleep deprivation with our babies, frustration with our toddlers, anxiety over what is best for our children, then worry with our teenagers, so why do we do it? Travelling with them is just the same. Sometimes you will look at your partner or your screaming child and wish you had never left your cosy home, but on balance the pleasures and the thrill of shared experience through innocent, wide eyes is worth every inconvenience and mishap.

We have made many mistakes and learned how to travel with a child the tough and gritty way. Paris had visited thirty countries before he was five years old, and regrettably we have suffered a few mishaps along the way. Because of my independent travel experience I was able to pick safe, hygienic and child-friendly destinations easily, but there are many things that I would do differently a second time.

It may seem unbelievable, but despite completing a physiology and pharmacology degree, I had no idea how vulnerable a young child is to relatively mild extremes of temperature and how quickly they can become at risk.

In my final year at university our practical sessions in the lab included extrapolated studies on the body's temperature-controlling mechanisms. I cycled in a closed room hotter than the Sahara until I fainted while thermometers measured my internal and external body temperature. My friend lay in a bath of iced water with a thermometer up her bottom while we timed her shivering fits and noted the colour changes in her black skin, until her internal temperature dropped to a dangerous level or she could stand it no longer. We controversially reviewed the deadly experiments carried out in the Dachau Concentration Camp, yet still Paris has suffered mild degrees of both hypo- and hyperthermia.

It didn't seem particularly cold when he caught his chill, and he had been in the shade all afternoon when he got heat stroke. I reproached myself bitterly and set out to uncover why it had happened, noting down the early signs so it would never happen again.

In this book I have discussed every situation I have encountered, and researched numerous others. I hope that it will be useful to all travellers with children, both in preparation for their holiday and while they are away. With all the advice to hand most parents should be able to deal with minor traumas and health problems without jeopardising their overall enjoyment of the holiday. Good packing, preparation and basic knowledge make travel safer, healthier and happier.

PART ONE

Deciding When and Where to Go

CHAPTER 1

Your First Holiday
with Children:
The Shock and
the Pleasure

Provided that you plan, prepare and pack well, travelling with a very young baby is infinitely easier than travelling with young children. Once our babies start to crawl we begin to childproof our houses. By the time they are toddling we have baby gates and plug socket protectors all over the house.

It is virtually guaranteed that when travelling with a toddler your holiday accommodation will be full of stone steps, slippery tiled floors, jagged furniture, self-locking doors and ancient electric points just at fiddling height. Outside your room there will be six foot deep swimming pools, balconies, scabby stray dogs and crowds. Your senseless toddler could be lost in a minute. You should be ready for anything. Until around the age of two, when toddlers cease to be classed as infants and become fare-paying children, travelling becomes increasingly challenging. By the time they reach the age of four or five, travelling with them becomes a pleasure, and we can then enjoy our holidays through their fresh and excited young eyes.

Holidaying with children of any age will be an entirely different experience. There will be no languishing on the beach for hours or enjoying a quiet dinner and a bottle of wine while watching the sunset. You will be up and down all day, checking their temperatures and sunscreen coverage. Then in the evening you will be fighting to get unfamiliar foods down them and falling into bed at ten o'clock, exhausted.

Children demand more expensive accommodation, more regular mealtimes and the constant relative proximity of a toilet, but if you are ready for all this you will share some of the happiest and most memorable times in your child's life. All too often bogged down in a world where we mothers don't even have time to peel our own vegetables, we can relax and devote to our children the time we do not have when the telephone is ringing and dozens of jobs need doing. When so many women choose to return to work, or are forced back for economic reasons, holidays are a time to indulge your children, discuss issues over dinner and expand their world.

I believe that travelling will enrich a child's life more than any other single factor. It will dispel the ignorance that contributes to racism, teach a love of different cultures, stimulate their imagination and give them wonderful memories. Whether it be a package holiday in Spain or a trek in Nepal, it will be something for your child to cherish.

Even if they are too young truly to recall the trip, seeing the photos or watching the videos will magic them back to a different time and place, then inspire them to imagine that they really do remember being there.

Travelling with New Babies

Coping with a very young baby abroad is not much more difficult than coping at home. They still wake up at all hours and demand to be fed at their convenience. They still want pampering, pandering to, changing, and their bottles, etc. sterilising.

It is worth waiting until after the first round of childhood immunisations before you travel abroad with your child. The triple vaccine (polio, tetanus and diphtheria) is given at about six weeks. This vaccination protects your baby from deadly illnesses still common worldwide.

Be aware that visiting friends and family in a familiar country where you can guarantee that hygiene levels should, in theory, be less of a risk, does not always work out this way. Even though you may have grown up safely in a particular environment, you will have lost your immunity to local disease, and your children will have none. In effect, your whole family will be just as susceptible to illness as any other travelling family, if not more so because of your extensive contact with local people. So do wait that extra one or two months until the first set of jabs are completed.

The diseases which have motivated world-wide immunisation programmes for three-month-old babies are very serious, highly contagious, life-threatening diseases, transmittable by sneezing and coughing. Due to the success of these programmes a whole generation of mothers has never known the horrors of polio and diphtheria, but still today, with all modern facilities and antibiotics, the death rate from diphtheria is 10 per cent. (Much higher in underdeveloped countries.)

Most mothers are now offered the option of the TB vaccination for their babies whilst in maternity hospital, so if you are going to do some early travelling with your baby, take it. If you have missed the opportunity, talk to your doctor about where to get your baby immunised.

Standard sterilising and feeding routines will protect against the common gastrointestinal complaints, but if travelling into a risk area with an unprotected baby you will not be able to protect them against highly contagious airborne diseases.

Once your baby has been immunised against pertussis (whooping cough), tuberculosis, tetanus, polio and diphtheria he or she will doubtless contract all manner of coughs, colds and fevers, whether at home or abroad, but they will almost invariably be mild and are unlikely to be life threatening.

You probably won't feel much like a trek abroad until your new baby is more than four months old anyway. It's hard enough going on holiday, breaking new ground and discovering new places without the added challenges of sleep deprivation, establishing solids and protecting a child during its most vulnerable first few months of life.

Holidaying with a four-or five-month-old can be a wholly pleasurable and relatively relaxing experience. There will doubtless be little hiccups – even the most preprepared of mothers makes mistakes – but be reassured that there are many easy ways of averting problems that could ruin a trip abroad.

My son's first trip was when he was five months old and we took him to Tobago in the Caribbean. His fare was £49 and, apart from discomfort on landing in the aeroplane and a mild case of heatstroke, we had a relaxing and enjoyable time. I found Paris easier in Tobago than I found him at home, where I had so many other tasks and responsibilities.

I had stopped breast-feeding when Paris was exactly five months old – just before we left – and although it would have had its advantages at times, bottle feeding was never a problem as the sterilising and feeding routine was exactly the same as at home. I bought bottled water and boiled it before adding the sterilising tablets. The hot water I used to mix with powdered feeds that I boiled twice; other than that there was no extra effort. (NB: Bottled/mineral water, although relatively pure, is not sterile so must be boiled for babies.) In many modern hotels there will be a kettle in your room, but the thought of endless trips to the hotel kitchen for boiled water was enough to provoke me to prepare myself.

Breast-fed babies are even easier travelling companions, and unless you are struggling or have dwindling milk supplies, there are many advantages to continuing breast-feeding until you return home. Babies will be easier to settle on long journeys and, as many babies will suckle for comfort even when not particularly hungry, you will be able to ease the pressure build up in their ears on take-off and landing very simply.

Beyond about seven months – around the time babies begin to roll around and crawl – journeying becomes more difficult. Babies will scurry over unsanitary floors and find filthy corners to grub around in, then put their fingers in their mouths or suck their thumbs.

By this time your own home will be crammed with all manner of things to make your life easier, but you will have had to leave them all behind. The lounge carpet you recently had specially cleaned is swapped for one in your three-star hotel room that looks as if it has been in place for twenty years and has recently been smeared with a mixture of honey and diesel oil. Your baby will cheerfully crawl all over it then return to you with dirty black hands, feet and knees. To combat this, request extra towels or bedding sheets and spread them all over any well-trodden, grubby sections of carpet or wherever your baby crawls the most.

If the floor is tiled, wipe it over with a cloth that has been soaked in Milton or any other sterilising fluid suitable for use with babies. A good dousing all over the floor and surfaces with one of the domestic, antibacterial kitchen or bathroom sprays will keep the population of germs in your apartment or hotel room down to a minimum.

You will have to be tireless in your attempts to keep your baby's hands clean. Babies' hands are constantly in their mouths and upset stomachs can easily result. Even after a bath or a swim in the pool I always cleaned my babies' hands with a wet wipe. President Franklin D. Roosevelt caught polio from his own swimming pool and was consequently paralysed – an extreme example, but something to think about. Polio and many other viruses are water-borne; even well-chlorinated pools can harbour germs, so take extra care not to let young babies, with their low levels of resistance, swallow any water.

At around ten or eleven months babies will pull themselves up on to their feet then fall backwards and sideways on to table corners and hard, ceramic tiled floors. You may have to do a full furniture removal job to make your room safe. If your baby develops a partic-ular fascination for an unsteady table or keeps toppling off a chair, ask your maid to remove it or stick it outside on the balcony.

Travelling with Toddlers and Very Young Children

It is important to have the MMR vaccine before travelling with a one-year-old. After visiting the A&E department in Praslin, the Seychelles, with Paris when he was fourteen months old, we returned home the following Sunday. On the Monday he fell ill, by Tuesday a rash developed and I was worried. On the Friday we were admitted into hospital and quarantined. He recovered well and the diagnosis was a 'measle-like virus'. He had already had the MMR, but must have picked up a less serious virus in the A&E department. These illnesses can be highly contagious.

As when travelling with new babies, check which other immunisations you will need before travelling to your destination. One of the most efficient and up-to-date ways to do this is by telephoning NHS Direct on 0845 4647. See Chapter 5 for more information about immunisations.

Between ten and twenty months is probably the most challenging time to travel with a child, so be prepared. At thirteen months they will totter unsteadily towards a lake or swimming pool and, if left unattended, may throw themselves in. Toddlers need watching every minute of every day.

When our son was fourteen months old, our trip to the Seychelles ended with a life-threatening incident in hospital. There were no high chairs in our hotel restaurant and he was constantly balancing on a chair and grabbing things off the table top. On the last day of our holiday he snatched up a glass ashtray and dropped it on to the floor where it smashed. He then fell off his chair, on to the broken glass, and slashed open his wrist. There was blood everywhere and it was one of the most terrifying experiences of my life. Somewhere at the back of our minds my husband and I knew to apply pressure around the wound and hold the arm up above his head to prevent excessive blood loss. A knowledge of basic first aid can be invaluable when travelling with a self-sabotaging toddler.

A trip we took to China when our son was eighteen months old was the hardest. Arguably, travelling with an infant is verging on masochism. The more mobile they are, the more you will have to cope with the danger and the stress, yet the challenge can be exhilarating and the rewards fantastic. We arrived in China to find that our luggage had been lost, leaving us without nappies, baby food, milk or clothes. We were all ill and suffered terribly from jet lag. It was absolutely exhausting.

However, because of our accompanying blond-haired boy, we saw another side to China. Young men offered us help constantly, and old women told us in broken English how beautiful our baby was. The tour guides saved us the best seats on the buses and even offered to look after him while we walked up the Great Wall of China. We returned to find a huge crowd gathered around him more interested in his blond hair than the Great Wall itself. In Tiananmen Square a young male student asked if he could hold our son and have his photo taken. Parenthood is an international condition that breaks down barriers and makes you far more welcome in many societies than you would be when travelling alone or as a couple.

Having broken the twenty-month barrier, we enjoyed a very pleasurable holiday to Margarita, Venezuela, when Paris was twenty-three months old. He had more confidence in the swimming pool and was more respectful of the sea. He was easier to feed and had a lot more sense in general. His jet lag, combined with my own, made sure we were all up at five o'clock every morning, but we went to bed reasonably early, so this wasn't an all-consuming problem.

On that occasion we holidayed with my mum and dad and I was interested to notice that other couples staying in the hotel with under-twos were doing the same. Travelling with an extra two helpers has many advantages, and it may be worth considering for an easier and more relaxing time. My mum and dad helped us watch over and discipline Paris. They even let us have a couple of meals to ourselves while they babysat. It also meant that we could take turns to go off on trips without leaving each other to cope with the baby completely alone. Out of the four of us there was always one who wasn't run ragged and willing to get a drink or meet any other demand.

Although it sounds great in theory, travelling with friends with their own children may not necessarily be the best recipe for a relaxing holiday. Even short trips I have taken with good friends and well-behaved children have been hard work. They all seem to take it in turns to wake up at three o'clock in the morning, need feeding, injure themselves and have crying fits. You may battle with your own toddler for fifteen minutes every hour, so in an apartment housing four others there is always going to be one who wants something. Provided that the children get on they will enjoy the holiday far more, so try it if you want to be self sacrificing, but be prepared to be very tolerant of other children's faults and demands.

Travelling with Young Children

Once a child has graduated from being an infant to a two-year-old, the fares increase dramatically. For most of us it is difficult to justify paying £700 for a holiday in the Caribbean for a twenty-five-month-old child when just four weeks before their fare would have cost £49. An adjusted budget now becomes more of an issue.

As the nappies are shed, there is a period of increased difficulty when a nearby toilet becomes essential. I gazed at my child with frustration as we neared the front of a fifty-minute queue at Disneyland Paris and a little voice demanded, 'Toilet, Mummy, toilet.' I didn't really have time to make a decision about whether or not to give up all our places before my son pulled down his shorts, thrust out his groin and sprinkled the air with his gesture. Thankfully, we were surrounded by a group of Italians, who always adore children. They laughed out loud and patted him on the head, slightly alleviating my acute embarrassment.

Then there are the battles next to the ice-cream stall. A two year old just does not comprehend that a delicious looking ice cream cone in India may half kill him. He may demand ice for his coke and be inconsolable when you refuse him. Still, what is the difference? At home he might be yelling down a supermarket aisle demanding a ten-ton bag of sweets or shouting for chicken nuggets every time you pass the dreaded red and yellow sign. You will doubtless find that as you relax into your holiday you will have more patience, so will be better able to try and reason with your unmanageable monster.

There will be all the time in the world to read together, gain confidence in the swimming pool and break bad habits in a relaxed environment without a guilty conscience, clouded with nagging images of washing, cleaning and phone calls to be made.

A three- or four-year-old may remember very little, but will have a sense of increasing enjoyment. They will appreciate being on the beach and digging sand castles and delight in the family atmosphere, taking walks together and being with parents who are away from all the usual pressures of life. What could be better?

Before you leave, remember to check whether all your children's vaccinations are up to date. Boosters are necessary for tetanus and polio. Also check which other immunisations you will need before travelling to your destination (see Chapter 5).

Travelling with Older Children

For children over the age of five, the family holiday will be as eagerly anticipated as birthdays and Christmas. Don't hesitate to book a trip with them, just concentrate on getting the most out it for the whole family. Children of school age are infinitely easier travelling companions and although more demanding in terms of where they want to go and what they want to eat, require far less effort to holiday with. You may want to choose your destination more carefully and pick a resort that caters well for children, or select a tour with visits to elephant orphanages rather than tea plantations. Avoid a series of museums and long treks round hot cities or ancient monuments. One is much the same as another to a six-year-old, and everyone will suffer. Opt for one or two at opposite ends of the holiday to achieve the most benefit. Don't let your children totally dominate your holiday. Negotiate a day in a theme park for a couple of hours of good behaviour while touring a vineyard, and go to the vineyard first.

Plan different things to do with your children before you go. Stimulate their imagination. Harness their individual interests and ask them to look up what different birds, insects, shells, fish or plants they will see. If you are travelling to the southern hemisphere, explain the differences in the positions of the stars. Ask them to help you learn some of the history and culture of the children who live in the country you will visit. What do they wear and eat? Promise to take them exploring either early morning on the beach or through the wilds of the countryside hunting for as-yet-undiscovered species. Even a ten-minute walk across a field next to a car lay-by will become a memorable adventure.

If you prefer to rely on the resort for entertainment, spend time comparing the different facilities offered by the hotels. As with all other ages, plan carefully, prepare for anything, pack well and you are destined to have a fantastic and unforgettable time.

CHAPTER 2

What Sort of Holiday?

It is likely that the major factor in helping you decide which country you will visit is the type of holiday you seek. Would you like hotel accommodation or self-catering? Do you want to experience adventure, safaris, camping, theme parks, or simply relax on a beach or by a hotel pool? Chapter 3 looks at each country and what it has to offer as a family-holiday destination, and features lots of great beach holiday destinations all around the world. But if all you are looking for is a sunbed by a clean pool, you can now go virtually anywhere in the world. Again, see Chapter 3 for details.

The more discerning you are and the lower your budget, the harder you will have to work to find your ideal holiday. However, the more you read and research before you go, the more likely you are to know what to expect, find what you are looking for and so enjoy the positive aspects of your destination.

Adventure Holidays and the Great Outdoors

For most of us, the wilderness is an incredibly exciting place. Horseback riding, caving, camping, climbing, cycling, rambling and canoeing can all invigorate an active family. However, it is important to remember that children find it much more difficult to control and maintain their body temperature than adults. As a result, don't go for energetic recreation in high temperatures with children, and be aware that low temperatures are even more dangerous.

High altitudes are always cooler but walking in high mountain ranges can seem much more difficult because the thin air means our lungs and hearts need to work much harder to get enough oxygen to all our working muscles.

If you're heading for the great outdoors, the best countries to make for are southern New Zealand and northern Britain. Both rarely get too hot, and as long as you avoid snowy seasons the temperatures should not be too cold for children either. The rivers are free from parasites and the woods free from snakes, bears, wild pigs and other dangerous animals. We can dress for our sport, not to fend off ticks and insects.

Scotland is somewhere we British tend to take for granted – it really is one of the last great wildernesses on Earth. In addition to this, on a sunny day the Lake District in the north of England is one of the world's most beautiful places.

Other good options are Canada, the US, Scandinavia and, for somewhere with a difference, southern Chile – although these countries will put you within range of tick-borne diseases and other parasites.

If you are interested in going on a cycling holiday with your family, you would be better off selecting a country with a predominantly flat terrain, such as the Netherlands, Denmark or Sweden. Also, be aware that if booking a horse-riding adventure outside Western countries, horses can be poorly kept and therefore dangerous to ride.

Before booking an activity holiday:

- Check your travel insurance carefully – many policies exclude sporting activities, even those considered relatively safe.
- Check which parasites and creatures are in the area – a canoeing holiday with children who are likely to fall into the water would be no fun in an area riddled with bilharzia. Caving amongst bats

where malaria is a problem is also dangerous, as there have been cases of people contracting rabies in such situations without having been bitten.

Camping

Many countries of the world offer excellent camping facilities for tents or caravans, but camping in France is hard to beat. The choice of campsites is huge, and in the summer it is hot without making you feel you are being slowly roasted in your tent. The only real negative is that many French campsite toilets are just holes in the ground and aren't particularly pleasant. However, it is possible for you to buy your own small chemical toilet and have it in its own separate tent nearby.

Most of the countries of Western Europe offer good facilities for campers in the summer, either travelling with your own tent or on organised sites where you can rent a tent.

Northern Europe generally offers perfect temperatures and woodland environments for peaceful country relaxation. Across Scandinavia, Belgium, Holland, Germany, Austria, and Switzerland, beautiful countryside is matched by warm welcomes and comfortable sites.

As you get into southern Europe, including Spain, southern Italy and Greece, camping makes it difficult to escape the heat and mosquitoes, and it is likely that the sun will force you out of your tent at 7.30 a.m. if you don't have a spot in the shade and want to avoid being baked. Tenting in these countries with children is more bearable in the spring, but if you do go in summer avoid the open, sunny spaces and try to find a pitch with plenty of shade.

In southern Europe the igloo tents with reflective silver flysheets are the best. They stop the tent absorbing the early morning sun-rays and don't get too hot inside until slightly later in the morning when the air temperature rises, allowing you to sleep-in longer.

Camping in northern Italy is preferable to camping further south, and there is a decent selection of very good sites a short boat ride outside Venice in Lido di Jesolo. It is reasonably easy to drive to Venice from the UK, and northern-Italian drivers are not nearly as crazy as those in the south and around Rome. If you want to fly, the Lido is well serviced by buses from Venice airport.

Summer camping in Spain is crowded and hot. With the huge choice of cheap, self-catering accommodation available, camping really doesn't offer any advantages unless you are touring, or as a back-up. Greece is even hotter and can be unbearable in a tent.

The national parks of the US offer fantastic camping, although those at altitude – including Yosemite in California – are very cold at night. The campsites here, and in Canada, are often huge and rarely get as crowded as those in Europe, and the scale of everything – including the trees and rivers – is much bigger. At night you will often be able to hear bears, but beware, they are dangerous and will rip into your tent on the hunt for food if you don't properly dispose of your rubbish. It is also important to remember that raccoons and other fluffy indigenous American mammals can be vicious and carry rabies, so warn your children to leave all wild animals well alone.

One of the great things about camping is cooking in the open, and you can really enjoy this in the US where camping shops sell fire-wood, barbecues, beef steaks, and marshmallows for toasting. By contrast, barbecuing is prohibited in many southern European campsites, but with good reason, as the foliage and grass becomes very dry in the summer, posing a real fire risk from sparks or dis-carded coals.

Camping in New Zealand and Australia is excellent. Scattered around all the campsites in Australia are fixed barbecues that are for everyone's use; the sports facilities are often good and many sites are near to the beach or have swimming pools. Camping is relaxing and the nights do generally cool down more than those in southern Europe, making sleep much more comfortable.

You should be constantly on the lookout for ticks while camping. They can be found all around the world, even in Australia and northern USA. They spread disease and are also responsible for some child deaths due to the fact that they pass on a lethal toxin as they feed. Insecticide sprayed on and around popular campsites keeps infestation and risk to a minimum, as although ticks are spider-like creatures, not insects, they can still be controlled in this way. Central and northern parts of Europe are host to ticks that spread a form of viral encephalitis; there is a vaccination which should be considered if you are spending time camping and walking in the countryside. See page 290 for more information about ticks and how to avoid them.

In many parts of the world, independent camping with a family is difficult, but not impossible. You will find sites from Zimbabwe to St Lucia, but their facilities and availability differ drastically. Escaping insects, which is very important when travelling in areas where malaria is drug resistant, is very difficult. No matter how hard you try to rid your tent of mosquitoes there is always one inside in the morning. If that one is a disease carrier, you may well suffer.

An easier, and very different option is to go camping with guides and porters on fixed treks or on fixed sites in national parks. The accommodation, although canvas, can be quite luxurious. Mosquito nets are provided and every effort is made to deter and diminish resident insect, arachnid and parasite populations.

For the more intrepid, you should make a very careful check of what the temperature, rainfall and humidity are likely to be when you visit, as you are more at the mercy of the elements in a tent than when you can retire to four walls and a hotel lobby!

Nature and the Environment

The most unique flora, fauna and wildlife is usually found on isolated islands such as Madagascar, the Seychelles and the Galapagos islands.

If you want natural beauty and rich, lush foliage, aim for the larger volcanic islands in hot climates, where the soil is fantastically rich in nutrients and minerals. The peaks of their volcanoes attract clouds and rainfall so that the trees, plants and flowers grow to awe-inspiring sizes. The negative is that the beaches are mostly black sand. Such paradise islands include Tahiti, Reunion, St Lucia and Hawaii.

Going on Safari

It is important to be aware that most children will probably not fully appreciate the wonders of a safari until they are about eight years old. Many tour companies will not allow you to book from the UK for younger children, enforcing strict age limits. However, once you reach your destination you will almost certainly be able to find more local – and possibly less arduous – options for shorter periods, that might be suitable for your family.

I recall a mother who took her five-year-old on a safari, quoting 'Oh, Mum, not another zebra!' and I think this would be the reaction of most young children. When on a safari, it isn't unusual to cover vast distances and see relatively little to get excited about, which can be tedious, hot and bumpy for very little ones, who would be more comfortable and much happier visiting more compact environmental parks, projects or zoos. But if your children are old enough to enjoy a safari, it really is a wonderful and most memorable holiday.

When selecting which safari to go on, it is important to be aware that not all safaris are the same, and that different parts of the world have different species of game. Kenya, Tanzania, Zimbabwe, Botswana, South Africa and Namibia are certainly the better safari options when travelling with children. Many other countries in Africa do have national parks and game reserves, but all those named above have a good tourist infrastructure, high standards of accommodation and do cater for families.

Kenya is generally the least expensive and has the added appeal of the white sandy beaches, which allow you to combine a safari with some time by the sea. The range of safaris on offer in Kenya is extensive, so you can choose one that will not be too long or arduous. In Kenya there is every opportunity to book a safari when you arrive, so if you are unsure whether or not the heat will tire your children too much, you can wait until you arrive at your beach resort and then decide when, for how long, and how far to go.

Safaris in Tanzania are more expensive, but probably a little more luxurious and less crowded than those in Kenya. From the game parks of Tanzania, the spice island of Zanzibar is just a short flight away. Alternatively, splitting the holiday between the beaches of Mombasa in Kenya and a safari in Tanzania tends to bring the price down, and is more likely to offer child discounts.

The Kruger Park in South Africa offers good game viewing, and the uncertain economy there means that at present you will get exceptionally good value for money. South Africa also has much more to offer besides its safaris, including beach resorts, mountains, vineyards and fantastic restaurants.

Zimbabwe offers good, high-class safaris, plus the wonder of Victoria Falls, but again, it can be pricey. However, the infrastructure is in place to allow you to book a basic deal to get out there, then arrange suitable trips and journeys to different lodges once you arrive.

Botswana has excellent game viewing, including the largest population of elephants left in Africa, big cats, hippos, grazing animals and many species of birds. All are well protected in the country's well-kept national parks. It is, however, significantly more costly for a family than eastern Africa and doesn't have the beaches. Nevertheless, Botswana does have the benefits of political and economic stability, which make for a more relaxing, refined and tout-free safari.

Theme and Water Parks

I took my little son Paris to Disneyland Paris just before he was two. He wasn't too impressed and cried fearfully any time one of the Disney characters in fancy dress tried to approach. He hasn't changed; he still doesn't like them anywhere near him and still refuses to have his photo taken with them. My second son Luca is less suspicious, more friendly and giggly. He expresses his enjoyment very loudly.

From the age of five, children really start to appreciate the theme park, but don't be disappointed if the kids aren't displaying their elation – they will all enjoy and remember it forever. Below the age of five they will have a lovely time, but probably won't remember much. Between the ages of six and seven they will get tired and need a buggy to really enjoy their time, while you might need to prepare eight- to nine-year-olds not to be disappointed if the height restrictions stop them going on a ride with an older sibling. Ten- to twelve-year-olds may find some of the rides too tame, and teenagers will be teenagers! It is important to try to find the balance between them being so young that they trudge round totally bewildered, and too old, when they just skulk round with their hands in their pockets, refusing to be impressed.

We best know our children and what they will enjoy, but try to include them in the decision making about which rides to 'fast track' and which ones they really don't want to miss out on and want to go on first. Many of the big, well-organised parks have introduced a system of 'fast tracking'. This is a wonderful concept that allows you to minimise the queuing for the more popular rides. If you 'clock in' your entrance ticket at your chosen ride, you will be given a ticket with a time to return. When you return you can then walk straight into the fast-track system and straight on to the ride without any, or minimal, queuing.

As mentioned above, because so many of the theme parks are vast, children of seven years and under will almost certainly need a trolley. It is possible that children of eight to ten years may need one too, depending on how used they are to walking. I always take our own buggy because it is so useful in the airport as well. In the better-organised, larger parks, you will be able to hire a single buggy for around £5 – 6 per day and double buggies for around £10 per day. Both are incredibly easy to push and have good sunshades already fitted.

Eating in the American parks is accessible both in terms of price and variety. Fries, hot dogs and burgers are readily available. Even the more refined sit-down restaurants offer inexpensive kids' meals. European parks are generally a little more pricey. If you want to take your own food, there are always plenty of benches and places to picnic. Virtually any type of sandwich, crisps and fruit will not spoil before lunchtime.

The greatest concentration of theme parks are in northern Europe and the US. However, the wealthier Asian countries, including Japan and South Korea, also have huge, clean, safe children's theme parks.

Florida

As everybody knows, Florida has the highest concentration of parks in the world, and is the perfect environment unless you go at the height of summer, when it is unbearably hot and humid. During the summer there is usually a rainstorm every afternoon. The skies suddenly open, the rain falls in buckets and you will be drenched right through, so take a light waterproof coat and/or an umbrella. However, the rain passes as abruptly as it begins, and as soon as the sun comes out, everything begins to dry. You can literally see the puddles evaporating into the air.

In Florida the range of parks ensures that you will find something to suit most most ages. Sea World has broad appeal, while Universal Studios and the Epcot Centre are more stimulating for older children. The three-, five- and ten-day passes to the Florida parks are of limited benefit unless you have time to visit all the parks on the pass, or unless you are going to Florida more than once. The passes do not expire and you can use them up on a future visit or even sell them to an agency when you leave. The passes are valid at a limited number of parks, so you must check whether or not they suit where you plan to go. The Disney theme and water parks are covered on one pass. Sea World, Universal Studios, Busch Gardens and a number of others are covered by another.

If you can't make a decision at home you can buy the passes easily in Florida – it is most likely that your motel or resort will be able to sell them to you.

Disneyland Paris

Disneyland Paris is well organised and the accommodation is very good and reasonably priced. The positive points of Disneyland are that your child will see all the familiar Disney characters and be enchanted. The firework displays are a must, although they are after dark, so quite late for young children. The negative aspects are that you will have to contend with unpredictable weather or the crowds of summer.

Disneyland Paris was basically a replica of Florida's Magic Kingdom, but with a new park opening in 2002 there is more to see and do. Some of the regional coach trips advertised in local papers are economical and hassle free enough to motivate the effort, but think about making Disneyland Paris part of a longer holiday to France, as the country has so much more to offer. Alternatively, book one of the short three- or five-day-break offers on the ferry and go camping for a few nights in Normandy, spending a long day or two at the parks.

Europe

Disneyland Paris is the best-known park in Europe, but there are many others. When Luca and Paris were five months and six years respectively, I was on maternity leave and money was tight. I didn't want Paris to miss out, so I booked a bargain coach trip to the parks of Holland and Germany for just the two of us, leaving the baby with his father. The coach travelled overnight to the south of Holland where Europe's oldest and biggest park, De Efteling, is situated. We also went to Phantasialand, over the border in Germany. The journey was tough going, but Paris didn't seem to care. He made friends with everyone and slept most of the night happily. As with planes, children seem to be lulled to sleep by the motion of coaches, and if they can spread out a little and use a toilet regularly, they are fine. The parks were perfect for young children. They were uncrowded, queue-free and virtually all the rides were suitable. I certainly enjoyed them more than the busy hype of Disneyland Paris.

General Pointers for a Theme Park Visit

- Remember to dress the children in cool clothes, comfy shoes and hats if they will wear one.

- Take sunglasses and sunscreen.
- Cameras, spare film, video cameras and batteries are all essential to bring home the memories.
- Instruct your child what to do if they become separated from you. Organise a meeting place for older children. Be vigilant – children do disappear from theme parks. I tell mine to walk into one of the shops, find a lady working there, and tell her you are lost. It may be a good idea to put your name and the address of where you are staying in your child's pocket as well as arranging the meeting place.
- Encourage your child to drink whenever you pass a water fountain, as these are cooling and refreshing in the heat. Take water bottles and fill them up regularly.
- The height restrictions on the rides are very strict and, even if you have queued for two hours, if you get to the end and your child is too small they will not be allowed on. This can be disappointing for an eight- to ten-year-old who wants to go on the bigger rides but is just too little. To avoid problems, make light of it and sweep them off to another ride. They soon forget. It's a good idea to take note of the height restrictions on the free park maps, so that you are forewarned.
- Often a board near the entrance of the park will give estimated queuing times for all the rides. This can help you plan your day.
- If your child takes a hand-held game or good book it will be useful in the longer queues.
- Toddlers and very young children who want to walk need reins or a lead attached to their wrist.
- Iced lollies, drinks, sweets and snacks are everywhere and need to be limited to an agreed level or they can mount up to become a huge expense. This isn't easy because when a child is hot and thirsty they don't respond to reason.
- Negotiate with your children how many toys or themed goods they will be allowed to buy during the holiday, as these items are expensive. I told Paris that he could have three treats while he was on his holiday. However, when our very kind neighbour gave him $20 to spend three became four over the ten days. This he

accepted, and when we were ushered into the toy shop at the end of each ride I was able to reason with him so that he did not choose the first things he saw and was prepared to wait in case he saw something he liked better.

Diving and Snorkelling

Children cannot scuba dive until they are twelve years old. However, you will often see as much – if not more – snorkelling, as many of the more colourful fish and corals live nearer the surface. A child who can hold their breath and is willing to put their face under the water can at least have a look under the sea, although it may not be until the age of seven or eight that they can really get to grips with snorkelling.

If you want to introduce your child to the wonders of the underwater world, the best snorkelling (and scuba diving) close to the UK is in the Red Sea, off Egypt and Israel. Further from home, good places to visit include Australia, the Maldives and Mexico.

The best way to increase a child's confidence is for them to wade out waist deep, put on their mask and fins and be able to see plenty of sea life a stone's throw from the shore. Don't try to teach your child to dive yourself. Leave it to the experts.

CHAPTER 3

What Type of Accommodation?

When travelling with children it is important to upgrade as much as you can and stay in the best place you can reasonably afford. Your rooms need to be free from cockroaches and the mattresses free from blood-sucking parasites, especially if you have a young baby. The younger the baby, the more essential it is to have a reliable electricity supply to boil water for sterilising and milk.

If you are on a very low budget, it may be better to consider tackling the wild and going camping, rather than trying to cope with the risk of disease in a flea-ridden one- or two-star hotel.

Camping and Caravanning

For years, whenever Simon and I went away we packed a tent. We would always travel 'flight only' and usually on a shoestring. The tent was security so that if we ran out of money we would always have somewhere to sleep. The first time we camped with our son, Paris, he was two-and-a-half. He loved it. He scuttled around excitedly as we erected the tent and cooked our evening meal on a camping stove. As the sun set, we snuggled up together for the night.

Most children love camping. It is adventurous and challenging, and they can get involved. There is the warm joy of sleeping with

Mummy and Daddy, plus the fun of the night-time open-air cooking and the midnight trek to the toilet. Camping isn't for every adult, but children will be content.

Camping on a site with fixed tents is straightforward and much the same as booking self-catering accommodation, without the air-conditioning. Camping independently is more difficult, but it does offer more variety and freedom: if you don't like your neighbours, you can re-pitch your tent; if you don't like the site, you can move. But if you are camping with a family you may struggle to move around if you don't have a car. The best campsites are usually fairly inaccessible and sited in beauty spots with poor transport links. Camping equipment on public transport is hard enough without children. The other bonus of a car is that if you don't have time to neatly repack your tent and deflate your airbeds each time you move on, you can bundle them into the boot and worry about it later.

If you enjoy camping, it is often cheaper to hire a car and camp in the countryside than pay for a hotel in a resort or city centre. If find your campsites in travel guides, you can check that they are still in existence and reserve your spot by fax anywhere in the world. If you don't speak the language, booking by telephone is an expensive nightmare, but by fax it is both efficient and cheap and you can request a reply back in English. Better still, if you can get a campsite's email address you can correspond easily and confirm details of site fees, accessibility by public transport and facilities. In the summer, sites in the South of France are often full. Space is limited and rather than open fields you will be assigned a numbered pitch. Camp sites in or just outside major cities fill up too, so it is a good idea to confirm availability before you set off.

In the heat of southern Europe, the igloo tents with reflective silver flysheets are the best. They stop the tent from absorbing the early morning sun's rays and don't get too hot until later in the morning when the air temperature rises, allowing you to sleep-in longer.

One of the negative aspects of a holiday in the open air is the toilets, especially in France. A potty or 'special' bucket may be more convenient and hygienic if disposed of properly, or you can even buy – or rent – a small chemical toilet.

Caravanning or travelling in a motor-home gives the fun, flexibility and variety of a camping holiday without the bugs, extremes of temperature and grubby toilets. It may not have a very glamorous image, but those who do it invariably enjoy it and do it again. Campervan deals to America offer good value. The van parks are of the highest standard, are easy to find and great for kids. For those on a budget, with spirit and a sense of adventure, camping with children is ideal. Even young babies will sleep well next to you and you can sterilise all the necessary equipment by boiling. (See page 19 Where to go camping.)

Hotels

If you can upgrade a little with a young child, particularly a child under four years old, you should. A low-class hotel with shoddy structure, dodgy electrics and a dangerous swimming pool is no place for a toddler. You would be safer and happier camping.

There are certain precautions you can take when choosing and booking a hotel, but there will always be something you could not have accounted for. In the Seychelles a thirty-foot drop on to the road from the hotel's breakfast restaurant was an ongoing concern for us. In China half the bars were missing from the cot provided and we had to position it against the wall in such a way that Paris could not slip, or fall, out between them. You will be lucky to find the perfect destination, but certain facilities will certainly ensure a more comfortable holiday.

In Europe, many tour companies have children's reps on site who run clubs, games, discos and other attractions for kids. However, be prepared that some are really only a babysitting service and won't be particularly enjoyable for your child. Many only operate for an hour or two each day or within limited times. Levels of stimulation and the variety of activities on offer vary between hotels, tour companies and even the reps, who vary widely in their energy levels and enthusiasm.

For children to sleep well, you really will need air-conditioning, but if your budget dictates that you either stay in Greece in a one-star hotel without air-conditioning or not go at all, you should go every time.

When looking through the brochures, try to pick your accommodation as carefully as you can. Alternatively, just book a flight with a civilised arrival time and you will always be able to find something on the day you arrive. You can then shop around to find a hotel that is suitable for your budget and needs. Don't forget that if you arrive at a hotel's front desk and they have rooms free, even five-star hotels will negotiate on price. Often the price first quoted will halve if you push and request a budget room.

You will often find that many good hotels allocate the more spacious rooms to young families. Whenever we travel with my parents, my dad always skulks around our room grumbling that it is bigger and better than his. I always suggest that he is welcome to swap if he would like to have the children sleeping with him.

So book into the best hotel you can afford and, when requesting your room, consider the following:

- In a small hotel in a safe environment, a ground-floor room is arguably the best, with fewer stairs to fall down and no treacherous balconies. It also avoids trekking up and down the stairs. When travelling with an infant, an even better ground-floor room is one which backs out on to the pool, as you can then leave your child sleeping peacefully while you laze by the pool a few feet away.
- With older children, or in malarial regions, the third floor and above may be preferable as there will be fewer insects and fewer threats from intruders or thieves.
- If your child is unlikely to settle in a strange cot alone and likely to end up nuzzled next to you, request a king-sized bed. If there is one available the hotel will usually oblige.

Booking Half Board (HB)

My dad once made the mistake of booking half board in a hotel on Jersey when travelling with my seven-year-old sister. She was a terribly fussy eater, but he was absolutely determined she should eat whatever was put in front of her, just because he had paid for it. Every mealtime became a battle, with my sister ending up in tears and my mum in despair. Thankfully I wasn't there, but Mum claimed that Dad, 'trying to get his money's worth', ruined the entire trip.

If your children are fussy, unless you know the hotel or can guarantee that it will serve food they like and will actually eat, be very careful about booking half or full board for them. You don't want to experience mealtime frustrations on your holidays. In my opinion, it all comes down to cost: if you're paying an extra £2 – 3 for half board per child per day, it's probably worth it. Anything more is probably a risk.

For a few pounds, most hotels around the world will cook a portion of chips, spaghetti or an omelette for a child and, done to order, your children's meals will be much fresher and safer than if they have been sitting on a hotel buffet for an hour.

Booking Fully Inclusive Holidays with Children

If you are planning on staying at an isolated resort or island that only caters for all-inclusive guests, then you probably won't have a choice – the nearest restaurant may be a £10 taxi- or boat-ride away, so feeding your children will prove very costly and tedious if you opt out.

In these instances, try to book a hotel with more than one restaurant. Even in destinations as luxurious as the Maldives or Mauritius, menus are often repetitive if there is only one place to dine. Many all-inclusive hotels offer a varied choice of bars and restaurants, and this is very important. If the hotel will let you book all inclusive for yourself and just bed and breakfast for the children, with a significant cost saving for the children, then do it. Booking all inclusive for children between the ages of two and ten years is usually poor value for money; their appetites will decrease in the heat and they will probably want to live off chips and Coke anyway. If you have paid an extra £200 for the week so they can appreciate the fantastically elaborate hotel buffet, it will drive you mad.

Under-twos are always virtually free. This is great. They need a plentiful supply of drinks (half of which they knock over), and it is a godsend having food available all day which your child can pick at whenever they are hungry, as this means you won't have to worry about every meal ime.

For the over-twos, compare the holiday prices for bed and breakfast and all inclusive. If you find that you can get the all-inclusive deal for between £5 and £10 extra per child per day, it is good value. Anything more will probably end up more costly than feeding them from the menu, unless they are very good eaters. (NB: All-inclusive hotels rarely have kettles in the rooms, so take your own.)

Facilities to Check for Before Booking a Hotel

1. Are a kettle and a fridge provided in the room? If there is no fridge available, the minibar is a useful substitute. Squash up the whisky miniatures and squeeze in the ready-prepared bottles, open baby foods or your own canned drinks. (NB: A few hotels may charge you for this, and some hotels now have fridges electronically rigged so it registers on your bill even if you move a can from its allotted place.)
2. Are cots available?
3. Are babysitters available at a reasonable cost? If you are relying on the babysitter promised in the hotel brochure, check the rates. A friend who recently married in Mauritius and took her one-year-old along, found out on arrival that the babysitter was £10 per hour. The £300 babysitting bill that she and her husband received at the end of their stay was quite a shock.
4. Can you get an early supper in your hotel? Will the kitchen provide children's meals outside hours?
5. Are highchairs available in the dining rooms?
6. Is there a crèche, playroom or children's activities available?
7. Are the beaches near the hotel? Children hate walking far in the heat. If so, are they safe, clean and free from dangerous sea life such as jelly fish, sea urchins or stone fish?
8. Is there a children's swimming pool or a shallow end to the main pool?

9. Are the grounds enclosed and, in more hostile African or Caribbean countries, are they protected by guards?
10. Will your child be the only one in the hotel and therefore a constant source of irritation to all the other guests?
11. How close is the hotel to local attractions?
12. Is there a courtesy bus to and from town and the airport?
13. How well is the hotel serviced by public transport?
14. If there is no transfer from the airport included, what is the hotel's proximity to and accessibility from the airport?
15. If your flight home leaves late at night and check out is at midday, will you be able to have the use of a room either free or for a nominal cost? You don't want to be hanging around the hotel grounds for twelve hours with a young baby and toddler in tow if you do not have access to a shower or air-conditioning.

Self-catering Holidays

A holiday in a self-catering villa, cottage, *gite* or apartment is probably one of the easiest, cheapest and least-risky options when travelling with children. You will have total control over what your child eats and drinks. You will be relatively free to rearrange furniture and juggle sleeping arrangements. There is more space for the children to amble around, spread out their toys and make themselves at home, without worrying about the wrath of the chambermaid. They can scatter food all over the floor and you have the tools to clean up. Many a time I have skulked out of a hotel room leaving lentils, crisps and dry noodles scattered all over the carpet and melted chocolate among the crisp, white bed sheets.

Washing facilities will cut down considerably on the packing and are essential if you aren't using disposable nappies. You can also wash all your clothes before you go home, which will ensure that your suitcase isn't packed with sicky bibs, pants and accidents, or clothing caked in sand and sea salt.

Individual apartments have far superior soundproofing between them than hotel rooms. I have often found myself responding to crocodile tears at 4.30 a.m. in a hotel room to save the neighbours from being woken up. Thus, self-catering offers more independence and privacy than hotels.

The only real disadvantages are that someone still has to clean, tidy and wash up, and it will probably be you. Also, self-catering apartments are usually rented by the week and don't generally offer the flexibility of hotels if you are planning to move around. However, they can be so cheap that you can book them for the week and just use them as a base. It is not uncommon that a package with an apartment costs less than a flight-only deal to many European destinations. As a result, even if you were only to stay just one night in the apartment it would still be a bargain, and you can take off and book into another hotel, or camp knowing that you have something to fall back on.

Facilities to Check for Before Booking Self-catering

1. Check washing, kitchen and bedroom facilities.
2. Are cots available?
3. Are babysitters or a maid service available at a reasonable cost?
4. Where are the nearest shops, supermarkets and restaurants? Can you walk there?
5. Are towels and bedding provided?
6. Will you need a hire car? If so, is there secure/adequate parking? In countries such as Spain, Portugal and the US the cost of your taxi fare to and from the airport could be more than an entire week's car hire. Couple this with having to buy all your provisions in the expensive resort shop instead of whizzing into town to the local markets or supermarket, and you may actually save a fortune by renting a car.
7. Are the beaches close by? Children hate walking far in the heat. If so, are they safe, clean and free from dangerous sea life such as jelly fish, sea urchins or stone fish?
8. Is there a children's swimming pool or a shallow end to the main pool?

9. Is there adequate security? Are the grounds enclosed and, in more hostile African or Caribbean countries, are they protected by guards?

10. How close is the accommodation to local attractions?

11. How well is the accommodation serviced by public transport?

12. What is the proximity to the airport?

13. Self-catering check out times are more likely to be compatible with flight times than those in hotels, which are usually more inflexible. However, it is still worth confirming that you will not be requested to leave mid-morning and have to sit on the street with your cases and children until midnight.

CHAPTER 4
Where to Go?

As the world becomes more accessible, both in terms of transport networks and affordability, it can seem that the whole planet is a huge tourist resort. Even the Himalayan treks of Nepal are well trodden and would be a safe destination for a family. The only places that are really out of bounds for the family are those which are war-torn and those with drug-resistant malaria or other outbreaks of serious illness. War-torn countries generally have a poor infrastructure, unreliable transport, unsanitary water supplies and food shortages. Drug-resistant malaria is voracious, and illnesses such as cholera or typhoid break out fairly regularly in pockets of Asia, Africa and Central/South America. It is a good idea to check with the World Health Organisation or NHS Direct if there are outbreaks in the area you are planning to visit.

Which Country?

- Choose a destination in line with your own experience, somewhere you will feel comfortable and safe. The children will sense your stress or discomfort and can easily become frightened if you are.
- Carefully consider any vaccinations you may need and whether or not they are indicated for your child's age group.

- Check whether or not you will need to give your children malaria tablets. If malaria is endemic you must follow advice – children and pregnant women are particularly susceptible.
- Think carefully about the weather and which season it will be when you arrive in your destination. Avoid monsoon seasons in South-East Asia, when there are more mosquitoes and contagious fevers around. Avoid the blistering heat of peak summer in Turkey, where most of the hotels and restaurants don't have air-conditioning. Consider that even in October, Spain and Portugal can be cold, particularly at night. Go prepared. Children are more at risk from the cold than they are from the heat, and so wherever and whenever you go take at least one thick warm jumper and blanket for them.
- Don't rely totally on travel agents; they will inevitably try their best but can not always guarantee your seat on the plane or the room you will be assigned to in your hotel on arrival. They may relay your preferences but a message to the airline may get lost in translation and a fax to your accommodation months before arrival can easily be overlooked.
- If your children are under school age, you will have the option to travel outside school holidays which is strongly advisable. The resorts will be less expensive and quieter. Also worth considering is the fact that less children around means less childhood bugs and contagious ailments for your children to catch.
- If you are relying on local baby sitters promised in the brochure check the rates.

Each country of the world has something to offer, especially if you are very familiar with the country or are staying with family or friends. If you like alternative holidays, consider joining a tour group. It may not be quite so adventurous, but the whole family will enjoy a much more stress-free trip. The guides will warn you about all the local tourist scams, which vary greatly from country to country. When travelling preoccupied with babies and toddlers, it is so much easier to fall prey to pickpockets. You will also feel more vulnerable.

Con artists will sense this and take advantage. Wherever you go be prepared, be aware; have a fabulous time, but be vigilant.

Never let your child out of your sight. It is a sad world that we live in when we have to monitor our children for fear of them being taken from us, and in many countries this would never happen. In Asia and the Caribbean, the deep love and respect for children is evident wherever you go. In Catholic countries, too, there is generally an attitude towards them that is caring and positive.

It is easy to get separated from your child in crowds. On one of my first trips to America I found a young girl wandering lost and alone in Disney World. I took her hand and asked her where her mummy was. She was either too young or too frightened to speak and just stared up at me. We stood with her on the spot expecting her anxious mum to run towards us at any time. After fifteen minutes I gave up and took her to the lost child station. She followed me with mute obliging and sat in the cabin tearless and bewildered. I am glad that I found her first.

A friend of my aunt's lost a child in one of the world's most famous and popular theme parks. She sold her house to fund the search but, devastatingly, has never found her. I have since heard stories about professional gangs that work in such parks – they snatch a child, then take it straight into the restrooms, change its clothes and put a baseball cap on its head to hide the familiar hair-colouring. They may cut or even dye the child's hair, making its appearance so different that its own mother wouldn't immediately recognise it. Incredibly, it has been rumoured that older children have been drugged to keep them quiet.

The tales may be sensationalist, but if you ever suffer the unbearable experience of a missing child, don't just look for familiar clothes and hair colour: scrutinise every child of a similar shape and size. Be aware but not paranoid.

Each country has been given a star rating for its suitability as a family holiday destination. The ratings are based on the following criteria:

1. Safe and unthreatening environment and low crime rates
2. Clean and hygienic environment
3. Free or low risks from parasitic diseases
4. Insect, spider, snake and scorpion-free
5. A child-friendly population that doesn't impose
6. Good medical facilities and emergency hospitals with English-speaking doctors
7. Good beaches or inland lakes and pools with safe swimming
8. Western-standard hotels and restaurants with reliable electricity
9. Entertainment available that is suitable for their age group. Water and theme parks.
10. Not too intolerable a journey or too many time zones away from home (although it is usually worth it)
11. Moderate temperatures and humidity
12. Low rainfall when you will be travelling – insects and diseases proliferate in the rainy seasons
13. Good, clean restaurants
14. Safe, clean seas without venomous creatures or predators
15. Low risk for rabies and attack by dangerous mammals
16. Safe roads with a low incidence of traffic accidents
17. Good transport infrastructure
18. Political stability

Key: ★   Very basic
          ★★   Adequate
          ★★★   Generally suitable
          ★★★★   Good
          ★★★★★   Excellent

Africa

Africa is certainly the most challenging continent to the traveller. Many countries suffer from a high incidence of parasitic disease and/or violent political unrest. The greatest attraction Africa has to offer families is the abundance and variety of well-run wildlife safaris all over the eastern and southern regions of this vast continent. Children love animals and what could be more spectacular and exciting for them than setting out to track lions, leopards, cheetahs, elephants, rhinos, zebras and giraffes?

Most of Africa would be hard going for a family. The intense heat, disease and the hostility of some locals mean that visits here can be hard work. However, the untamed nature of Africa can be enjoyed in several countries which have settled their turbulent histories and now enjoy stability. The places you will stay will be as memorable as the wildlife. The comfortable lodges or camping safaris all have appeal.

Below is a list of African countries which, in my opinion, are the only ones suitable as a family holiday destination, based on the criteria outlined at the beginning of this section. For clarity, a list of the countries to avoid can be found at the end.

BOTSWANA ★★★

Flight time: 12-14 hours
Best time to visit: March-April

Botswana is where wealthy South Africans head for on safari. Almost 20 per cent of Botswana's land is set aside as national parks or game reserves, which is one of the highest percentages of protected land in the world. Environmentalists abound, and the government is keen to attract tourists and trophy hunters. The Okavango swamps and delta are an inspiring taste of wild Africa. The largest collection of elephants remaining in Africa come to bathe alongside a mix of drinking and grazing animals that is unmatched anywhere else.

Feeding off the concentrated game are legions of predators, including lions, cheetahs, leopards, hyenas and wild dogs. There are eighty species of fish, turtles, hippos, crocodiles, fishing eagles and waterfowl. A family of wildlife lovers will be in clover and what child isn't fascinated by animals? Significantly more costly for a family than eastern Africa, and without the beaches, Botswana has the benefits of political and economic stability. which make for a more relaxing, refined and tout-free safari.

Parasitic disease has been tackled aggressively in Botswana. The tsetse fly and the associated problem of sleeping sickness has been virtually eliminated, although this was done more for the protection of cattle than humans. Respiratory diseases are common and care must be taken with hygiene. Malaria tablets should be taken in the northern areas between November and June.

EGYPT ★★★

Flight time: 6 hours
Best time to visit: March-April

The terrorist attacks specifically aimed at tourists take the shine off the pyramids. Your children will have a lifetime to visit them and so there is no real point travelling in troubled times, although the give-away holiday prices are attractive and it is unlikely that your family will be involved in any trouble. However, I would not take any child to Egypt until they have reached the age of seven.

Mini-cruises from Limassol in Cyprus deposit you in Egypt for a day or two and are a good option if you would really like to show your children the site of the most ancient of civilisations. If you do travel from Cyprus or opt to take advantage of the present bargain-holiday prices to Egypt, you must visit the Egyptian Museum in Cairo to see the contents of Tutankhamen's tomb, which are fascinating for both adults and children. The colours and detail are stunning.

Egypt's food-hygiene standards are somewhat lacking and stomach bugs are common even on the Nile cruises and at the best hotels. The chefs may do their best, but if the produce from the local markets finds its way to your table you are likely to suffer. A trip to an Egyptian market may put you off feeding your children anything but crisps and chocolate.

In addition to the amazing sightseeing that has been attracting travellers for centuries, the Red Sea resorts offer excellent scuba diving, luxury hotels, good water sports and great beaches.

There is a great deal to attract and entertain the family, but this should be carefully considered on balance with the risk of stomach upset and terrorism. The time of year you visit should also be taken into account. The summer heat can be oppressive for children and the winters can be surprisingly chilly in the north. Spring or autumn would be the best time to take advantage of all the different aspects of the country with a family. Combining time at the beach with a stay in Cairo and/or Luxor would be the best way of discovering Egypt.

GAMBIA ★★★

Flight time: 7-8 hours
Best time to visit: February-March

The Gambia is a fairly characterless destination. It is relatively developed, so accessible for families, but it is basically just reasonable hotels and beaches. If you have a passion to try Africa it is one of the safer options to head for. The beaches are broad and sandy, every effort is made by the hotels to keep food hygiene standards high, and there are trips along the river to break up your stay.

GHANA ★★★

Flight time: 8-10 hours
Best time to visit: February-March

Ghana is one of the more hospitable African countries. The government is keen to attract tourists and it views development of the tourist industry as a key to economic strength. The standards of the hotels are high, although the choice of food and its quality is very variable.

There are some good beaches but these are on the Atlantic ocean, which is cold. You will receive a warm welcome and be encouraged to travel to other regions of the country to visit rainforests. The horrifying evidence of the slave trade and places where slaves were held before transportation are still intact, and a visit to them is offered as a tourist attraction.

The culture of true Africa is still undiminished, and if you want to experience the 'dark continent', it may be somewhere to put on the list for when the children are older.

KENYA ★★★★

Flight time: 10-12 hours
Best time to visit: January-March

Bandits, operating mostly in the north east, have meant that many safaris have been accompanied by armed guards. There are flare-ups from time to time. In spring 1998 many tour operators advised tourists to cancel their trips. The trouble seems to have settled again and thousand of tourists each year enjoy trouble-free bargain safaris.

Kenya offers many short safaris combined with time relaxing at the beach. This is better for young children, who may tire of the early morning awakenings and long days spent in a bumpy minibus, trekking miles looking for elusive game, elephants or big cats. A few days may be a great novelty, especially if they have the beach to look forward to. Older children are likely to enjoy the longer safaris, but the combination with time spent on the beach is more fun for all the family.

Kenyan safaris are generally good value and considerably less expensive than in many other African countries. However, cheaper prices have brought the Kenyan safari within the price range of many tourists, so in some parks you may find yourself in a race with several other vehicles to be first to the kill.

Resistant malaria is a concern and tablets must be taken. Other health risks include respiratory and diarrhoeal illnesses.

Many hotels are of a high standard but service is generally very laid back. Take snacks such as cereals, and raisins for your child to nibble on just in case.

LESOTHO ★★★

Flight time: 14 hours
Best time to visit: November-February

Spectacular mountain scenery is the main attraction for tourists. In May, June and July the mountains are cold, with snowfall. Much safer than South Africa, which surrounds Lesotho, but of limited accessibility.

MADAGASCAR ★★★

Flight time: 12-14 hours
Best time to visit: March-June

Madagascar is a huge island off the east coast of Africa. Its geographical isolation means it is home to many unique animals and plants. Protection programmes for lemurs and other animals are helped by the revenue of visiting tourists, and are an interesting experience for young travellers.

There are thousands of miles of tropical beach and much to explore in Madagascar. However, malaria is endemic.

There is a good, inexpensive domestic air network that compensates for the difficulties of getting around by road and rail over the long distances involved. The country is relatively poor but the people are not hostile towards tourists and so a family who are confident travellers could enjoy a nature-orientated trip.

MALAWI ★★

Flight time: 12-13 hours
Best time to visit: September-October

Malawi is a small country dominated by the eponymous Lake Malawi which attracts anglers and nature lovers. National parks, mountain lodges, good hotels and watersports are readily available, but resistant malaria is a problem and, as young children are so vulnerable to the disease, it would seem pointless to risk it.

MAURITIUS ★★★★

Flight time: 12-14 hours
Best time to visit: March-April

The main problem with Mauritius is the price tag. Eating, sleeping and baby-sitting in Mauritius costs a small fortune. The beaches are spectacular, and the wooded mountain peaks and turquoise waters make for a romantic and idyllic holiday for a couple. However, as your child trips up the honeymooners too busy gazing into each other's eyes to watch where they are going, you may wish you had chosen somewhere cheaper that was more geared towards family fun and relaxation. Also, be aware that July and August in Mauritius can be chilly and rainy.

MOROCCO ★★★★

Flight time: 4-6 hours
Best time to visit: March-May

Child mortality is high, so if you do go and your child falls ill, get home. Crime levels are low but be a little careful with blond children, as they are very attractive to Moroccan men. The difference in culture makes Morocco a very popular destination for fair homosexual men, where they find they are very much in demand.

Morocco is basically all beach resorts and beggars. Having said that, the beaches are good, hotels standards are reasonably high and Morocco is cheap and near the UK. If you are careful with what you eat and avoid the water you should enjoy your family holiday. The bazaars and belly dancers are interesting for even the youngest members of the family, while Marrakech offers culture and luxury.

NAMIBIA ★★★

Flight time: 10-14 hours
Best time to visit: September-October

Sand-dune skiing and desert ecology are the main attractions, plus there are some good, self-drive safaris on offer. However, Namibia is generally more expensive than other African countries and there is less to entertain the children. The western 'skeleton' coast (so named because of all the shipwrecks scattered along the coastline) is usually shrouded in cold, thick fog.

SEYCHELLES ★★★★★

Flight time: 12-14 hours
Best time to visit: March-April

The Seychelles offers nature at her best and her most beautiful; the islands support unique flora, fauna and wildlife. Thousands of spiders spin webs between the overhead telephone lines, hundreds of huge fruit bats weigh down the boughs of the mango trees and giant tortoises amble around hotel grounds. It really is a nature lover's and a children's paradise, the perfect place to teach them about the environment and stimulate their imagination by exploring deserted 'real' pirate coves.

The beaches are among the best in the world. They are quiet, the sand is soft and white, they are safe, shallow and a real taste of paradise.

Prohibitive pricing and the distance from Europe, America or any other rich society is possibly what has kept the Seychelles more unspoilt and quieter than the Caribbean or the Mediterranean. Now prices have come down to relatively affordable levels it is a good time to visit, and the Seychelles' attention to protecting the environment will hopefully mean that it can be enjoyed for the foreseeable future.

If you can afford luxury on the Seychelles you will find it. At the other extreme there is some budget accommodation available which is better value than some of the bigger medium class hotels, which are expensive breeze block and concrete creations rather than hibiscus and turtle dove havens.

The health care is good and free. We were unfortunate enough to end up in hospital on the main island of Mahe after our fourteen-month-old son slashed open his wrist deeply. He was treated faultlessly and well stitched up. The pharmacy shelf was a little sparse but the doctors were efficient and confident and the nurses were sensitive to our concerns. I was just grateful to have been staying on one of the main islands rather than a more remote one.

SOUTH AFRICA ★★★★

Flight time: 10-12 hours
Best time to visit: October-March

Times are still changing in South Africa and who knows for how long it will be safe to visit. Crime is still escalating and Johannesburg is already the murder capital of the world; in fact South Africa is the most dangerous country in the world outside the war zones. You are forty times more likely to be murdered in South Africa than you are in the UK and twelve times more likely to be murdered there than in the US. Big international hotels in downtown Jo'burg have simply shut down.

Cape Town is less hostile and infinitely more interesting, and so if you want to see the country you should head there. There is plenty to do and see around Cape Town for everyone. The Cape of Good Hope is a daytrip worth taking. There are good hotels, beaches and pleasant sightseeing. Table Mountain towers over the city and you can take trips to the top by cable car.

If you simply want beaches, Durban is an option. North-west of Durban are Zululand and the Drakensberg Mountains, both worth exploring.

The excellent wildlife reserves in north-east South Africa are a good safari option. In the Kruger park there are 140 species of mammals and 450 species of bird. The lodges are of a high standard.

At the moment South Africa is incredibly cheap. The whole family would be able to eat out constantly at bargain prices. The food standards and range of choice are high.

A fly-drive would mean you could take in much of what the country has to offer, but be careful: many impoverished black South Africans drive without a licence or insurance and road deaths are common.

A few days on safari, a few days in the Drakensberg Mountains, then a week on the beach would be perfect, but organised tours from the UK are relatively expensive when you consider the cost of living and how cheaply you could do it yourself.

The health care in the cities is good but in rural South Africa access to care is limited and black children suffer tragic 20 per cent death rates. Political uncertainty is unlikely to resolve itself at least within the next five to ten years, so if you want to sample what South Africa has to offer, stay clear of Johannesburg and go now.

TANZANIA and ZANZIBAR ★★★

Flight time: 10-14 hours
Best time to visit: September-October

Tanzania is a fantastic destination for a safari. One third of the country is national park or game reserve and offers amazing game-viewing opportunities. It is considerably more expensive than Kenya, but the lodges and camps are first class. To bring down the price, you could spend part of your safari in Kenya, and part in Tanzania on an organised tour.

If you want to head for the beach for part of your holiday with the family, the beaches of Mombasa are just a short flight away. Alternatively, the spice island of Zanzibar is an option.

Zanzibar was built up on the slave trade and so has a strong history. It is undeveloped but offers good hotels, deserted beaches and warm, reef-protected waters.

Whatever you decide to do be careful what you eat. The health care is good by African standards, but in many areas it is provincial. There is also a high incidence of malaria, diarrhoeal and respiratory diseases.

TUNISIA ★★★★★

Flight time: 4-6 hours
Best time to visit: March-May

Tunisia is one of the Mediterranean's cheapest holiday destinations. It is marketed as a winter-sun destination but, as in Egypt and Morocco, it can be chilly in December, January and February. In the summer it is very hot. The choice of hotels is wide and you are sure to get good value for money. Like other North African countries, there is little here but sand and sea. Children may enjoy camel rides and desert safaris, and there is a tiny theme park in Port El Kantaoui.

Tunisians developed a bad reputation in the 1970s when tourists started to arrive; hassle was common and the men were very forward. Two-and-a-half million tourists now descend on the locals each year and have become an accepted and natural part of life. Tunisians are generally easy going, the men are friendly but not overpowering, and they are very kind to children.

Food hygiene levels seem to have improved since Tunisia became a popular tourist haunt and health-care standards have improved dramatically. Wine is made in Tunisia and is sold in all the local restaurants for just a few pounds. Even Chateaubriand, the finest joint of fillet steak, is just £5 per person. Camel rides and tours into the desert are popular and enjoyable for all the family.

ZAMBIA ★★

Flight time: 10-14 hours
Best time to visit: September-October

Victoria Falls, the Zambezi river and safaris are the reasons to visit Zambia, but all this and more can be found over the border in Zimbabwe and, for a family, Zimbabwe is a better choice, with a better tourist infrastructure and standard of hotels. Corruption at the borders is an issue.

ZIMBABWE ★★

Flight time: 10-14 hours
Best time to visit: September-October

Zimbabwe is a beautiful country with some good game viewing and the natural wonder of Victoria Falls and the Zambezi river. The hotels and game lodges are generally medium class but the famous colonial style Victoria Falls Hotel is fantastic.

Temperatures can soar in the summertime but, because of the higher altitude, they are still generally more bearable than on the plains of Tanzania and Kenya.

Action holidays are developing. White-water rafting has been set up on the Zambezi, but is too dangerous for young children. Canoeing on the Zambezi is good for older children but make sure you tell them to keep their mouths closed tight should they fall in. Parasitic illnesses are common in Zimbabwe, and as so many are water-borne you don't want any member of the family with a tummy full of the Zambezi.

Zimbabwe also offers a number of cultural attractions and ruins, and even though you won't get the beaches or the bargain-priced safaris so readily available in Kenya, you will get more peace and atmosphere.

The following African countries are, in my opinion, best avoided as family holiday destinations for many reasons, including war, political instability, poor health care, the absence of any tourist infrastructure, and violent- and high-crime rates:

Algeria, Angola, Benin, Burkina Faso, Burundi, Cameroon, Cape Verde, Central African Republic, Chad, Congo, Djibouti, Equatorial Guinea, Eritrea, Ethiopia, Gabon, Guinea, Guinea-Bissau, Ivory Coast, Liberia, Libya, Mali, Mauritiana, Mozambique, Niger, Nigeria, Rwanda, São Tomé and Principe, Senegal, Sierra Leone, Somalia, Sudan, Surinam, Swaziland, Togo, Uganda, Zaïre.

Antarctica ★

Flight time: 25-35 hours
Best time to visit: December-January

Great if stepping off a cruise ship to view the penguins for half a day, but with ice, blizzards, fog and temperatures as low as −75°C, Antarctica is not really the place to stay for a holiday with young children. It is too cold and windy with the risk of hypothermia, frost-bite and possibly snow-blindness. If visiting from a cruise ship your family will almost certainly be supplied with suitable clothing that will protect against the biting cold. December and January are the 'warmest' times of year, with average temperatures around −4°F.

Asia

South Asia

BANGLADESH ★

Flight time: 10-14 hours
Best time to visit: December-March

The environment is harsh, there is a high incidence of parasitic, diar-rhoeal and communicable diseases, and the climate can be cata-strophic. Tropical monsoons from June to October create floods that can cover two thirds of the country, devastating a whole season's crops and so creating famine, disease and extreme hardship. Cyclones in April and May and after the monsoons can lead to huge death tolls.

BHUTAN ★

Flight time: 11-13 hours
Best time to visit: April-September

Tourism is not encouraged by the government, and the country has only recently been open to visitors at all. For centuries the tiny king-dom remained tucked away in the Eastern Himalayas, secret from the outside world. It is possible that Bhutan gave rise to the myths of Shangri La.

The land is of outstanding natural beauty; 70 per cent of the country is forested and the bird life is exceptional. The treks are less well trodden than those in the more popular destination of Nepal. The people are deeply religious and gentle.

Organised tours would be the best way of visiting Bhutan, as tourism and prices are strictly controlled by the government and you won't have the choice or flexibility you need with a family if you don't prearrange your visit.

Exceptionally high infant mortality, poor health care and a high incidence of fatal communicable diseases are major concerns when travelling to Bhutan with vulnerable children, but your tour or trekking guide will offer all the advice you need to keep your family safe.

BRUNEI ★★★

Flight time: 15-17 hours
Best time to visit: September-October

The Sultan of Brunei was once the richest man in the world. He lives in the biggest palace in the world and is still enjoys the third richest. Vast oil and gas reserves ensure that the people of Brunei enjoy one of the highest living standards globally. The government encourages tourism and there is a Western-standard free health service.

Brunei is a small country and 75 per cent of it is covered by rainforest. The beaches are good, crime levels are low and the standards of service are high. Perhaps visited in combination with Borneo, Brunei could be a good family travel destination with a difference.

BURMA (Myanmar) ★★★

For a family on tour

Flight time: 12-15 hours
Best time to visit: December-April

Visiting Myanmar is like stepping back in time. It is one of the least-developed countries in South East Asia, rich in ancient customs and traditions. Pagodas, temples, lakes and stunning scenery are commonplace. The road to Mandalay, Rangoon and the legendary Irrawaddy River are all major attractions.

The government encourages tourists to stay in the five-star hotels and take the luxury cruises on the Irrawaddy. The prices paid in hard currency are in no way proportionate to the cost of living. As a result, visiting Burma is expensive.

If visiting the country with a family it is a good idea to join a tour group. Travelling independently with children in Myanmar would be tough and tiring and, although a fraction of the cost of an organised Western-tourist-fleecing trip, it is regrettably the better option, as your guide will ensure you are sensitive to the totalitarian regime that is still in place.

There is a lot to see, but getting around alone is difficult. The atmosphere and variety between boat trips and golden pagodas is likely to stimulate children, and it would be a shame to arrive and stay in Rangoon.

The Burmese people are gentle and remain constrained; sadly human rights records are poor and they will be 'encouraged' to stay away from the tourists and may smile softly at you from a distance. Be respectful of the police and the military.

Avoid the tropical wet season in the summer, especially with children, when fevers can run riot. Take extra care to avoid diarrhoeal illnesses and be aware that malaria is on the increase. Leprosy in Burma is more common than in the rest of Asia.

CAMBODIA ★★

Flight time: 12-15 hours
Best time to visit: September-October

Although a great destination for the adventurous, independent traveller, the occasional tourist kidnappings and uncertain politics should direct most families to neighbouring Thailand or Vietnam.

If you really want to visit Cambodia as a family, then it would be advisable to join a tour group. You will see more and be able to relax and enjoy the trip, instead of battling with transport, hoteliers and even the police.

INDIA ★★★

With careful preparation and choice of destination

Flight time: 10-14 hours
Best time to visit: November-March (Dependant on region)

Despite all that India has to offer it remains, in the mind of the tourist, a place for an experience rather than a relaxing, enjoyable holiday. It is certain that you will never forget your time there, but concentrated attention to hygiene and careful choice of destination can ensure a happy, and not just a memorable, trip.

Whether or not to take your children for the real Indian experience is not an easy decision, especially when they are young. The roads are lethal and the terrible reputation for infestations such as 'Delhi belly' are all true. It may even be that is not worth showing your children the splendours of India when they are too young, because they could not truly appreciate them and there must be some corners of the world left for them to discover themselves. Seeing the Taj Mahal and the palaces of Jaipur too young may take the wonder out of it. However, children under the age of seven or eight may appreciate the country's atmosphere and they will be inspired by all the local fables and stories. Buy local books which tell children's stories, as many are in English.

If you do want to go and do not know India well, it is better to travel with a tour group when travelling with children. The heat in the summer is insufferable and journeying independently by road and rail is exhausting – even with a group it is tiring. Your tour guide will usher you through crowds to the right train platform, take you to hotels and restaurants where hygiene standards do not jeopardise the sensitive tourist-stomach, and protect you from scams and the multitude of over-zealous touts.

The best family holidays in India would be in the north where it is cooler and civilised colonialism is still strongly in evidence. New Delhi is surprisingly sophisticated, with spacious boulevards, manicured gardens and 'gentlemen's' clubs where you can eat cucumber sandwiches watched by a picture of the Queen. Old Delhi is a mass of temples, mosques and bazaars. Sacred cows wander around in the main streets unmoved by deafening beeping horns.

Alternatively, if you do want to relax on your holiday and have just a taste of India, choose a beach holiday in Goa. The influence of a Portuguese colony, golden beaches and welcoming local people ensure an enjoyable experience. You will get incredible value for money and the hotels do make every effort to ensure the tourist's stomachs are not upset. Be careful, take all the usual precaution –

avoid salad, ice and ice cream, and brush your teeth in bottled water – and your family should have a cheap, trouble-free trip.

INDONESIA

General suitability for a family holiday in Bali ★★★★
In other regions of Indonesia ★★

Flight time: 12-16 hours
Best time to visit: April-October

Indonesia consists of 13,667 islands. The main islands are Java, Bali, Kalimantan (approximately 60 per cent of Borneo) and Sumatra and Sulawesi.

The best of these islands to visit with a family is undoubtedly Bali, although the recent bombing in October 2002 shocked this tropical paradise and a repeat attack – although unlikely – is possible. Bali is beautiful, relaxed, safe and geared towards tourism. The five-star hotels in Nusa Dua are among the best in the world, but are still affordable compared to the price you may pay for a room of an equivalent standard in a hotel in a European city. There are plenty of reasonable, lower-budget options too. The beaches are good and the island is easy to explore in a hire car. On Bali the roads are not too crowded, but as always be careful. The gentle Balinese temperament is reflected in their driving but be wary of mopeds and animals in the road.

Indonesian food is delicious and in the tourist hotels and restaurants it is quite safe. Even children usually eat the skewered meat or chicken satay and rice. American and Continental food is also widely available in the hotels.

The island of Borneo is becoming more accessible, although tourism is developing mainly on the northern Malaysian side of the island. Orang Utans are a popular section of the island's inhabitants. Java is really for the more-experienced traveller. Its capital, Jakarta, is one of those cities where as soon as you step out of the airport you need your wits about you. Passports can disappear before you get to your hotel, and it is likely that your taxi driver will try and extort every last penny of your holiday money. The recent economic problems have really hit Java, and you will see a great deal of hardship. It can be heartbreaking, especially when you witness the effects it has had on the children, who have to do whatever they can to feed themselves.

LAOS ★

Flight time: 12-15 hours
Best time to visit: September-October

Health is a concern, sanitation is poor, and dengue-fever and malaria are an increasing problem. The infant mortality rate is more than 10 per cent.

Even travellers familiar with South-East Asia may have a more enjoyable holiday in one of the neighbouring and more developed tourist destinations if travelling with children.

If you take the easier option of visiting Laos with a tour group, you will doubtless have a trouble-free holiday, but how enjoyable it will be for young children is debatable.

MALAYSIA ★★★★

Flight time: 12-15 hours
Best time to visit: January-September

Malaysia is South-East Asia's major tourist destination. It is a beautiful place to visit, but is mainly sun, sea and sand. It is civilised and easy to get around, so even with children you could base yourselves in Kuala Lumpur or one of the beach resorts and still explore without a guide. The beaches are stunning and many of the resorts are set in beautiful, tropical gardens. The roads are good enough and car hire is reasonable enough to opt for a family fly-drive.

Kuala Lumpur is safe and civilised, although a few days in the capital would be enough with a family. From Kuala Lumpur you could then visit Singapore, which is only a short train trip away and has attractions for the whole family. The Malaysian islands of Penang and Langkawi and the many beach resorts on the mainland are stunning, and the hotel standards very high. Children are readily welcomed. The cool climate of the Cameron Highlands is a break from the heat of the coast and a nice chance to see working tea plantations.

Health standards are high in the cities. Malaria is only a concern in certain areas and western Malaysia is one of the few places in the world that does not host the threat of rabies.

Food hygiene standards are high, but as always be very discerning if you decide to risk eating from street stalls. Check the food is being cooked fresh and not just reheated.

MALDIVES ★★★★

Flight time: 10-12 hours
Best time to visit: October-March

The only concern I would have about taking a child to the Maldives is what would happen if they had an accident on one of the outlying islands. It is unlikely, but I have experienced the panic of having to rush to a hospital with a bleeding baby, and my blood freezes at the thought of having to wait for a seaplane or a boat to take you to a hospital that is hours away.

Aside from this unlikely event, a trip to the Maldives is total escapism. Good hotels on uninhabited islands offer white sands, clear waters and total relaxation.

The food standards vary between resorts, and meals are often repetitive. Bear this in mind if booking an all-inclusive with fussy children. You may not have much choice, but you are often better going all-inclusive yourselves and opting for pay-as-you-go with the children. Pack cereals, instant noodles and long-life bread for crisp sandwiches, then supplement this with chips, fresh fish, rice and fresh fruit when you arrive.

The water sports are better on some islands than others, which is worth considering. Older children could learn to water-ski or windsurf while you bury your nose in a book, happy that they are being entertained. The snorkelling and diving off the Maldives is also good.

NEPAL ★★★

Flight time: 10-12 hours
Best time to visit: October-March

Nepal's treks are becoming well trodden. Parents with a love of the mountains, and who know what to expect, may opt for a gentler trek and travel in Nepal with confidence.

Even for first-timers there should be few problems, as the guides will help you cater for your children's needs and even offer to carry them if they tire. But a trek is a trek, with all its proverbial connotations, and is likely to be easier with either small children who are easily carried and happy to be wherever you are, or older, stronger children who can adapt to long walks and cold nights without being miserable. For a five- or six-year-old, the beautiful surroundings may not balance out the hard work of a trek. Therefore, if you want to witness the stunning scenery of the Himalayas with a young family, you are probably better to book a tour in an air-conditioned vehicle, especially between May and September.

Nepal is one of the most dangerous countries of the world to give birth in and in remote destinations good health care is limited and cannot be trusted. Emergency first aid followed by a quick return to the nearest big city would be imperative in the case of an accident. Severe diarrhoeal illnesses are common, so be careful what you eat – particularly in Katmandu.

PHILLIPINES ★

Flight time: 15-18 hours
Best time to visit: November-February

Manila would be tough to tackle with accompanying children because it is a tough city. The poverty of the country is reflected in the capital, where high crime rates mean armed guards are a common feature.

Outside the cities, the country is poor but beautiful. The beaches are as idyllic as you will find and the hotels are built to satisfy American standards. Tourism is underdeveloped relative to other regions of South-East Asia, possibly due to the image of corruption and poverty and the presence of American military bases.

Booking a package in one of the pleasant island resorts or touring with a group would ensure that you enjoyed your family trip. It is easy to be overwhelmed if you arrive in the bustle of Manila without preplanning where to go. The people are genuinely friendly with a warm, genuine attitude to Westerners, but there is a predatory side to the capital and tourist kidnappings are a threat. Spend one or two days in Manila and then get out into the remote, but beautiful, provinces.

Malaria has been eradicated in all but remote areas, however there is still a significant risk of respiratory or diarrhoeal illness.

SINGAPORE ★★★★★

Flight time: 12-15 hours
Best time to visit: Year round

Singapore is as safe as it gets. There are severe punishments for relatively minor crimes, including the sale of chewing gum and for not flushing the toilet, but this – and perhaps the fact that Singapore is so small and easily managed – make it a very easy destination to enjoy without a hint of a worry or risk to your family.

The city doesn't really have an oriental feel, and when standing looking down Orchard Road you could be excused for comparing it to any other Western city. Even many of the department stores sell and advertise the same brands as the shops in London and New York.

The best place to stay in Singapore with a family, especially if staying for more than a couple of days, is Sentosa Island. It is linked with Singapore by causeway and cable car and is serviced by ferry. The island is one big fun-packed resort, with many attractions and activities such as theme parks and water parks. The hotels are excellent and there are good, albeit manmade, beaches to relax on. It may not be an adult ideal but the children will really enjoy the time spent there. It is then easy to pop into Singapore for shopping or a barbecue at Raffles. Even at night you needn't worry about being out with your family.

SRI LANKA ★★★★

Flight time: 11-13 hours
Best time to visit: October-March

If it weren't for the civil war, which is a very real threat in Colombo and the north of the island, Sri Lanka would be top on the list of tourist destinations. Sadly, terrorism is a threat and has, on occasion, been targeted specifically towards tourists although the usual targets are politicians. Even children can be involved and persuaded to become suicide bombs, often by their own families. The war has had a serious impact on tourism, which has resulted in many hotels becoming run down. However, the infrastructure is still in place and you can tour the country in your own private car very cheaply.

There are magnificent caves, an elephant orphanage and beautiful windswept beaches for the family to enjoy. The elephant orphanage is a joy. Children are invited to ride on the elephants and watch the babies being fed from giant bottles. Mid-morning the whole herd is guided down to bathe in a huge river nearby. It is a beautiful sight; there is a pathetic looking three-legged elephant who lost a leg on a land mine and who limps along at the back of the herd, but he is well-looked after and happy.

The beaches are stunning and even around the more popular hotels there is masses of room in which to spread out. The beach sellers call over to attract your attention and haggle good humouredly.

Sri Lanka offers some of the best holiday deals available long-haul and, because of the worries in Columbo, bargains are constantly available. The hotels in the packages are of a very high standard and generally uncrowded, and the local people are wonderfully friendly. Tours are relatively expensive because of the distances involved, but for a family to travel comfortably in a private car it is an affordable deal. If you can get your hotel reception to arrange a driver for you for the day this will probably be cheaper.

Health care is accessible and reasonable. Malaria is not of the resistant strain.

THAILAND ★★★★

Flight time: 12-15 hours
Best time to visit: October-March

Thailand is a fascinating country, but when you first arrive in the heat, traffic and smog of Bangkok, it is easy to be disenchanted. It will probably take you a good few days to acclimatise and begin to relax and enjoy this city heaving with humanity. The traffic and noise never stops, and if you look out of your hotel at 4.30 a.m. you will still witness a traffic jam as dense as those in London's rush hour.

Many of the hotels in Thailand, and particularly Bangkok, are among the best in the world. They are luxurious, if not opulent, with abundant staff, orchids for your pillow and excellent food, yet they are cheaper per night than an English three-star hotel.

Shopping and eating out are fun for the whole family. The Thai people are friendly and gentle, but they drive a hard bargain, and even in the grocery stores you will need to barter. Build up your children's confidence and let them barter for you. It is a wearying process that you will soon tire of, but children seem to treat it as a huge game and thoroughly enjoy it.

The beaches are among the best in the world, and most are safe for children. Nice islands to visit are Koh Samui and Koh Chang, while Phuket is busier, but enjoyable and very popular. Out in the provinces tourists are encouraged to enjoy contact with elephants and the local wildlife, which is wonderful for children.

Don't buy any beachwear before you go. You will get better-quality cotton goods in Thailand at cheaper prices for the entire family. Also good value are tapes and fake watches.

Couples are seeking out the less-developed resorts and islands, which are harder to reach but well worth the trip for their remote, tropical appeal.

The food in the hotels is excellent, and standards of hygiene are high – but don't be tempted to feed your family from a street stall however good the food looks and smells. The locals will have higher levels of resistance to the stomach bugs that could easily ruin your holiday.

The cooler season in Thailand is from November to March, which is a much better time to visit with children. It is also outside the monsoon season when fevers are more common.

The sex districts in Bangkok around Patpong are safe during the day and some of the city's best market shopping is to be found in the surrounding streets. At night it is best avoided with your family as it is somehow more seedy, hostile and serious than Amsterdam. You will find yourself answering very awkward questions.

If you don't have much time it is better to bypass Bangkok altogether, unless you simply want to visit the Grand Palace, which is stunning. If you are there for one or two nights you won't have time to get your bearings, and having two centres will bump up the cost of your holiday for little extra enjoyment. It would be better to head straight for one of the beaches or islands on arrival. Put Pattaya at the bottom of your list, as it is dominated by the sex industry, which has followed the single male tourists in search of prostitutes of both sexes and all ages.

In many of the busy resorts, drugs are also a problem and friends have told me about having seen used needles on beaches. Be vigilant, and if your hotel is seedy, upgrade, even if you have to pay for it out of your own pocket. It won't cost a fortune and it isn't worth the hassle of waiting for your tour rep to get the authority. On balance it is very unlikely that you will find yourself needing to upgrade, as most of the tourist hotels sold in packages are first class.

VIETNAM

Vietnam is one of the more difficult South-East Asian countries to travel in with a family. Transport is unreliable and a lot of the tourist industry is built on the ravages of war. The tunnels the Viet Cong used are still in existence and visited on tourist trips, as is the Vietnamese war museum, although this is probably unsuitable for even older children.

The bustle of the cities and excellent inexpensive hotels make the destination an evocative and achievable destination with a family, but without a tour group/guide going can get tough and hot.

North Asia

CHINA ★★★

Flight time: 12-15 hours
Best time to visit: April-June

China is a fantastic place to visit. Most of China is now open to tourists and you can be assured of safe, free conduct in this fascinating country. Organised tours of China are available in abundance, but even with a family in tow you could safely explore alone.

The only major problem travelling independently is the language barrier, and the fact that when you arrive in China you will find yourself totally illiterate – even train station names will be unreadable. Very few people in China speak English, so if you do intend to do it alone you must at least take a phrase book and a list of common Chinese characters for, for example, the toilet.

It is unlikely that you will see as much if you don't go with a group, and journeying will be tiring – but the cost savings will be enormous. Many tourist activities and shops are run by the government and are very expensive. A tour from Beijing to the Great Wall of China is likely to cost more than £50; if you travel alone it is more likely to cost £5. This obviously makes a huge difference for a family of four.

If travelling to Beijing with children, the Holiday Inn hotel outside the centre is a very good choice. It has all the facilities you will need as it has a complex for Western expatriates within its boundaries which provides everything to service them, including a wide choice of good restaurants, a well-stocked pharmacy and an excellent supermarket that sells everything from fresh milk to Pampers (although the Chinese-branded nappies are much cheaper and very good). There is also a constant stream of courtesy buses into the centre.

The main problem in China is the water, and the fairly unhygienic conditions in many of the restaurants. Be careful. Even the water put in your hotel room and labelled as drinking water should not be used as such. Buy bottled water and always check the seal. The food in many of the hotels and restaurants on the tourist trail is relatively safe, but again be sensible with what you choose from the menu, and if you want to be adventurous be prepared for the worst. Many menus include mice, wasps, rats, dogs, cats, and sadly even tiger. Diarrhoeal illnesses are very common and be aware that you can catch serious food poisoning from plain boiled rice that has been sitting around for twenty-four hours at room temperature. It can harbour a bacteria that is well recognised in the UK and any Health and Safety officer will tell you that Chinese restaurants in the UK are major offenders of this type of tummy bug. If the rice doesn't taste or smell fresh, don't eat it.

A visit to a Chinese acrobatic show is a must and a pleasure for the whole family. A Chinese opera may be an acquired taste but the screeching will certainly drown out any children who don't like it. The zoos are a little sad, as the animals are kept in fairly poor conditions.

There are over one billion Chinese people and many of their heritage sites are crowded and very tiring to visit. Pace yourself and be very careful about the time of year you choose to go. On the Great Wall the temperatures may vary from -20 to $+50°C$. It is a challenging climb if you wish to walk beyond the crowds, but certainly worth the effort. The Forbidden City is a maze with its thousands of steps, and taking a pushchair around is exhausting, even in the spring, so trying to do it when temperatures are at $50°C$ would be impossible. But, unless the heat is prohibitive, all China's principal sites are well worth the effort.

Hong Kong

The buzz of Hong Kong is wonderful, but to a child it is basically shopping and restaurants. However, seeing how the fishermen and their families live on the water in the harbour is an imaginative experience. From Hong Kong you can go to China to visit the local schools. The night food markets are wonderful and the safety of the city is relaxing.

JAPAN ★★★★

Flight time: 12-15 hours
Best time to visit: April-June

There are no real tourist beach resorts in Japan – the hot-spring resorts are their alternative for a relaxing break. There is a Tokyo Disney though, which is identical in every respect to those in the US and France, except for the fact that everything is in Japanese.

Japan is as safe as it gets. Even in Tokyo, if you lose a purse or leave a camera on a train there is a very good chance you will get it back. If you want to visit Japan with children there is absolutely no need to join a tour. There are few families that could afford the price ticket for four on a guided tour around Japan, but if you go alone you could spend less than you might in the Caribbean or Europe.

Even language is no longer a barrier. The streets are crammed with Japanese youngsters anxious to practise their English and to help a disorientated family. The main cities now have underground maps, train stations and even street names written in English, so you should be able to tackle the transport system comfortably. There is no need to fear anything other than driving on the roads, which are confusing, dangerous and fraught with congested traffic.

Japan is also spotlessly clean. The health and hygiene standards are among the highest in the world. You need have no fear of visiting a hospital in Japan; you would be among some of the safest hands in the world.

As for the food, don't worry. My eldest son is so fussy he will only eat certain brands of frozen sweetcorn, yet he adores Japanese food. But you do need to choose carefully. The best dishes for children are tempura, sweet chicken skewers called yakitori, rice, and ramen or udon noodles. Japan also has McDonalds and other fast-food restaurants everywhere. Look out for a big red lantern hanging outside the restaurant, which indicates that the restaurant is inexpensive.

Western-style hotel accommodation can be horribly expensive but there are many 'Ryokan', or Japanese inns, in which a family room is very reasonable. The etiquette is rather complicated, but don't be put off. It is an adventure and a fantastic experience for all of you. Follow your children's uninhibited lead; they will doubtless adapt to your hosts' instruction with enthusiasm. Because Japan is so safe and honest you need never fear arriving off a train and heading for tourist and hotel information to book your accommodation. They will offer you a range of Ryokan, whose hosts will be well accustomed to the clumsiness of Western tourists.

Staying in a Ryokan is an experience in itself. You will be shown to your room where you will wonder where you are going to sleep, as the beds are generally made up each night and put away each morning. You must take off your shoes when you enter the Ryokan. Your host will offer you slippers which you may wear everywhere except in the toilet area. Inside the toilet area you must put on a different set of slippers that are only used inside this area. It takes some getting used to but you will be helped and your host will tolerate your oafish behaviour with resolve and a slight smile.

Train travel is the best way to get around Japan, but it is very expensive unless you get a rail pass which you must buy <u>before</u> you arrive. The cost of the rail pass for a fortnight is approximately the same as one return journey between Tokyo and Osaka. It even covers travel on the bullet train (Shinkensen), the fastest train in the world. It runs on time, down to the second, and glides through Japan with breathtaking efficiency.

For children and adults the best sites in Japan are in Kyoto. The Golden Palace is beautiful and the gardens and shrines of Japan feature ponds full of massive Koi carp that are fascinating for children. In nearby Nara, the deer parks and Great Buddha of Nara are also worth a trip with the family.

In Osaka, the castle and surrounding park are crowded with children on school trips. The views from the top floor of the castle are amazing. The Sony Tower and the Osaka World Trade Centre are interesting, as are the streets downtown, which are alive and a mass of neon until late into the evening, yet still completely safe.

The humidity in July and August is stifling. Spring is the best time to go. Cherry-blossom season is a time for celebration and picnicking under the trees.

There are also volcanic and hot spring areas which are great fun, if not a little touristy. Mount Fuji can be seen from the bullet train and the aeroplane on descent into Tokyo if you are lucky, but the Japanese say that 'She, (Mount Fuji) is very shy.' I have been to the foot of the great mountain four times, but have never seen her because she has always been shrouded in thick cloud.

Japan is becoming more and more Westernised, but thankfully old traditions, respect for others, and family values are very much intact.

KAZAKHSTAN

Kazakhstan has little to offer the family on holiday.

MONGOLIA

Mongolia has little to offer the family on holiday.

NORTH KOREA

Tourism is banned by the government in North Korea, but you can travel from South Korea to the border, where you can see the North Korean guns aimed disconcertingly at its neighbour.

SOUTH KOREA ★★★★

Flight time: 12-14 hours
Best time to visit: March-May

Like Japan, South Korea is spotlessly clean. This attracts many Japanese visitors who travel for the golf, nightlife and excellent shopping in Seoul. There are huge, safe, children's theme parks outside the capital, which make it attractive for families, and in the southern city of Pusan, which is easily reached by ferry from Japan, there are good beaches and shopping. Crime rates are low, but the country is constantly under the threat of aggression from the North, which is perhaps why South Korea has remained off the list of many Western tourists, although any Korean will tell you that their country is clean, beautiful and safe for a family to travel in independently.

TAIWAN ★★

Flight time: 14-16 hours
Best time to visit: March-May

Health facilities are among the best in the world, but manufacturing, the rise in sex tourism and the dense population on the coast makes the island feel crowded, sprawling and slightly grimy. The cities have grown quickly, without any planning or any regard for the environment, which has attracted industry but repelled tourists. There has been some effort to upgrade hotels and tourist facilities but Taiwan still attracts more businessmen and sex tourists than families on holiday.

In central Taiwan there is the opportunity to see quiet serenity, lakes, mountains and temples.

Avoid the monsoon season between July and September.

Western Asia

It would take a more adventurous spirit than mine to tackle a war zone with a precious young family in tow. There are very civilised regions of western Asia, but there are also a number of very dangerous ones.

AFGHANISTAN

Terrorism, political unrest, poor sanitation and extremes of temperature, from -50 to $+50°C$ are what to expect and prepare for.

ARMENIA

Armenia is at war with neighbouring Azerbaijan and, even accepting this fact, there is little to attract a family with young children.

AZERBAIJAN

A long tradition of oil exploitation, the simmering war with Armenia and strong anti-Western feeling have kept all but a few business visitors away.

BAHRAIN ★★★

Flight time: 7-8 hours
Best time to visit: December-March

Tourism is important to Bahrain, particularly as its oil reserves are now almost depleted. Between December and March is the best time of year to visit, when the weather is pleasantly warm. In the summer months the temperatures are uncomfortably high for even the hardiest adult. As a stop over or as a short break in a Western-standard hotel with air-conditioning, the liberal lifestyle of the main island could be enjoyed by families who were respectful of the heat and intense sun, but there is basically just sea, sand and more sand to entertain you all.

IRAN

The reasons you may want to visit Iran may not be of particular interest to your children. Bazaars, mosques and history are important to expand a child's mind, but they will also love to relax with you in-between times. Iran is not a place to go to relax right now.

IRAQ

Iraq is effectively closed to Western tourists.

ISRAEL ★

Flight time: 5-6 hours
Best time to visit: March-April

Sadly, the threat of terrorist attacks is very current and very real. Suicide bombings have become an increasing problem that Israelis have to live with. If you accept that the odds of being caught in a terrorist attack are statistically very low and are not a worrier, Israel is fascinating. Even for those who have no religious beliefs, it will leave you thinking deeply. You can visit the river Jordan where Jesus was baptised, see the stone where Jesus was sitting when he performed the miracle of the loaves and the fishes, then travel to Nazareth to visit a church built on the site where Mary was visited by the Angel Gabriel.

The country is under constant threat from its neighbours, which is evident from the truck loads of eighteen-year-old boys and girls in army uniforms with guns over their shoulders. Every Israeli is trained to protect their country.

There is so much to see and do. Health care is good and health standards are high. The road system is good, so hiring a car and driving east of Jerusalem to the Dead Sea and/or south to the Red Sea is easily feasible.

As in many countries of the world, keep a keen eye on your blond children, boys and girls. There are some stories to be heard.

JORDAN ★★★

Flight time: 5-6 hours
Best time to visit: March-April

Jordan attracts as many tourists as Israel. Like Israel, it borders the Red Sea and offers fine beaches, water sports and some of the best sub aqua diving in the world – without the political unrest. Travel agents describe the sightseeing as superb. One of the most spectacular sites is the ancient rose-red city of Petra carved into the mountains. Or follow in the footsteps of Lawrence of Arabia and visit the Wadi Rum, where the famous film was shot.

The tourist infrastructure is limited, so it may be better to join an organised tour. Travelling with children can be gruelling in the heat.

KUWAIT

Postwar Kuwait has little to offer the family on holiday.

KYRGYZSTAN

Kyrgyzstan has little to offer the family on holiday.

LEBANON ★★

Flight time: 6-7 hours
Best time to visit: April-May

In the past, Lebanon was known as the playground of the Middle East. Fine beaches, historical sights, superb cuisine and spectacular sightseeing attracted millions of tourists every year. The Civil War and the corresponding kidnapping of tourists in the seventies made Beirut and Lebanon a no-go area for Western tourists. However, Lebanon is beginning to restablish itself as an exciting tourist destination, though the threat of terrorism still exists. Cruise ships are beginning to stop in Beirut again, which is encouraging.

OMAN ★★★

Flight time: 7-8 hours
Best time to visit: January-March

The home of the Arabian Nights and alleged home of Sinbad the Sailor. Take the books with you and stimulate your children's imaginations.

Oman offers great beaches, a spotlessly clean environment, and luxury hotels at affordable prices. Combine this with great weather and a rich cultural heritage for a good family holiday destination with a difference, although it will be too hot at the height of summer.

PAKISTAN

The rich cultural heritage and unspoilt beauty is not enough on balance with the high levels of crime – including murder and rapes – poor health standards and a high risk of fatal diarrhoeal infections.

QATAR ★

Flight time: 7-8 hours
Best time to visit: March-April

Qatar is all desert and, although there are some good beaches, the temperatures in the summer are scorching.

SAUDI ARABIA

General suitability for non-Muslim families ★

Flight time: 7-8 hours
Best time to visit: March-April

Saudi Arabia does not encourage Western, non-Muslim tourists.

SYRIA ★

Flight time: 6-7 hours
Best time to visit: March-April

Historical Damascus may be worth a trip, but hospitals lack modern equipment and services.

TAJIKISTAN

There is nothing to offer the family on holiday.

TURKEY ★★★

Flight time: 5 hours
Best time to visit: April-June

Turkey is cheap, its standards of accommodation in line with Greece and the cheaper Spanish resorts. However, the summer in Turkey is inescapably hot. The best beaches are in the south and there aren't many. Some of the popular, busy resorts either have no beach (Bodrum), or man-made ones with imported sand (Marmaris). Most offer water sports and boat trips, many of which are well worth doing as the sea is clear and turquoise with good, safe snorkelling.

Food standards are variable and care is needed when feeding children both in the hotel and the restaurants. Upset tummies are common and serious diseases such as hepatitis A are a concern.

Turkey is basically a hot beach or poolside holiday, but there is a lot of history there if you're prepared to cover the distances, including the Temple of Artemis, one of the Seven Ancient Wonders of the World, which is near the historical site of Ephesus. Istanbul is a fascinating, sprawling city, but make sure you take a tourist guide.

TURKMENISTAN ★

Flight time: 6-7 hours
Best time to visit: March-April

There is the potential for tourist appeal. It is one of the more politically stable countries of the region with warm, dry springs and a border on the Caspian Sea. At present it may not be the most diverse or interesting destination, but it does enjoy relatively low crime rates, and many of the historical monuments are being restored.

Most of the country is desert and temperatures soar in the summer. Health care and hygiene standards are low. Highly polluted water is a major health hazard.

UNITED ARAB EMIRATES ★★★★

Flight time: 7-8 hours
Best time to visit: December-February

For year-round sun, deluxe hotels and first-class service the UAE is becoming an increasingly popular choice. Dubai is the first stop and probably the best choice for most tourists who are attracted by fantastic beaches, duty-free shopping, watersports, good sightseeing, a fascinating culture and hotels which really are exceptional.

All the buildings in the UAE have a short life span and are constantly being knocked down. As a result there is a succession of brand-new hotels in which everything is sparkling, modern and luxurious in the extreme.

The gold souks in the main town are interesting, but not as crammed with bargains as they once were.

There is a safe, calm, crime-free atmosphere in the country, the health care is good, and hygiene levels are generally very high. The only real enemy you will face when you visit with children is the intense heat.

YEMEN

Threats of terrorism and tourist-family kidnappings would reasonably deter all but the most determined and experienced traveller.

Europe

Western Europe

ALBANIA

Sadly, now is not the right point in history to visit Albania, despite its scenic beauty.

ANDORRA ★★★★

Flight time: 2-3 hours
Best time to visit: May-June

Twelve million tourists flock to Andorra every year, mainly from France and Spain, for duty-free shopping, and in the winter 500,000 skiers descend. In a tiny country, 180 square miles in area and with a population of just 58,000, the impact of the tourist is in evidence everywhere.

There is a slightly tacky feel to the duty-free shopping areas on each border and in the main town of Andorra, although this won't bother the children who are often attracted by garish signs and neon banners.

Good, reasonably priced skiing in the winter and hiking in the summer are both enjoyable pursuits with older children. The negatives are that in the summer the ski runs blight the beautiful Pyrenean landscape and the mass of day-glo orange adverts stating the prices of duty-free booze everywhere look unpleasant.

Another consideration if driving to or through Andorra with kids is that the roads often become heavily congested in peak season. Roads in the main town of Andorra La Vella and the border shopping areas may be at a standstill. The open mountain roads need concentration.

On the other hand, there are plenty of reasons to visit Andorra. You and your children should be as safe as you would be at home. Interesting bird-life, wildlife and unique mountain flowers are fun to discover, with the added advantage that the altitude ensures that the weather in the spring and summer is relatively mild, so walking is a pleasure and not a hot toil.

AUSTRIA ★★★★★

Flight time: 2-3 hours
Best time to visit: May-August

Austria is beautiful and serene. In the summer the places to head for are the scenic Tyrol and the Austrian lakes. You are more likely to find good-value winter skiing in Innsbruck, but in the summer Salzburg is the better destination. Salzburg is the birthplace of Mozart and home to the internationally famous summer music festival. It is also where the famous children's favourite *The Sound of Music* was filmed. You can tour and visit many of the sites in the film, such as the gazebo, the baron's house next to the lake, and the fountain. Outside Salzburg, around the lakes, you can enjoy the quiet, tranquil beauty in the surrounding mountains or, alternatively, try water sports and sunbathing.

The roads are good, although a little windy if you have to contend with children who get car sick. If you take your own car you will be able to search out better hotels for your budget than in the main towns at the lakesides.

There is an unhurried feel about Austria, and it is very much somewhere you can clean your lungs and relax. Health care is good and crime rates are low. Hotel prices are reasonable, especially when compared to neighbouring Germany and Switzerland. Even eating out is affordable, thus sampling the relaxed Austrian city life does not come with too high a price tag.

Furthermore, children are made to feel much more welcome here than they are in the UK and the US. We seem to try and steer our families out of good restaurants and into raucous 'family restaurants', whereas in Austria this is not so. Even fine restaurants and theatres in Vienna treat children as if they were a mini person, offering them drinks and trying to please them as well as their parents.

Vienna is a sophisticated city of dancing horses, palaces and interesting museums. The natural history museum is an excellent place for families to spend a rainy day.

If you are in Vienna for a few days and feeling adventurous, Prague and Budapest are within reasonable distance by train. A good way of visiting all three cities and saving a night in a hotel would be to travel from Vienna to Prague on the early train. Spend the day in Prague then travel on the overnight sleeper to Budapest. Spend the day in Budapest then back to Vienna. It will be an adventure which is interesting, enjoyable and affordable.

The disadvantages when travelling with young children in Austria are that the dry cold in the winter can reach deceptively low temperatures. Also, as we have seen for the first time recently, although there is excellent skiing in the winter, it can be treacherous if snow falls too long and too deep.

BELGIUM ★★★★★

Flight time: 1 hour
Best time to visit: May-August

Bruges is an easy hop from England and a city of canals, swans, horse-drawn carriages and chocolate shops. A pleasant stop or short-break destination to relax as a family.

Historic cities in the north and pretty countryside in the south are Belgium's main attractions. Good roads and a hospitable, tolerant population make Belgium an enjoyable part in the route of a European driving holiday.

Unreliable weather and cool summers, with a higher average rainfall in July than that in the UK, mean that booking a fortnight's holiday could be a gamble for those wanting to escape the British weather. Hotel prices are similar to those in the UK.

CYPRUS ★★★★★

Flight time: 5 hours
Best time to visit: April-June

Cyprus was aggressively divided when Turkey invaded in 1974. It remains under Turkish control in the north and Greek control in the south. The Greek Cypriots, who were forced to flee, claim that most of the country's best beaches are in northern Cyprus, where tourism is growing, but it is to the south that most overseas arrivals are bound.

The strangest thing about Cyprus is that it is promoted in all the winter sun brochures, yet temperatures in January and February can average only 5°C. Good hotels cost next to nothing after Christmas, but many of the resorts have an out-of-season Blackpool feel about them and are more suitable for the retired than the family. In contrast, the summer temperatures can reach the high thirties. Again, not ideal for children without air-conditioning and other cooling comforts.

Fifty per cent of Cyprus's tourists are British, so if you want British food, newspapers or English-speaking company then you won't be disappointed. The friendly Cypriots welcome the British with refreshing hospitality. With their own strong, family culture, they always seem to be willing to help make your family holiday more comfortable and relaxing.

Egypt is easily accessible if you take a mini cruise from one of the ports in southern Cyprus. The cruises are good value and your children will be able to spend the day at the pyramids without having to tackle the grime and possible dangers of Cairo.

The hotel standards in Cyprus are generally good. There are a number of deluxe tourist-class hotels and those with three stars are generally run with care by local families. Everything in between should be acceptable as long as you make your choice as carefully as you would in any other tourist resort.

Health care is good and crime rates are low.

DENMARK ★★★★

Flight time: 1 hour
Best time to visit: July-August

Legoland and Hans Christian Andersen's Copenhagen may be the main destinations for a family trip, but Denmark offers much more for the family. Summertime is the best time to visit, as winter in Denmark is cold and grey and the days are short.

There is a great choice of affordable cottage accommodation in the Danish countryside which can be booked in combination with a ferry crossing at prices within the budget of most families. Cheaper still would be the well-kept, excellently situated campsites. There are also plenty of touring inns, hotels and manor houses which have opened up as first-class hotels. Self-contained holiday centres in the Centre Parcs style are equipped with facilities such as indoor swimming pools and children's playgrounds – all the things that make a childhood paradise and fabulous for families.

Denmark is perfect for touring in your own car. The country's small size means that anywhere is within a day's journey. The beaches are good, English is widely spoken and health-service standards are high. Getting around locally is easy on a bicycle as Denmark is very flat.

You can book excellent deals with Scandinavian Seaways and get free child places for more than one child if you book early enough.

FINLAND ★★★★★

Flight time: 2-3 hours
Best time to visit: July-August

An increasingly popular reason to visit Finland is to see Santa at Christmas time. It is apparently in line with a trip to Disneyland on the scale of major events in a child's life. When you ask anyone who has been there with their children what it was like, they become a little hazy and a warm glow comes over them as they recall the look on their children's faces. It is best to book one of the special one- or two-day trips, as these are very good value and smoothly run. The flight time is approximately four hours to the Arctic circle, where you will be greeted and taken by coach, reindeer and then sleigh to a wooden village where Santa is housed in a post office surrounded by the thousands and thousands of letters he receives each year. Every child gets a special present from Santa, often a reindeer bell.

It can be bitterly cold, so to ensure a perfect day you should travel prepared. The best age to take most children is between six and seven years old. They are young enough to still believe, yet old enough to remember the trip for their lifetime.

FRANCE ★★★★★

Flight time: 2 hours
Best time to visit: June-September

France is perfect for family holidays. It is just a hop away across the Channel and there are endless choices of the types of holiday on offer. Touring France by car is the ultimate freedom holiday and the options for accommodation en route are endless, ranging from excellent camping facilities to luxury château hotels. All are flexible and welcoming. Combine a few nights of fun camping with the children as priority, then a few nights of sophistication for yourselves.

Every region of France has something fascinating to explore. In many ways the north-west of France and its resorts are similar to those on the south coast of England. Even the architecture is familiar. So for those who enjoy Brighton or Bournemouth, why not pay a few extra pounds for the ferry fare and try Deauville, near Le Havre, famous for its beaches, lovely harbour, luxurious hotels, casino and racetrack.

Disneyland Paris is predictably fun, and the pleasure it gives the children is worth the trip, especially if you are on a driving holiday. A one- or two-day stop off will be an enjoyable thrill for the little ones. Disneyland is well-signposted from the motorway system, but is more difficult to find from the centre of Paris. However, once you get on to the periphery of the city and out of the dense traffic it becomes easy to follow the right direction. A regular, direct shuttle service runs to the park from the airports and, from the city centre, the RER has a direct service that takes approximately thirty-five minutes. All the hotels in the park are good and, as you would expect, the more you pay, the higher the standard of rooms, the better the facilities and the closer you are to the parks. However, even the hotels further out have good inter-connecting transport. (See Chapter 2 for more information about Disneyland Paris.)

Paris holds many delights for every member of the family. You can ascend most things in Paris, including the Eiffel Tower, the Arc de Triomphe and Notre Dame. While the views of Paris from the Eiffel Tower are magnificent, looking down over the city from the steps of the Sacré-Coeur is certainly another memorable vista. A short cruise along the Seine is a lazy pleasure but don't think you've got the cheap seats if you skip lunch; it is not for children's tastes.

The Louvre is fascinating for adults and interesting for older children, but the museum is huge and a trek around it with younger ones may be a test of endurance for you all.

The best way of getting around Paris with a family and seeing most of the sights is by car. If you are on a driving holiday anyway don't be put off by tales of traffic jams and crazy drivers. But if you want to avoid it all, go in at night and see the wonders of Paris when fully illuminated. This is a stunning way of seeing the city and it is much easier to find your way around when it is quieter. Even if you do get stuck in long queues, though, you can still take in the flavours and pace of one of the world's most fantastic cities.

The Palace of Versailles is a short distance outside the centre and worth a visit. The grounds are beautiful and the children can be kept entertained with stories from its macabre history, while you enjoy its spectacular architecture.

Most other cities in France are worth visiting if you are driving through. The French countryside in the summertime is gorgeous. Fields full of sunflowers and sweetcorn can be found up and down the country, while in the south you will pass vineyards and cherry orchards between quaint villages and scattered farm houses. The

French love their food, and local markets are a delight, as are the bakeries and patisseries.

In the south you will find the cosmopolitan style that people the world over have tried to mimic – invariably without success. It comes with a price tag, but there are excellent campsites and not-too-extortionate villas for rent just outside Nice and Monte Carlo. St Tropez is the place to people watch and spot the yacht. It is a much smaller resort than its other famous neighbours, but with that it has managed to retain a little more charm. Marseille is basically a port and host to many of France's racist clashes and criminals, with little to attract the family.

In the summer many campsites next to lakes have water sports on offer, which are a far less-expensive alternative to the south and the sea.

The winter skiing in France is also excellent but expensive. It is best to avoid French skiing holidays, because the slopes are so crowded.

If you do need to see a doctor or visit a hospital it will be costly, and so check out insurance before you go. Otherwise an E111 form is essential. Also take a phrase book – the French tend to be as reluctant to learn English as we are to learn French, and although there are more English-speaking Frenchmen than vice versa, without a word of the language you may struggle outside the cities or in an emergency.

GERMANY ★★★★

Flight time: 2 hours
Best time to visit: June-September

The reason why we see so many Germans abroad around the Mediterranean is because, like us, their northern beaches are freezing for most of the year and they want a glimpse of sand and sunshine, too. So if you want beaches, Germany is not the best place to head for in Europe. Germany is a good alternative destination for a driving holiday, though, as the roadways are efficient and the autobahns (motorways) are toll free.

Germany has a number of holiday centres, such as Centre Parcs, which are always ideal for children, while the Bavarian Alps and the Black Forest are beautiful and have an aura of rich folklore amid fairytale castles.

Sensibly, you don't have to pay train fares or entrance fees in many areas for children until they are three years old. The choice of affordable accommodation along the routes is good and you will find all the services, comforts and health care you have at home.

GREECE

General suitability for travelling with children:
Spring and late summer ★★★★★
Peak summer ★★★★

Flight time: 5 hours
Best time to visit: April-June

Greece offers many choices of holiday destinations. There is the mainland and Athens with its history, and the islands, which offer a total contrast between remote subsistence, with a small population and few visitors, to bigger islands where the whole economy is centred around the tourist industry. Corfu, Crete, Rhodes and Kos are the most popular, and with that you can expect a mass of hotels, restaurants and nightclubs. Many of the resorts are clusters of high-rises lacking air-conditioning and adequate balconies. The popular beaches are crowded and the hotel pools are rarely heated. On the positive side, Greece is cheap to get to, hot, sunny and relatively nearby.

Although Greece is very cheap to travel to, you should budget for the fact that in many places, like Spain, eating out is expensive. Parents may be surprised to learn that a meal for four in popular tourist resorts on the Greek Islands can cost more than it would in a restaurant in the Caribbean, and certainly more than in America or Australia. All these considerations are important if you are not self-catering and are on a budget. The good points are that you are guaranteed beating sun and scorching heat, even into the night.

Greece is not the cleanest destination in Europe, and you are likely to see your restaurant chef with filthy overalls picking his teeth and smoking in a corner, so take care what you eat and drink.

If you plan to get to bed early and sleep, you really do need to check the situation of your hotel on a map of the town before booking. With children, try to book somewhere just outside the main shopping and disco area and, if possible, right next to a beach. The walk to the beach in the Greek summer is too long and too hot for children, especially when returning at the end of the day.

Health care is of a variable standard. A friend told me of an experience in Greece when a doctor, who was smoking at the time, stabbed a lance into her unanaesthetised groin and fished around in the wound while two nurses held her down. If you do need medical treatment, ask your hotel for an English-speaking doctor. If you can at least communicate, you have a good chance of getting decent care.

Greece is great if you are on a budget, but if you have a little more money to spend on your family holiday look at offers in the Caribbean before you decide, where the only real negative is the long flight. The safety, hygiene and general standards in Greece are lower than in many places, which is not ideal for children. Touring and sightseeing is hard in the intense heat and because the country is so arid the scenery is limited to olive groves, vineyards and craggy mountain sides. Although you may have had the time of your life in your teens dancing all through the hot summer nights, I would avoid the summer in Greece with a young family. Spring is a much better time to visit, when it is cooler and infinitely more pleasant.

HUNGARY ★★★

Flight time: 3 hours
Best time to visit: May-August

Budapest is a pleasant cosmopolitan city and I am certain a family who based themselves in the capital would find plenty of cultural and enjoyable ways of passing their time. Cruise on the Blue Danube, explore the museums or head out from the city towards Lake Balaton, a popular summer destination for many Eastern Europeans. Your money will go a long way.

ICELAND ★★★★

Flight time: 3 hours
Best time to visit: July-August

Nobody would travel to Iceland seeking sunshine, but if you want snow, ice, fjords, hot springs and spectacular glaciers, Reykjavik will be keen to accommodate you. You can then settle in and travel to the more adventurous regions at leisure. The wind in the winter is biting – even the babies' prams have real fur covers instead of woollen blankets – yet you will still be enticed into bathing in hot natural springs in the open air, as Paris and I were.

Civilised but expensive, Iceland offers an experience as far removed from the Med as is imaginable. The terrain of the country in winter is evocative of images of the moon.

IRELAND ★★★★★

Flight time: 1 hour
Best time to visit: July-August

The only factor going against Ireland as a tourist destination is the weather, as the climate is mild but wet. The average temperature even in summer is just 20°C. The beaches on the west coast are among the best in the world; sadly it is usually too cold to enjoy them.

Ireland is one of the ultimate driving-holiday destinations. Driving in Ireland is how it must have been in England twenty years ago, when people went out for a Sunday drive to relax. Unimaginable. The Irish countryside is scenic, unspoiled and uncongested, although if you head off the beaten track, the roads can be in poor condition.

The lifestyle is incredibly relaxed, and wherever you go to drink. Guinness no one looks at your children as if they should be in bed. The pubs are very welcoming and have wonderful musical sessions, but note that there can be plenty of swearing.

Throughout Ireland you can visit historic castles and parks, and explore the mountains, lakes and rivers on beautiful walks. The best places to visit are close to the coast, and you will find that most places of interest are well signposted because of the number of motorists.

Ireland is a perfect destination for taking a caravan, and you can even hire horse-driven Romany caravans and see the country travelling at a horse's pace. You can stay on farms where you will be welcomed and even the horse will be catered for. Cycling holidays are also a good option with older children.

Accommodation is available in every price bracket. You can stay in spotlessly clean hostels which have family rooms, stop at a farm house every night as part of a spontaneous motoring holiday, or book into a plenitude of bed and breakfasts, small hotels or five-star hotels in converted castles.

ITALY ★★★★★

Flight time: 2-3 hours
Best time to visit: June-July

Italy is Europe at its best and most sophisticated. It is atmospheric, historic and romantic.

The camping in Italy is excellent and definitely the cheapest way of seeing the country, as accommodation can be very expensive. Without air-conditioning, summer driving holidays are a very hot experience, and Italian drivers can be incredibly dangerous. You will regularly come out of a blind corner to find some hothead coming towards you on your side of the road. By contrast, the motorways are quiet and much safer, but the tolls are expensive.

The beach areas are built up and often unattractive, crime levels are high and holidaying in Italy with a family can be pricey. Sorrento is a very popular destination, so it is therefore a surprise that there are no beaches in the area. The better beaches are in Rimini and Lido di Jesolo, which is very close to Venice. Both offer decent budget hotels and good camping, but are very touristy.

Many of the hotels offer full board at incredible savings. The lunch and dinner menus are usually at least five courses and the food standards are very high. Swimming around Rimini is safe and the sea has been cleaned up, while an artificial rock surf breaker stretches for miles along the East coast to keep bathers safe in relatively shallow waters.

The cities of Italy are historic and amazing but can be very hot and tiring in the summer, especially for children. The cost of ice creams and drinks around Venice, Florence and Rome are extortionate.

LIECHTENSTEIN ★★★

Flight time: 2 hours
Best time to visit: June-September

Liechtenstein is a tiny country at the western tip of Austria, where you and your children would be as safe as you are at home. The weather in the spring and summer is mild, with beautiful alpine scenery, but there is little to attract a family for a long stay.

LITHUANIA ★★

Flight time: 5 hours
Best time to visit: July-August

Health and hygiene standards are OK, but there is little particularly to attract a family on holiday.

LUXEMBOURG ★★★★

Flight time: 2 hours
Best time to visit: June-September

Luxembourg is a small country of mountains, forests and castles. It is dominated by the city, which is pleasant but not very memorable. It is nice to pass through on a driving holiday, but differs little in terrain and atmosphere from its dominating, more charismatic neighbours.

MACEDONIA

War tensions make Macedonia less than ideal for a family holiday.

MALTA ★★★★

Flight time: 4-5 hours
Best time to visit: April-May

Malta is well developed as a tourist resort, but is geared towards the older visitor. Over half the tourists who visit Malta are British, and you can sometimes feel as if you are in Llandudno in a heat wave. It's not quite cosmopolitan or cultural, but comfortable, crowded and familiar. English is widely spoken and the health care is of Western standards.

There are few beaches and the summers are very hot for children, but Malta is friendly and relaxing. It is also excellent value for money.

Neighbouring Gozo is quieter and prettier but more difficult to get to and, like Malta, can be windy, especially early in the season.

MONACO ★★★

Flight time: 2-3 hours
Best time to visit: June-July

Monaco may be a little stuffy for a family trying to relax. It attracts the rich, who travel for the James Bond-style casinos to wear their diamonds. The hotels are glamorous, probably too glamorous for sticky fingers and grubby faces.

It is great for a short break or a stopover on a driving holiday through Europe, but in terms of making it the main destination for your annual family holiday, when you should be having fun together, you are more likely to enjoy other destinations in Europe.

NETHERLANDS ★★★★

Flight time: 1 hour
Best time to visit: July-August

The flat terrain of the Netherlands is ideal for family cycling holidays through tulip fields and windmills, although you won't find warm beaches.

For a city break, Amsterdam is certainly fascinating, with many aspects that make it appealing for a family. Anne Frank's house, museums and art galleries provide the culture. The restaurants and accommodation are good and affordable. You can hire a boat by the hour and tour the canals alone, or join an organised trip, then hire bikes for the afternoon and explore.

Amsterdam has a safe feel even at night, but whether or not you choose to wander around the red light district with your children is something only you can decide. A friend of mine walked through the area with her parents when she was about eleven years old and commented on it briefly when she returned to school. It certainly didn't do her any harm, but stay clear of the sex-shop windows with accompanying children, as they can have the power to shock even the most streetwise adult.

Outside Amsterdam, Holland is excellent for touring by car although the attractions vary little from those in England and they are smaller and fewer. Accommodation standards are high and reasonably priced.

NORWAY ★★★★★

Flight time: 1-2 hours
Best time to visit: July-August

Skiing and fjord trips on cruise ships are the main reason many tourists visit Norway. Its greatest attraction is its scenery, which is so dramatic even children may appreciate it.

The country is mountainous and some of the roads are challenging. You will need your concentration and if any of the children are likely to get car sick, make sure you travel prepared.

The history of the Vikings and the folklore are fascinating for children. In Oslo you can visit Viking ships, and in south-east Norway you can find the home of the world's largest troll.

There is plenty of affordable country-cottage accommodation, which can be booked in combination with a ferry crossing at prices that would be within the budget of most families. Good camping, holiday centres, touring hotels and resort hotels are also available.

Norway is also host to the midnight sun.

You can book excellent deals with Scandinavian Seaways and get free child places for more than one child if you book early enough.

PORTUGAL ★★★★★

Flight time: 2-3 hours
Best time to visit: May-June

Holidaying in southern Portugal is as easy as it gets. Even someone who had never been abroad in their lives and was travelling with ten children would be unlikely to get unstuck in the Algarve. The villas are perfect for families – spotlessly clean, pretty, built to high standards, well equipped and tastefully furnished, they are the real lazy man's choice. Be aware that there will be little adventure in the Algarve, as the real sense of Portugal has been gradually nudged out of the south, but if you just want to relax in the sunshine, then put the kids to bed and drink by the pool, the Algarve is perfect. If you opt for a hotel, you will generally find high standards and good value for money.

The other big bonus is that Portugal is a stone's throw from the UK. Easy, cheap and abundant flights from all UK airports make it accessible to everyone. The only slight negatives are that the sea is a little cold and rough, as it is the Atlantic, and there are also lots of large mosquitoes.

Portugal can get very hot in the summer, and from October onwards the evenings can get very cold. If visiting later in the year, you will find that there is little heating in the villas, so make sure you pack jumpers and warm clothing.

Be careful on the roads. The main road between Faro airport and the majority of the main tourist areas is the most dangerous road in Europe, and has the most fatalities. If you hire a car, get used to the controls and gears before you get on the main highway, then go steadily. Don't let anyone hassle you into making a decision – if you get lost, what does it matter? You'll soon be on track again, unless you try to veer off from the outside lane. Let someone map read, or stop the car to follow the route.

Lisbon is more of a challenge and harder to find your way around than many other European capitals, but it is interesting with fantastic seafood restaurants. It's great for a short break or stopover.

In Portugal, the public health system is free and, although standards lag behind those of the UK, they are adequate. Portugal still enjoys lower crime rates and cheaper prices than Spain and Italy, and has good shopping and excellent golf courses.

SAN MARINO

General suitability for a short family holiday ★★★

Flight time: 2-3 hours
Best time to visit: May-June

San Marino is a tiny republic in the centre of Italy. Perched on the top of a mountain, you can see for miles from its fortresses, which is surely how it has managed to maintain its independence. It is pretty and worth a day trip or an overnight stay, but there would not be enough to entertain a family for an entire holiday.

You must also beware of the precipitous drops down sheer mountainside.

SPAIN ★★★★★

Flight time: 2-3 hours
Best time to visit: May-June

The fact that British families flock to Spain to holiday in their millions is an indication of how easy it is to cope with family on holiday there. The tourist infrastructure is well developed and in place to cope with even the tiniest traveller. Many hotels offer babysitting at reasonable rates and many tour companies have children's reps on site who run children's clubs, games, discos and other attractions. However, you shouldn't rely on the clubs to entertain your children, as some are little more than a babysitting service and many only operate for an hour or two a day. Levels of stimulation and the variety of activities on offer varies between hotels, tour companies and even the reps, who vary widely in their enthusiasm.

Spain offers a huge choice of destinations virtually along the entire length of the southern coast. In addition there are the Canary and the Balearic Islands, each of which offers a choice of quiet or lively resorts. For culture, head for Madrid, Seville, Granada and Barcelona, all of which are energetic and fascinating cities, but be aware that in the summer Seville can be the hottest place in Spain with temperatures over 50°C, and children will be miserable.

Throughout the resorts you will find accommodation for every budget. Many are a mass of apartment complexes and multi-storey hotels. Few are pretty and they have not been planned to stay in keeping with Spanish architecture, which is an indication of how quickly tourism has swept and dominated much of the Spanish coast. Some of the newer and more attractive hotels are set back a little from the main beaches, because most of the prime coast was snapped up years ago and cluttered with grey towers. You can save a small fortune in the summer if you opt for an apartment or hotel a car journey from the beach and town and hire a car for the duration of your stay. Car hire is very good value in Spain and will often cost you the same for one week as the return taxi fare from the airport. You will often find that you get prettier accommodation for your money, as the nicer hotels on the beachfront are very expensive in peak season, which unfortunately coincides with the children's school holidays. The added bonus is that you will be able to sleep away from the noise of town nightlife, which is unceasing in the height of the season.

The greatest attraction is that the sun, heat and lack of rain are guaranteed all over Spain in the summer. However, be aware that in the winter and often in the spring and autumn, Spain and the Balearic Islands are cold. The Canary Islands remain generally warm, but the weather can be terrible and very rainy, especially during January and February, despite the fact that it is heavily promoted for winter sun holidays.

The downsides in the summer are the crowds and an abundance of childhood illnesses. Many children will pick up something at this time of year, whether it be a mild tummy bug, a cold or an ear infection. Spain's water and hygiene standards are a little unsanitary, which has led to the much-publicised outbreaks of food poisoning. In the heat bacteria multiply at an alarming rate, so be wary of the hotel buffet and only drink bottled water.

The other concern is that building regulations and safety standards vary from those in the UK: balconies can be positively dangerous and always check that your door is locked properly. Many of the locks are at the same site as the door handle, so with a brief fiddle your toddler could be roaming in hotel corridors or, even worse, could be loose on the road. Some hotel rooms have child locks well out of reach but most do not, so either lock the door with your key or use the security chain.

SWEDEN ★★★★★

Flight time: 1-2 hours
Best time to visit: July-August

Children may enjoy a Scandinavian driving holiday more than one in southern Europe, because you won't be battling to keep them cool in the car. Swedish roads are toll free and uncrowded, which relieves the anxiety faced on some of the French and Spanish roads.

The extensive choice of affordable accommodation can be booked in combination with a ferry crossing at prices that would be within the budget of most families. Choose from country cottages, well-situated campsites or touring inns and hotels.

You can book excellent deals with Scandinavian Seaways and get free child places for more than one child if you book early enough.

SWITZERLAND ★★★★

Flight time: 2-3 hours
Best time to visit: June-August

Switzerland offers excellent skiing, but it is expensive when compared with other European resorts. A positive consequence of this is that it isn't as crowded and overrun by snowboarders as some of the cheaper destinations tend to be.

Switzerland in the summer has a sleepy beauty. Even the cities are relatively quiet, all except Zurich, which is lively but has a drug problem. In Zurich the authorities are fighting a constant battle to clean used needles out of the parks, so always watch where your children are playing. Berne and Geneva are a peaceful contrast.

The countryside is stunning with its alpine flowers and Swiss chalets. Mountain walks are breathtaking, and are a wonderful opportunity for a family to enjoy each other's company in a serene environment.

Switzerland suffers from the stiff competition and cheaper prices in Austria but if on a driving holiday, why not visit them both?

Eastern Europe

BELORUSSIA

After being arrested at the border and deported with a train full of people anxious to flee the country, I feel confident in claiming that there is little here to attract a family on holiday.

BOSNIA and HERZEGOVINA

Many of the roads, railways, bridges and historic sites have been destroyed. Little infrastructure remains.

BULGARIA ★★★

Flight time: 2-3 hours
Best time to visit: July-August

Most of Bulgaria's tourists arrive from Eastern Europe, so if you want a family holiday away from English breakfasts, why not try Bulgaria? Family resorts are trying to attract Western visitors, so parents who are prepared for basic tourist standards will certainly benefit from cheaper sea and sun on the Black Sea than most Mediterranean countries, although the safety and quality of the beaches is variable, especially towards the end of the tourist season. The culture and heritage is still largely intact, too.

The skiing in Bulgaria is acceptable for families, though may be lacking in challenge for the more experienced skier. Once again the benefit is that it is cheap.

Be wary, food standards are variable and hotel food can be inedible, although a family of six can apparently enjoy a fantastic meal in a local restaurant, with wine, for around £20.

Unfortunately, tourists in the major resorts are targets for muggings, but to no greater extent than in Spain or Italy.

CROATIA ★★

Flight time: 2-3 hours
Best time to visit: July-August

Croatia has acquired much of Former-Yugoslavia's Adriatic coastline, and has encouraged a creeping recovery of the tourist industry. Sadly, beautiful cities such as Dubrovnik were shelled during the country's break up. If you decide to visit and support the tourist regeneration, the northern seaside resorts are the best places to head for, although the quality of the hotels and tourist infrastructure is still underdeveloped and variable.

CZECH REPUBLIC

For a long city break ★★★★
For a full holiday ★★

Flight time: 2-3 hours
Best time to visit: July-August

Prague, the capital of the Czech Republic, is the main reason most tourists choose to visit the country. It is one of the most enchanting cities in the world and well worth a visit. However, if you would rather experience a two-centre holiday, an overnight sleeper train runs between Prague and Budapest. Due to the fact that Prague escaped being bombed during the wars, the evolution of architecture through the centuries is still apparent on an impressive scale. It has a fairytale feel. The tiny dwellings built into the castle fortifications on Golden Lane look like they might be inhabited by Thumbelina or Tom

Thumb, while the central squares in Prague ring with the sound of horses' hooves, bringing to life notions of the Emperor parading through the streets naked in his imaginary new clothes. Even Wenceslas Square was named after the real life 'Good King Wenceslas'.

Food is variable but cheap. Much of it is stodgy stews, and quite often the attempts at other dishes are quite bland. However, Western tastes are catered for.

If your family are music lovers, Vienna is a tolerable distance by train (five to six hours), which will give you the chance to view the Czech countryside and experience the more expensive Austrian capital from your less expensive hotel room in Prague.

Health service standards lag behind those in Western Europe and infant mortality is high in some of the outlying polluted towns. However, the Czech Republic is quite close to home and flights are frequent enough to whip straight back if you suspect your child is becoming seriously ill.

Prague gets very cold in the winter. Even in late April, the easterly winds can be icy, so travel prepared with thick socks, coats and mittens.

Be aware of your belongings all the time, as pickpocketing is rife.

Driving out into the countryside, away from Prague, is like stepping back in time. Old Eastern European values are still in place, and slow economic growth means many of the towns have a provincial feel.

ESTONIA ★

Flight time: 3-4 hours
Best time to visit: Juky-August

Estonia offers a gentle introduction to Eastern European life. The capital, Tallinn, is the main attraction, whose architectural beauty, with its perfectly preserved buildings, spires and twisting lanes, has been compared with Prague. Like Prague, Tallinn escaped being bombed in the wars, and has remained virtually unchanged over the centuries.

GEORGIA

Political strife has pushed tourists to other destinations around the Black Sea region.

LATVIA

General suitability for a city break with children ★★

Flight time: 3-4 hours
Best time to visit: July-August

Latvia is very cold in the winter and warm in the summer. The capital of Riga is the destination of a number of cruise ships attracted by its medieval centre. The landscape is unspectacular, so a full holiday may be a little unremarkable and unrewarding for children.

MOLDAVIA ★

Flight time: 3-4 hours
Best time to visit: July-August

Crime is low and there is a relatively well-developed infrastructure in the country. However, health care is rudimentary and doctors are poorly trained.

POLAND ★★

Flight time: 3-4 hours
Best time to visit: July-August

Poland in the winter is grey and bleak. Even the historic areas of Warsaw have a dreary feel. By contrast, the summer is good for hiking, but the food and hotel standards are perhaps more Russian than Western, which make it difficult when travelling with children. This would probably be an unremarkable and unrewarding holiday for children.

ROMANIA ★

Flight time: 3-4 hours
Best time to visit: July-August

Romania is worth a visit to explore Dracula country. Transylvania and the Carpathian Mountains are steeped in historical heritage.

Other attractions in Romania are the Black Sea and the mouth of the River Danube.

The negatives are that the availability of hotel accommodation is limited, and standards of health care are among the lowest in Europe.

RUSSIAN FEDERATION ★★

Flight time: 3-7 hours
Best time to visit: July-August

Tourist trips to Moscow and St Petersburg are on the increase again. Both offer overwhelming history. A short break in either city would be a fantastic cultural opportunity for an older child of either sex. There is the ballet and the palaces, or they can take a tour in a MiG jet and drive a Russian tank!

Crime is a huge problem; tourist extortion and muggings are commonplace. It is not a safe tourist destination for families, and there are many more enjoyable world experiences to be shared with young children.

SLOVAKIA ★★

Flight time: 3-4 hours
Best time to visit: July-August

Slovakia was half of the former Czechoslovakia, which split the Czech Republic and Slovakia in 1993.

Slovakia is the less developed of the two countries, and has a poorer health service. The main attraction is the Tatra Mountains, which attract families for skiing, caving and hiking.

Snowfall is heavy in the winter, and summer temperatures are warm.

SLOVENIA ★★

Flight time: 3-4 hours
Best time to visit: July-August

Slovenia is trying to attract village tourism to the farms as well as mountains and beaches. It is still off-track development-wise, but there are mediocre places where you could stay cheaply. Food standards are unreliable.

UKRAINE ★

Flight time: 3-4 hours
Best time to visit: July-August

The warm resorts in the south are the main potential attractions. However, crime rates are rising and foreigners are a target for muggers. The Mafia, corruption and a poor economy would not make for a cheerful holiday.

UZBEKISTAN

Uzbekistan was on the silk route and is famous worldwide for its architecture. However, culture in isolation is often dreary to children.

YUGOSLAVIA (Serbia and Montenegro)

Sadly, the provocation and political unrest is ongoing and tourists should avoid the country.

The Caribbean

Most of the Caribbean islands rate quite highly in their suitability for travelling with children. There are a few exceptions, but generally the only disadvantage when travelling from the UK is the long journey.

If you shop around carefully you may well be able to get a week in the Caribbean in the school holidays for around the same price or less than in the Med – the reason being that the Caribbean is out of season in our summer, whereas in the Mediterranean it is peak time.

Varying between the individual islands, June through to November is the hottest, rainiest time. Heat and rainfall deter the American tourists to such an extent that many hotels offer all sorts of incentives to attract visitors. The temperatures and humidity are child's play compared to the intense, sweaty heat of the Greek summer, and the rainfall on many Caribbean islands is brief and refreshing – so when you consider paying double the rates in the sweltering Mediterranean, research the options across the Atlantic too.

Caribbean women love children. When we travelled to Tobago with five-month-old Paris, the waitresses would often squeal with delight when we entered a restaurant, and our chambermaid spent more time talking and playing with him than she did cleaning our room. The hotel staff would laugh and fuss at our table. Nothing was too much trouble. Few restaurants have highchairs, but we were welcome to help ourselves to as many chairs as we needed to pin the baby carrier, complete with baby, in a safe place.

The Caribbean environment is safe and free from tropical diseases. The abundance of white sandy beaches with warm shallow seas are a delight for even the tiniest baby, sitting and watching the gentle waves tickle her toes. You can relax watching your unstable toddler gaining the confidence to take successive steps into the water. Even the mosquitoes are less prolific than in Spain, Portugal or Italy.

The hotels and restaurants are accustomed to dealing with the sensitive American stomach, which is suitably intolerant of upset. Standards of hygiene and cleanliness are well above those in many

Mediterranean destinations, where we Brits seem to accept falling ill as part and parcel of our holiday.

Throughout the Caribbean you can get decent American and continental food. Generally, at breakfast there is plenty of fresh fruit, cereal, eggs, toast, bacon and cheese. Lunch, room service and evening menus will doubtless include one or all of the following: chips, burgers, omelettes, sandwiches, pasta, pizza, deep-fried chicken, rice, peas and garlic bread – so you will always find something in the majority of restaurants to feed your children.

On most of the islands it is better to secure your accommodation before you arrive, as the package deals negotiated by tour operators are invariably good value and, with the added incentive of the cheap child places offered by many of them, the prices in the summer are hard to beat. Pick the accommodation that you are comfortable with. If it would stress you out dressing three children and yourself for dinner, don't bother with a deluxe hotel. Opt instead for a motel-style or less-elaborate hotel where you can walk through reception with sandy feet if you wish to.

All the islands are easy to get around by hire car. Most of them are small enough to tour in a day or two and so it is doubtful that you will need a car for longer. The roads are good, uncrowded and many of the systems are similar to that of the British – that is, they drive on the left.

Jamaica is the most challenging and dangerous destination to drive around independently, as many drivers have no insurance and may not have even passed their driving test, so be careful.

Hurricanes may occur from July to October, but they are usually nothing to write home about and, because they come with good warnings, there are few fatalities. The most important thing is to follow advice. The winds can whip up suddenly, so if you are instructed to stay in your hotel for the day, make sure you do.

For stimulating a child's imagination, the strong history of pirates, sugar plantations and slaves is too powerful to go unmentioned.

ANTIGUA and BARBUDA ★★★★

Flight time: 8-10 hours
Best time to visit: November-May

The disadvantages relative to some of the other islands are that it can be expensive to stay and eat on Antigua and Barbuda, plus there is a little hostility towards tourists. However, the standard of living on the islands is high, which keeps most of the locals free from animosity.

The advantages are that Antigua is safe, clean, hygienic and disease-free. The medical facilities are good and, as the island is English speaking, so are the doctors. Many of the hotels and restaurants are of the highest standard. An added bonus is that Antigua is less humid than other Caribbean islands, so if you are travelling to the Caribbean in the children's summer holidays you are likely to be treated to less heat, less rainfall and milder hurricanes if they do hit!

BAHAMAS ★★★★

Flight time: 10-12 hours
Best time to visit: December-April

Six tourists per inhabitant visit the Bahamas each year, and the consequence of this is inevitable. The main islands of the Bahamas serviced by major airports are a mass of casinos, hotels and tourist trips, and there is some animosity between the local population and the holidaymakers. To add fuel to the fire, the Bahamas are in the path of the main narcotic drug routes between South and North America, so on some of the islands you will encounter some of the associated crime, mugging and the occasional tourist shooting – possibly the accidental result of a bungled mugging. As a result, the Bahamas can be disappointing.

For the average family, staying on Paradise Island – which is isolated from Nassau except by access over a significant bridge – is the best option. This island has a wide choice of accommodation from luxury villas and hotels, to apartments and rooms. Its relative detachment from the capital brings security and safety. There are plenty of water sports on offer and safe, shallow beaches. Most of the hotels have a number of good swimming pools, too. Orientation towards short, casino-bound, American budget trips ensures that the prices are reasonable and the service is to a good standard.

There are high standards of health and hygiene in the resorts and the locals and the doctors are all English speaking. Typical American-orientated menus feature all the foods children love.

The Bahamas may not be the ideal of the Caribbean you imagine, and the Caribbean culture seems a little watered down by the strong American influence, yet on balance the Bahamas offer a comfortable, child-friendly environment, with reasonable value for money *if* you are careful and choose the right spot.

Sailing to the outlying islands is out of the reach of most pockets, but if you have your own yacht it would be a perfect destination. Just avoid hurricane season from July to December, and prepare for high temperatures and uncomfortable humidity in the summer months of July and August.

BARBADOS ★★★★★

Flight time: 10-12 hours
Best time to visit: December-April

The British visitor will not experience a drastic culture change in many of the resorts. Lovers of Barbados tend to be those who like their very British, pampered home comforts, or children who can revel in luxurious familiarity. Expensive hotels, exclusive members' clubs and elitist control of business has resulted in a disparity between the local Bajans and the more affluent residents of the island. This has led to some resentment and clearly not every local welcomes the tourists with open arms, as attacks on tourists are on the increase. There is an intrusive degree of local hawking and touting all over the beaches and tourist spots of Barbados.

The real beauty of Barbados is its serenity and natural exquisiteness. Just inland, behind the busy public beaches and multitude of hotels, huge ginger lilies, hibiscus and sugarcane fields decorate a tidy, pretty island. Ask a local to cut a piece of sugar cane from the field for your children to taste. The tropical gardens are memorable, as is Harrison's Cave, Barbados's number-one tourist spot. Aboard an electric tram you can view a beautiful, natural underground world of stalactites and stalagmites, which is fantastic for even the youngest of children. The wildlife reserve would be another enjoyable family day out as a change from the miles of pink and white beaches.

Magnificent beaches, hotels and facilities will ensure an easy and relaxing holiday, but it is wise to choose your hotel bearing in mind that with accompanying children you may find a budget-class hotel far more restful than a more exclusive one where pretentions can run high. Your children just want to have fun and run around screaming, not dress for dinner and mind their manners so that you can avoid other people's condescending stares. There is an increasing number of very good-value holidays to Barbados on offer, especially during our summertime. Many hotels, faced with increased competition and the downturn in trade at the end of the high season, offer free child places, and it usually follows that these hotels are the ones most likely to be child friendly.

Health care and hygiene standards are good, and English is the official language.

Beware of the sea on the east coast, as it is rough, with strong currents and high waves. Many fatal accidents have occured on the east coast beaches.

CAYMAN ISLANDS ★★★★★

Flight time: 10-12 hours
Best time to visit: December-April

The Cayman Islands are pleasant, if more barren, than many of their lush, mountainous, volcanic neighbouring islands. There is not a great deal to do with children other than relax in pleasant hotels and enjoy the sea.

The diving is good in deeper waters, but this is of little use to children under the age of twelve. The snorkelling is good by Caribbean standards – virtually all the coral just off many of the islands is dead, but in certain areas of the Caymans it is still intact.

Seven Mile Beach is a vast expanse of gleaming white sand that in parts is totally deserted. Instead of being clumped together, the hotels are spread along the beach giving relative seclusion between them. The sea is gentle and crystal clear. Service is excellent and the choice of restaurants close to Seven Mile Beach is perfect for families. Fast-food restaurants do blight the landscape, but they are the cheapest way of feeding the children. Slightly up-market American-style diners are also a good option for a clean plate. In Georgetown, patisseries and big American supermarkets sell everything you are likely to need, and gourmet cuisine is easily found, too.

Sightseeing on the island is limited to a long day trip. You can travel to picturesque Rum Point with its shallow, turquoise waters and silver-white sand, then turn around and drive to the other side of the island to visit the turtle farm – all in one day. Car hire is good value and Jeeps are a cool option with older children.

Health and hygiene standards are excellent.

There are some very reasonable deals available for families in the British summertime, but it can be very rainy in June. As life in the Caymans revolves around the sea, there is little else to do when it is wet.

CUBA ★★★★

Flight time: 10-12 hours
Best time to visit: December-April

The image of Cuba as a military regime or communist stronghold is still in the minds of many would-be tourists, but it is now largely an untrue impression. Cuba is completely unique, with an intriguing history, culture, a spectacular mix of scenery and excellent beaches.

The hotels are very good and the 'all-inclusive' deals are good value. There are some incredibly cheap child offers available with major tour operators. The islands off the north coast are reputed to be for tourists with more money than sense, but this no longer appears to be true, with deals on offer that match those of any of the more popular islands. The beaches both on the islands and on the mainland are lovely.

Health care is good and crime rates are low.

DOMINICA ★★★
(Do not confuse with the Dominican Republic)

Flight time: 10-12 hours
Best time to visit: December-April

The airports on Dominica can only take small propeller planes, not commercial aircraft. This, and possibly the lack of easily accessible beaches, has kept many tourists away. There are flight connections from a number of surrounding islands including Martinique, Guadeloupe, Barbados and Antigua.

Dominica is the most unspoiled, untamed and rugged of all the Caribbean islands. There are waterfalls, green grottoes, clear rivers and hot springs to bathe in instead of the sea. Nature lovers and child explorers will relish trekking up mountainsides and through safe, tropical rainforests.

Accommodation at a reasonably high standard can be secured at bargain prices. Food is more traditionally Caribbean than American or continental. The local delicacy is mountain chicken – more commonly known as frog! Health care is very much small-town.

For the more earnest searcher of paradise, the inaccessibility would be well worth the trouble.

DOMINICAN REPUBLIC and HAITI (Hispaniola) ★★★

Flight time: 10-12 hours
Best time to visit: March-September

Haiti is the poorest country in the Americas. The political instability has sent most tourists east of the border and into the neighbouring Dominican Republic.

The Dominican Republic has received a lot of bad press recently with claims that the hygiene standards are very low. Foods tested in even the best hotels in the resorts were found to contain levels of food-poisoning bacteria which would certainly cause illness. This is the very last thing you want when travelling with children. There can be few things more torturous than tending a vomiting child in the heat of the Caribbean when you feel ill yourself. If one of the family gets sick with an ear infection it is bad enough, but if the entire family goes down with food poisoning you'll wish you had never left home. Health care and hospital treatment is improving every year though, because of tourist income.

The positives are good beaches and cheap prices. If you are vigilant there should be no problem. Ask other hotel guests who arrived before you if they have been OK. If not, ask them what they think caused the problem. Ice? Salad? Seafood? The swimming pool?

For families seeking out reminders of Spain in the Caribbean (including the tummy bugs) the Dominican Republic is perfect. Although it is still very much a beach resort destination, attractions are popping up.

GRENADA ★★★★

Flight time: 10-12 hours
Best time to visit: December-March

The Spice Island of Grenada is as tranquil and pretty as it gets. The beaches are good and health care has improved since the restoration of democracy. Tourism is still lagging behind that of other Caribbean islands, but in a positive way. Food is good and the locals are friendly, if not a little money wise. It may turn out a more expensive holiday than a similar one taken on a more developed neighbouring island.

JAMAICA ★★★

Flight time: 10-12 hours
Best time to visit: December-May

Jamaica is a tough place. Inside the 'all-inclusive' resorts you may find the paradise you seek, but outside the gates you will be subjected to constant hassle. The Jamaicans rely heavily on their tourists but don't treat them well. They target you the most before you get a tan, as they know that the whiter you are, the greener you are.

My own experiences in Jamaica – thankfully before any children – amounted to a holiday from hell. I left smiling, but my husband spent the last week of our holiday wishing the time away.

In the first week we were robbed twice. My passport then disappeared, and we were forced to travel to the British Embassy in Kingston before I could get home. When I got home I received reverse charge calls telling me that if I sent some money I could get my passport back.

My husband and I went on a horse-riding tour, but the horses were so poorly kept that mine collapsed and fell on top of me. Luckily he started to get up before he crushed me. In addition, a motel owner tried to trick me into signing a credit card slip that stated two nights stay would be US$600 instead of Jamaican $600. If I hadn't noticed, two nights in a dingy motel would have cost £400 instead of £60. We had headed for Jamaica with images of a colonial Caribbean that is no longer in existence. Life in the slums around Kingston is as tough as it gets with its dons, gangs, guns, drugs and violence.

Jamaica is basically a third-world country. If you decide to go, make sure you book carefully. Go into an enclosed beach resort if you have the budget – you will still be able to venture out on trips and see some of the beauty of the island if you choose, but you will also have the security and protection for your family at night and when you want to relax without constant harassment.

ST KITTS and NEVIS ★★★★

Flight time: 10-12 hours
Best time to visit: December-May

A little off the traditional Caribbean beaten track, St Kitts is historically and scenically fascinating. The beaches are stunning and prices are more reasonable than on some of the other islands, probably as a result of the island's relative inaccessibility. Nevis is just a ferry ride away. Between them the two islands have everything typically Caribbean to offer except the crowds.

ST LUCIA ★★★★

Flight time: 9-11 hours
Best time to visit: December-April

St Lucia is lush, green and beautiful. It is a volcanic island, which ensures that its flora and fertility are spectacular. It also means that you won't find the powdery white beaches to be found in many other parts of the Caribbean. It is also pricey when compared to many of the other islands, although an increasing number of good-value packages and unbelievable child offers are making St Lucia more accessible.

There is some hostility towards tourists but the local people are generally welcoming. Ruled by the British and the French at different times, St Lucia retains some of the character and cuisine of both.

The hotels are good and many are positively luxurious. Health care is also good.

Getting around is relatively easy and there are many sites and coves to explore. There is plenty to see including a 'drive-in' volcano and some of the finest tropical gardens in the Caribbean, although you can explore most of the island in a day.

Because the island is a tropical paradise, most of its visitors are couples rather than families. Prices are falling, but it would still be very costly to feed a family on St Lucia because of the tilt towards the luxury holiday market.

ST VINCENT and THE GRENADINES ★★★

Flight time: 10-12 hours
Best time to visit: December-April

The Grenadines offer the finest yachting areas in the Caribbean Sea, and have an atmosphere of sleepy beauty. However, there is very little to do and see on the tiny islands.

St Vincent has more to offer a family, but it is still more orientated towards the jet set. As a result, prices are higher than in other parts of the Caribbean and there are few child reductions available.

Most of the islands are too small to do anything other than escape from the real world. Other Caribbean islands with more variety may be a better option with children.

TRINIDAD and TOBAGO ★★★★★

Flight time: 10-12 hours
Best time to visit: December-April

Tobago is purported to be the legendary island of Robinson Crusoe. It certainly fulfils the image. Life in Tobago is quiet, simple and very relaxing. The beaches are lovely, the seas are warm and the country-side is rich in tropical flora and fauna. Both Trinidad and Tobago have rainforests.

Crime is a problem in Trinidad and, sadly, this is spilling over on to sleepy Tobago, However, the major targets are the bigger, more popular hotels, so the smaller, cheaper, family hotels without much beachfront remain unsullied.

Tobago is a lovely destination but it is hard to get to. Most tourists must change in Trinidad and board a smaller plane with propellers and a handful of seats – a tedious connection after a transatlantic haul with an extra one- to two-hour wait for just a short thirty-five minute hop. However, the extra hassle does mean extra exclusivity. You won't find the crowds or the shopping that you would on the other islands and it also keeps the prices down – there needs to be some tangible incentive for tourists if they are to travel an additional three hours to get there.

Apart from the extra connection to reach it, Tobago is excellent for families. The people are friendly and welcoming, the beaches are soft, safe and clean, and the food is good and hygienic. The health care is of a high standard, and if there are any major mishaps, Trinidad is host to a major teaching hospital, ensuring the availabil-ity of some of the best medical facilities in the Caribbean.

It is an island you will want to go back to if you just want to enjoy the laid-back image and shoeless lifestyle of the Caribbean Sea.

North America

CANADA ★★★★

Flight time: 10-14 hours
Best time to visit: June-September

Canada is massive and beautiful. The winters are cold and the summers pleasantly warm. The roads are good and the accommodation
is world class. Vancouver, on the west coast, is apparently the most
wonderful city in the world in which to live.

As a holiday destination, the greatest attraction is the outdoors
and the national parks. The Rockies are breathtaking and the experience changes between seasons. Early fall, when the trees change to
rich autumnal colours, is stunning, but the summer is probably
better for a family because it does get cold later in the year, which can
make it difficult to get involved with outdoor pursuits. In addition to
this, being cold when camping is a totally miserable experience.

Canada is probably not a holiday destination that every child will
enjoy, unless maybe including a visit to friends or relatives. Not many
children truly appreciate scenery, and most get fed up on long journeys. However, mature, nature-loving kids will love the experience.

If going it alone, don't try to be too ambitious with the distances
you set out to cover, as this may make the trip into a challenge rather
than a pleasure. Organised tours can be tiring and with few decent
discounted offers available for children, they can work out to be very
expensive and outside the price range of most families. If you can
balance the sums, a tour would give you the time to talk and share
the experience without the challenge of driving miles in the wilderness.

Skiing in Canada can be bitterly cold, too cold for young children
who cannot gauge when they are at risk. At its worst the cold will
make eyes stream, and it makes everything seem much more of an
effort. Children will definitely need specialist ski wear and balaclavas
should to be worn to stop the face freezing in the wind.

THE USA ★★★★★

Flight time: 9-11 hours (East coast)
Best time to visit: March-May
Flight time: 12-14 hours (West coast)
Best time to visit: June-September

As the price of airfares has fallen dramatically the trans-Atlantic routes have become affordable for most families to get to the US at least once. A trip to Disneyland is no longer a wild dream, but an achievable ambition within the reach of the family with an average income. It needn't be an expensive holiday option because so many tour companies offer packages to Florida from the UK – even during the school holidays a good standard hotel for two weeks in Orlando often costs the same for a family as a villa in Portugal.

If you are still toying with the idea, start comparing prices on teletext, the Internet and the Sunday papers. Even if you aren't a seasoned traveller, America is an undaunting and relaxing environment for a family holiday. Most parents and children will highly recommend the experience and many will say it was their favourite holiday ever and the trip of a lifetime.

Packages are easy, but not always the best way to travel, especially to somewhere so accessible and full of choices. If you are on a tight budget going it alone will add to the experience and can save a fortune.

Fly-drives

If your children are good travellers by car, a fly-drive in the US offers freedom, flexibility and variety. Petrol is unbelievably cheap, road signs are good and, although you will be driving on the other side of the road, it is very easy to get around. The pace on the roads is much steadier and slower than those on the roads of Europe – generally the speed limits are lower, and hassle on the freeways is less than on our motorways.

Car hire prices are reasonable, but the insurance costs are high. There are all manner of extra options for insurance, but unfortunately you will need it, as a car accident in America would inevitably be costly and it just isn't worth risking the strain of the consequences. Even if you usually travel without health care insurance, get it for travelling to the US and check how comprehensive it is, as medical costs are extortionate, and people in America love to sue.

Picking up a pre-booked car from an airport in America couldn't be simpler. The hire companies offer 24-hour pick up and telephone help for directions, etc., and with a credit card and your driving licence ready you will usually be driving away in minutes. If you have an option of companies choose one that has branches all over the states in which you intend to travel. We once picked up a car in Los Angeles, and after driving to Las Vegas we started having a few minor problems that made us uneasy about driving into the heat of Death Valley. We felt a little foolish, but when we telephoned the hire company in LA they told us to go immediately to the local branch where they changed the car, without question.

Accommodation

Accommodation is easy to find within every budget. The charge per night in motels is per room, not per person, which makes travelling with a family in America very good value. You can arrive in a town late at night and find a bed for the night quickly and easily. The vacancies, prices and facilities (cable TV, swimming pool etc.) are usually advertised on bill boards, easily readable from the roadway, which makes it simple to choose what will suit you within your budget.

Don't be embarrassed to ask to see the room before you check in, and if you don't like what is on offer, don't feel awkward about walking away. Be polite and explain that it isn't quite right for the family but never feel that you should stay where you will not be totally comfortable. Be especially cautious if you see a sign in the foyer stating that your money will not be refunded under any circumstances, as that should undoubtedly serve as a warning of noisy air-conditioning, bed bugs, sticky carpets or cockroaches. To check for cockroaches, turn the light on at the last minute and look under the beds quickly, as they will scurry to escape the light and disappear until you turn the lights off again.

Hotels and apartments are more expensive but more secure if you want some privacy from the children. Motel rooms always have direct access on to the outside, so you will need adjoining rooms with through access to keep them safe if they want to come and find you. A reasonably priced motel room would be $40-50 with two double beds. An apartment with two bedrooms should be roughly $120.

Don't be too shy to walk into the plushest apartment block around – Americans are good negotiators and shrewd business people, so if they have vacant accommodation, they won't let it lie empty if you are prepared to make a reasonable offer.

Eating out

Eating out is generally much cheaper in the US than it is in Europe, and often costs the same or less than shopping in a supermarket for two weeks. Service standards are generally high.

Fast food is predictably cheap, quick and absolutely everywhere. For children, eating rubbish all holiday is bliss, and for two weeks won't do them any harm. On the road it is difficult to avoid the multitude of signs, and it is such an easy and reliably clean option. I never feel too guilty about junk food on holiday but always supplement it with lots of fruits from supermarkets and fresh juice that is available everywhere.

The portions in the restaurants are huge, and an extra-large drink is literally the size of a child's bucket. Children's meals are about the worst value and least nutritious items on an American menu, so ordering a full-size meal and sharing it will usually work out better.

As well as hot dogs and fried chicken, Mexican food is widely available and reasonably priced. Japanese is almost as popular as Chinese and much healthier. If you like familiarity, Pizza Hut, Dominos Pizza, TGI's, the Hard Rock Café and Planet Hollywood seem to be everywhere.

Don't take hygiene standards for granted or let down your guard. Fresh, hot food and bottled water is still important. The only two cases of serious food poisoning that I have ever had were both in America, and each time it was after a day in a theme park.

Camping

Camping in the great outdoors and the expansive diversity of the US is amazing. The way they tend to do it in America is by campervan, but tents are allowed in many gorgeous campsites amidst massive trees and the sound of bears. The national parks are the best places to camp and in many you truly have a sense of being in the wilderness. Stunning natural beauty, flora, fauna, smells and sounds are new and exciting. Good road infrastructure in the parks means they are very accessible and easy to get around.

Summer camp in the US is almost a national institution, and is geared around outdoor pursuits, fresh air and fun, so a taste of this on holiday is thrilling and memorable for a family.

Shopping

The malls are bigger versions of our indoor shopping centres, housing restaurants and shops selling everything you could imagine. American clothing, videos, CDs and books are all much cheaper than those in Europe, so it is better to wait for your holiday before you buy jeans, sunglasses and beachwear. Trainers are a little bit cheaper too, while American cotton is of a good, heavy quality and lasts for years.

Theme and water parks (see page 23)

The Americans do theme and water parks better than anyone else in the world. Aside from the Disney parks there are many, many others with a mixture of thrills, daring and sheer terror on offer. Children often have less fear than parents and love the fact that they are not too scared when you might be. Watch out for special cautionary notes and age or height restrictions on each ride. If you adhere to the

American guidelines you won't go wrong. The only other concern in the US is that children do get abducted from the parks. Go over and over with your child what to do if they get separated from you (see page 247), and don't let them stray or go to the toilet on their own.

Generally the parks are crowded, and as a consequence the queues are a nightmare. However, you will usually be shaded for most of your queuing time, plus there are accurate guidelines at interim stages as to the length of time you will have to wait. As you are fore warned of the length of time it will take and never seem to be standing still for long, the frustration is minimised. In these circumstances children often have more patience than adults, but be prepared – if you relax and adjust your mindset it will be bearable.

Most of the parks are expensive, and the child price is virtually the same as the adult so it can become very costly. In Florida, the Disney theme and water parks are covered by one pass and a separate pass covers Universal Studios, Busch Gardens and Sea World. For most of us it is prohibitively expensive to buy both. Three- and five-day passes don't offer much of a saving and aren't flexible enough, but the ten-day passes may be useful from one year to the next if they don't expire, but they will definitely be too much for one visit. It can be overwhelming for children if they spend every day traipsing round park after park, and they can soon become blasé, which will spoil the overall experience for all of you. I would avoid buying any tickets or passes until you are there, unless there is a major price incentive. You can buy exactly the same passes all over Florida from your hotel reception and ticket agencies in the shopping malls.

Beaches

The beaches of California and Florida are gorgeous and a whole culture exists around them. In California this is surfing, posing and strutting around looking toned and beautiful. On Florida's east coast it's all about music, wheels, chilling and being cool.

The beaches expand broadly in width and depth. Most of the famous beaches are crowded, but there is plenty of room for everyone to do their own thing, whether it is a full work-out in front of everyone or having a tattoo.

The Ten Most Popular Things to do in America with a Family

1. Florida Theme Parks (see page 25)

Florida is the world leader for theme and water parks. However, there are too many of them to visit in one holiday. Generally, the most famous parks have the most to offer but, as you would expect, they are the most crowded.

Disney's Magic Kingdom is great for small children but for kids over ten years old it can seem a bit tame. One friend told me they left it until last and it ended up a huge disappointment. Make sure you don't miss the parades and the night-time fireworks.

Disney's Animal Kingdom has a few thrilling rides for older children and the mini safari is excellent. It is a comfy, compact ride, which is reminiscent of the real Africa, complete with imported fauna and man-made massive trees. There are several tigers that you can see up close enough to be awed by what spectacular creatures they are. There is also plenty to keep younger children entertained.

Disney's Epcot Centre, based around a large lake, is a cultural as well as thrilling experience for children of any age. It is very well done, interesting and pretty. The idea is that you can sample a flavour of several countries around the world. The different countries achieve an atmosphere of where they are supposed to be, from the market in Mexico to the band playing Beatles' tunes in Great Britain outside the English pub. The 360° cinemas in Disney's Canada and China are educational and fascinating. All countries sell traditional food and goods.

There is a little play table in each country where young children are given a mask to colour and decorate. Every country has their own passport stamp and something to attach to their mask. In Italy it is a Venetian paper mask, in Norway a tiny paper Viking ship. The children will have great fun collecting all the bits and pieces.

At Disney's MGM Studios, not many people opt twice for the Tower of Terror ride. It was the only ride where I saw children screaming to get off if they were seated ready for a second go and knew what was coming. A replica studio of *Who Wants to be a*

Millionaire? often evoked the cute response, 'I can't believe we are really here.'

The Disney water parks – Blizzard Beach and Typhoon Lagoon – are excellent fun with thrills for children from approximately ten years and upwards (depending on height) in the form of precipitous water slides, while everyone can enjoy the gentle, pleasant rides on rubber rings and dinghies. A $10 themed soft-drinks cup is refillable all day for free, but buy one between the children, as they will probably still want slush ices and lollies, too.

The only negative to be aware of is that it can become chilly in the late afternoon until mid June, and overcast days outside peak summer can be cold. Between October and April, depending on the temperature, you may need to persuade your children to come out of the water on a regular basis so they can warm up. However, no doubt they will insist through little blue lips that they aren't cold at all.

Busch Gardens proves to be a consistent favourite of older children, and of all of the parks it is often the one children ask to go back to a second time.

Universal Studios is probably better than MGM Studios if you have been to other Disney parks, as the rides are more thrilling and the sets just as impressive.

At Seaworld the dolphins and whales are the stars of all the shows. The sea creatures are cared for impeccably but it is difficult not to feel a twinge of sadness for them. If you don't want to get wet, make sure you don't sit in the front rows. The trainers assured us that the dolphins enjoy performing their tricks, and I have to admit that, on the keys, I have seen wild dolphins leaping into an enclosure every morning for tricks and breakfast with the hotel guests before disappearing back to sea until the next morning, so the possibility that there may be pleasure in the performance is not unfathomable.

2. Florida Beaches and the Kennedy Space Centre

If you base yourselves in Orlando for one or two weeks, the beaches and the Kennedy Space Centre are easily accessible. If you don't have pre-booked accommodation, heading from the airport or from the Disney parks into downtown (city centre) Orlando you will find plenty of motels on the main thoroughfares that cost $20-$30 for a decent, clean, family room.

If you have had enough of the parks, both the east and the west coasts of Florida have stunning beaches. On Daytona beach, cars and Harley Davidsons drive on to the sands. Cocoa beach is close enough to the Kennedy Space Centre to watch shuttle launches, and people gather there to watch the spectacle despite the fact that most scheduled launches do not take place for a host of different reasons.

If you go to the Space Centre on the day of a scheduled launch, tours are interrupted and finish running several hours before take-off. When the time for take-off approaches, all the roads are closed, so you must arrive early in the day to be allowed access to the Space Centre for the duration of the launch.

From Fort Lauderdale to Miami beach on the south-east tip of Florida, the atmosphere changes. A major international drug-smuggling route seems to grip the area with quadruple locks and spy holes on motel doors. I couldn't relax on Miami beach, so wouldn't take my family there.

The Florida Keys are pleasant, and on the Florida's west coast the beaches are geared towards families. Naples, Sarasota, St Petersburg and Clearwater are all nice, easygoing beaches with pelicans and tourist shops.

3. Florida Keys and the Everglades

The Florida Keys are a string of tiny islands that stretch from the tip of Florida and are linked by a series of bridges. The shopping and dining on Key West is pleasant, and a hint of Caribbean atmosphere is all around. Water sports and sailing are available.

Beautiful and memorable, the everglades are swamps abundant in bird life with alligators and millions upon millions of savage mosquitoes, so long sleeves and insect repellant are essential before setting foot out of the car. The warden can then tell you the choices of trips that would be best for the season and the ages of your children.

4. California Beaches

Stretching south from Los Angeles to San Diego the motels are plentiful and cheap. Finding new accommodation is easy, even if you want to move most nights. Many motels have pools, but the beaches are too good to miss. California borders the Pacific Ocean, which is warm, with high waves for surfing. There is, however, a real threat of sharks.

Heading north from LA, the costal drive is pretty but the temperature drops steadily, so that by the time you reach San Francisco, the weather is significantly cooler all year round. Even the summers are temperate.

Of the most famous beaches, Malibu beach is a mass of private accommodation. Venice beach is where the beautiful people strut their stuff while jogging, playing volleyball and even doing workouts with full weights. Most of what is going on will be uninteresting for the children, so for them the Californian beaches will seem sunny, pleasant and vast. Volleyball nets are free for everyone to use so take your own ball to the beach.

Long Beach and Santa Barbara are up-market resorts. You will often see night fires on the beach where teenagers congregate at night to socialise in the warm air.

As with most places in the world, it is best to leave your valuables in the motel safe and carry small amounts of cash for drinks and ice cream.

5. California Theme Parks

Sea World in San Diego, Disneyland and Universal Studios near LA,are the most popular theme parks in California. These are plenty for most families, and you will still have time to enjoy all the other things the US has to offer.

6. California Cities and Yosemite

The crime in the cities is something to be conscious of and the racial tension is apparent between most minorities. By world standards in

Britain we are very tolerant of each other. In America things are not the same, and you need to be aware that you may not be welcome to walk or drive in every district around a city. In San Francisco, homosexuality is evident everywhere, so you should be prepared to answer questions however you see fit.

Outside the cities there are fruit groves, nut trees and vineyards, and Yosemite National Park is definitely worth the trip inland as the scenery is spectacular and the camping facilities good. Be aware that it is very cold at night due to the high altitude, and car engines misfire because of the low oxygen levels.

7. Skiing

As in Canada, skiing in the US can be freezing cold, but the advantages are the lack of crowds, good organisation and better value for money. Accommodation and eating out is cheaper than in the European ski resorts.

8. Yellowstone Park

Unrivalled natural beauty in the wilds and perfect camping.

9. Grand Canyon

The Grand Canyon has the most wonderful vistas, and the deepest rocks were around at the time of the dinosaurs. Trekking down into the canyon is possible with a guide, but is exhausting on foot, so donkeys might be a better option for children.

Flights into the canyon are very turbulent and can make delicate stomachs very sick. It isn't worth the expense with children.

10. Las Vegas

Las Vegas hotels are excellent and cheap because they are subsidised by the casinos. There are a lot of attractions in the city, with shows in all the big hotels. Swimming pools are luxurious to encourage you to stay there in the sunshine for as long as possible. Las Vegas is slightly tacky, and seeing the gamblers pouring coins from paper buckets into the slot machines at nine o'clock in the morning is depressing, but the gloss and glamour overrides the downside.

The US offers plenty more for the family on holiday. Tours cover most states by bus, inter-state driving is straightforward, and accommodation is easily found all over the country. Travelling coast to coast would be a fun challenge with older children who can appreciate the changing landscape and history of an area.

Central America

BELIZE ★★★★

Flight time: 12-15 hours
Best time to visit: March-April

If you want to visit a Central American country with a family, Belize should be your first choice. It has everything to offer, from Jaguar sanctuaries where big cats roam free, to pristine rainforest, Caribbean beaches, excellent diving and tiny cays offshore where there are no tarmac roads and few people wear shoes.

You should take malaria tablets, but the strains of malaria are not resistant so the tablets your family needs to take are the tried-and-tested medicines that have been in use for over forty years and are not even contraindicated in pregnant women.

One major problem with Belize is that travelling around the country is a challenging task and very hard by road. Car hire is unbelievably expensive: the same journey that will cost you $3 by bone-jerking bus will cost you up to $150 by dilapidated taxi. It is incredible. In addition, there is no rail system. To deal with these problems, a network of short, reasonably priced flights has built up between the cays on the reef, the resorts on the south-east coast and the interior of the country.

Packages to Belize are very expensive. They offer few reductions for children, although the flights do offer a nominal discount. However, if you go it alone you will save a fortune. Flights are relatively cheap and so is the accommodation if you pick well. On the quieter cays a cabana on the beach that can host a family could cost just $20-$30. On Ambergris Cay, which is by far the most expensive, there are cheap rooms in the reasonable standard main street motels, and if you wander around or hire a golf cart and drive around the sandy streets you may pick up a condo for a bargain.

Health care in Belize is limited on the Cayes, but the presence of the British Army means that good-standard army medics are available.

Everyone speaks English and everyone appears to live a comfortable enough lifestyle to sustain themselves honestly. Belize is a refreshing, unspoilt haven.

COSTA RICA ★★★★

Flight time: 12-15 hours
Best time to visit: December-March

Costa Rica offers the family cable-car journeys through spectacular rainforests, rich and varied countryside, volcanic mountain ranges and delightful beaches. The government is keen to attract tourists and secure their safety. Crime in the country is mostly limited to petty theft and Costa Rica is considered the safest country in Central America. The health system is one of the best in Latin America, and the country is a good introduction to the atmosphere and land of the tropics for a family. Rainfall is lowest in January and February. The accommodation is generally of a high standard, the people are gentle and helpful, and the tourist infrastructure has rapidly improved to a reliable level.

EL SALVADOR ★

Flight time: 12-15 hours
Best time to visit: March-April

El Salvador is a small country on the Pacific coast. It offers unspoilt beach resorts in the region of the Costa del Sol, and now the civil war has ended you will enjoy safe transit around the country. However, despite its beautiful beaches, El Salvador has not made great efforts to attract tourists. As a result, neighbouring Costa Rica may be the better choice when travelling with a family.

GUATEMALA

Flight time: 12-15 hours
Best time to visit: March-April

Guatemala has problems with terrorists and aggressive muggings, so tours to the fantastic Mayan ruins of Tikal are accompanied from

Belize by armed guards. Most of the crimes are carried out by boys in their young teens, but when they are armed with guns and machetes who is going to argue with a hormone-strung juvenile?

The scenery in the south is dramatic jungle, once used as the backdrop for the Hollywood movie, *Tarzan*, but despite this, the mosquitoes in the region carry dengue-fever as well as malaria.

Health standards are limited and poverty dictates that hygiene standards are generally low.

Guatemala is a fascinating and a beautiful place and well worth a visit for a day or two when based in a neighbouring country. However, when considered on balance, there is little to attract a family for the full duration of their vacation .

HONDURAS ★

Flight time: 12-15 hours
Best time to visit: March-April

The devastation caused by the last hurricane to hit Central America will take a long time to recover from. The whole infrastructure of Honduras was hit hard and many priorities need to be fulfilled before the people can focus on drawing tourists back into the region.

MEXICO ★★★★

Flight time: 10-12 hours
Best time to visit: December-April

Mexico has recently become much more accessible and affordable from the UK and has much to attract visitors. It offers powdery white sands on fabulous Caribbean beaches, mixed with a rich, colourful culture. It is a lively place of fun and excitement for each member of the family.

Mayan and Aztec archaelogical sites, if introduced with enthusiasm, can be fascinating for older children. Read about the topic with your child before you go, to stimulate their interest and excitement.

There are many luxurious hotels, good restaurants and there is excellent shopping.

A stay on the mainland at Cancun or Playa del Carman is preferable to Cozumel when travelling with a family, as the mainland offers a much greater variety of activities and sightseeing.

Private healthcare is good and you only need to take malaria tablets if travelling inland to certain areas.

NICARAGUA ★

Flight time: 12-15 hours
Best time to visit: March-April

As with Honduras, the devastation caused by the last hurricane to hit Central America will take the country a long time to recover from. Again, its whole infrastructure was hit hard and it will be a long time before the people will be able to focus on drawing tourists back into the region.

PANAMA ★★

Flight time: 12-15 hours
Best time to visit: December-April

Panama is purported to be the most underrated tourist destination in the world – but perhaps not when travelling with children. Cruise liners sail the Panama Canal and give a cosseted taste of the rainforests with limited exposure to disease.

The north coast of Panama is known as the Mosquito Coast.

South America

ARGENTINA ★★

Flight time: 14-16 hours
Best time to visit: December-April

Buenos Aires is one of the safest cities in South America and there are more doctors per capita in Argentina than there are in the US. Older children may appreciate the history and atmosphere of city life in Buenos Aires, which is arguably one of the most chic cities in the world. It has such an air of smart sophistication that it is often referred to as the 'Paris of South America'.

Older children will also enjoy horseback riding in the pampas, a stay on a cattle ranch and the good skiing available in the highlands.

Outside the capital head for the Iguassu Falls, as they are spectacular. However, you must aim to see them in the wet season, because otherwise they may be no more than a trickle.

The troubles in Argentina and the struggling economy have led to an increase in poverty and crime throughout the country, so do be careful.

BOLIVIA ★

Flight time: 16-18 hours
Best time to visit: December-February

Bolivia is one of the poorest countries in South America and geographically one of most inhospitable places on Earth. La Paz is the highest-altitude capital city in the world.

You must not drink the water and diseases such as Chagas infest the population. Although once the most politically unstable country in the world, Bolivia is now a country of elected governments and growing economic stability.

Despite the negatives and the poverty, La Paz is one of the safest cities in South America and tourists do not have to be constantly on their guard as they would, for example, in the cities of Peru or Brazil. Plaits, bowler hats and ponchos are not just for the tourists, and colourful markets and well-fed boot-shine boys with toothy grins are all around.

Lake Titicaca is well worth the trouble it takes to get there. A site of serenity, history and legend, it is the highest navigable lake in the world, settled between distant snowy peaks. There is plenty here to stretch a child's imagination, from frog men in the lake to the island birthplace of the sun according to Inca mythology.

BRAZIL ★

Flight time: 12-14 hours
Best time to visit: January-February

Life is cheap in Brazil and the grinding poverty in the cities horrific. The dramatic splendour and natural beauty of Rio and its Statue of Christ is thrilling, but you can't even carry a handbag in the streets because of the risk of theft. When I visited Brazil, a fellow traveller was wrestled to the floor of a busy public bus by a youth attempting to steal his camcorder. All the shops will make arrangements to come to your hotel to deliver the goods you want and receive payment, because they know that it would be dangerous for you to carry money or credit cards with you when out and about. I have even heard stories of women being forced to strip in the streets – rape isn't the objective; what the thieves want is the money you might have hidden in your underwear. This constitutes the type of hassle you can do without when travelling with a family.

The internationally famous Rio carnival can be viewed from inside the *Sambodromo* for a price. Here you can sit in grandstands in relative safety and comfort and watch the thousands of people parading all through the night, but it is still an exhausting, repetitive and claustrophobic business, and any child could be excused for falling asleep in the seat for which you have paid a fortune. A visit to the carnivals of neighbouring Bolivia offers a greater and safer opportunity to join in and have more family fun.

The rainforest region around the massive Amazon River covers one third of Brazil, which itself covers half of South America. Manaus is the best place to head for with children. The tourist-class jungle lodges are exciting, hospitable and pleasant. The treks around them are safe and well trodden.

For viewing wildlife the best place is not around the Amazon but near to the border with Bolivia in the Pantalan. Sadly, as is common throughout Brazil, man's activities are threatening the region.

Accommodation is stunning, health care is excellent.

CHILE ★★★

Flight time: 16-20 hours
Best time to visit: December-April

Chile is perhaps not the destination you would choose if you were to put your children first, but it is a country that can be enjoyed by the family whose objective is to spend time together and relax while surrounded by diverse and breathtaking scenery.

Chile is an untamed country with a clean and tidy Europeanness about it. There are fjords that even the Norwegians admire, turquoise lakes, stunning Andean mountain vistas, glaciers, geysers and desert. Rich Argentinians flock there for a taste of its wild nature.

Skiing, hiking, biking, canoeing and general delight of the outdoors can be fun for all the family.

Accommodation is excellent. Health care is of a very high standard.

COLOMBIA

Many tour groups have pulled out of Colombia, political instability, narcotic-related crime, kidnappings, violence and the killing of street children being five good reasons. It is the most violent society in Latin America and one of the most violent in the world. Murder is one of the major causes of death, alongside cancer and heart disease.

The Caribbean coastal resorts offer some appeal for the family, but there are so many safe and beautiful beaches in less dangerous surroundings, and more accessible parts of the Amazon rainforests, that it is pointless to risk Colombia if you are not familiar with the country.

ECUADOR ★

Flight time: 14-16 hours
Best time to visit: November-March

Ecuador is one of those places where serenity seekers go to find themselves amidst soul-enriching mountains. Malaria is a problem but resistant malaria is not. When compared to other countries around the Amazon Basin this is an advantage. The drugs you will need to take have been used for forty years, and it is reasonably safe to say that even pregnant women should suffer no adverse effects, and provided you can get your children to take the tablets they will be fine, too. Stronger, newer drugs need to be taken, for example, in Brazil.

Tourism is well developed and accommodation is easy to find and incredibly cheap. If you intend to go trekking into the mountains, where health care services are scarce or non-existent, read up about first aid and carry a basic medical kit complete with drugs to combat any intestinal infections you may pick up.

GUYANA

Guyana has no significant tourism because it is generally the most dangerous place to visit in South America. Muggings are aggressive and narcotic smuggling is a major problem. Head to its western neighbour, Venezuela, instead.

PERU ★

Flight time: 16-18 hours
Best time to visit: February-May

Peru is fantastic, but not the best place to take children. The food is risky except in the very best hotels and tourist restaurants, and the mortality rate for children is estimated to be as high as 25%, many from infective illnesses, which is a major concern for a family. The ocean isn't really safe for swimming: it is thought that a major outbreak of cholera came from the Pacific. There is also a sewage issue, especially off Lima.

However, the Inca ruins at Macchu Picchu are a good reason to visit Peru with older children. Climbing to the summit is a good challenge, and the aura and serenity of the place is amazing. Train rides across the Andes and safe science research havens on the Amazon, open to tourists, are stunning with wildlife all around to see.

A very careful family watching what they ate and not letting any local water pass their lips (even for teeth cleaning) would have a wonderful time, although a non-Spanish-speaking family would probably have a more pleasurable trip with an escorted tour, which can be expensive.

PARAGUAY ★

Flight time: 16-18 hours
Best time to visit: February-May

The breathtaking Iguassu Falls would be a good enough reason to visit Paraguay, but to see them you do actually have the choice of staying in Brazil or Argentina, too, as the falls border all three countries. The border town of Ciudad del Este is where South Americans from the bordering countries go to buy cheap electrical goods and designer copies.

URUGUAY ★

Flight time: 16-18 hours
Best time to visit: February-May

Uruguay is a safe, hassle-free country, particularly by South American standards. It has good beaches, mainly occupied by Argentinians who flock there from Buenos Aires, only a ferry or short plane ride away. The small capital of Montevideo has a quiet, colonial feel, but the charm is in the countryside which is virtually devoid of people, being home to nine times more cattle and sheep than humans.

It is easy to get around the country, but driving is treacherous. Two thirds of accidents are caused by drunk drivers. Crime levels are low, and the health services are good, ensuring that the Uruguayans enjoy a high life expectancy. Malaria is not a concern.

VENEZUELA ★★★★

Flight time: 12-15 hours
Best time to visit: February-May

Venezuela is stunning and wild, but safe. The economy is reasonable, the climate is pleasant and the national parks are well run and beautiful. Canaima National Park is one of the most accessible. It is easy to get around and has its own runway for incoming planes. It is home to Angel Falls, the tallest waterfall in the world, as well as stunning plateau mountains, lakes and other waterfalls under which you are invited to walk. However, climbing amongst the slippery rocks means young children have to be watched rigorously.

Canaima is easily accessible from Margarita, the Venezuelan island in the Caribbean, probably the best place for a family to stay when visiting the country. From Margarita it is also easy to get to Venezuela's pleasant capital, Caracas. Both excursions could be done as a day trip by plane.

Margarita is hot and dry and the low humidity makes it a more pleasurable environment for children than some of the prettier, greener Caribbean islands. Tourist standards are high, many of the hotel packages are all inclusive, and the food is excellent. There is little outside the resorts to interest the family. Nightlife is usually centred around the hotels which often have good entertainment, and children's discos are sometimes held early in the evening.

Australasia

AUSTRALIA ★★★★★

Flight time: 24 hours
Best time to visit: November-February

Australia has something to attract the majority of travellers and offers abundant attractions for every member of the family. It is a vast country as diverse as any other, and is now very accessible from most parts of the world. There are impressive, well-managed national parks, mountain ranges, tropical rain forests, incredible coral reefs, deserts, wilderness and exotic white beaches while good sailing, swimming, snorkelling, diving, trekking, camping and skiing abound.

Unique wildlife is clearly visible all over, from kangaroos racing your car, to koalas, possums and flocks of wild budgerigars in the trees, and giant clams and brilliant-coloured fish in the turquoise seas – everything children love. After all of this there are aquariums, zoos, water parks and fast-food takeaways amidst colourful city life. Add in a splash of Aboriginal culture, a host of stories about runaway convicts and there is little more a child could wish for.

The standards of aircraft and service on the flights between Europe and Australia via Asia are excellent and good value for money, and the wide choice of accommodation will suit every budget: good camping facilities with municipal barbecues on most sites can offer a family a real taste of adventure, while clean, well-run motels and deluxe hotels by even the highest international standards are all better value than those in many other parts of the world.

Eating out with children will never be a problem, and health care standards are as high as you will find anywhere else in the world.

Despite all these wonderful reasons to take your family to Australia, you should be aware of certain elements that can catch some tourists out:

1. Australia is home to ten of the most dangerous creatures known to man. There are poisonous toads, deadly snakes, deadly jellyfish whose sting is so poisonous it can kill, dangerous spiders who live

under toilet seats in the cities, sharks and crocodiles. However, most Australians manage to survive, so it is more than likely that you will too, especially if you warn your children and prepare yourself.

2. The sun is very strong and, inland, the central desert temperatures can reach 50°C. This is uncomfortable and dangerous for babies and young children.

3. Despite the high standards of aircraft and flights to Australia, it is a long, arduous journey and the jet lag is horrendous. It is said that it takes one day to adjust per hour of time difference, so after a fortnight in Australia you will have enjoyed only a few good nights' sleep before it's time to come home and adjust all over again.

4. The distances between cities in Australia are huge. Internal flights would be preferable and, if booked at the same time as international air tickets, can be bought cheaply. Often one or two internal flights may be included free. Cars are relatively expensive to hire and with days on the hot road and children complaining you have to make careful, well-prepared decisions.

5. When driving, be respectful of the roads. The Pacific Highway on the east coast is host to many fatalities. In more rural areas collisions with wild animals, including kangaroos, can cause serious accidents on the road, particularly when driving at night.

As long as you are aware of these potential pitfalls, your Australian holiday should be wonderful. Australia always seemed tame to me when I was looking for excitement in my earlier travel days, but with a family it is an exciting destination.

NEW ZEALAND ★★★★

Flight time: 24 hours
Best time to visit: November–February

New Zealand has the feel of 1950s England. It is one of the safest and most peaceful countries in the world. The roads are quiet and the countryside is unspoilt. You can travel for miles and miles without seeing another car. There are a number of popular attractions scattered over the country, but they are not close together so you will need to make choices.

If you travel from Auckland with the children in mind, head for the Waitomo Caves. Travelling through the illuminated stalactites and stalagmites in a little boat is a joy. Inside the roof of the caves is a mass of glow bugs which look like tiny stars covering the ceiling. You can also try river rafting in the area. Rotorua is a popular destination. The children will wrinkle their noses at the smell of sulphur, but enjoy the boiling mud pools and geysers.

There is also skiing and bungee jumping. Lake Taupo is the place to bungee, but there is a minimum height, so children under the age of twelve would be unlikely to be allowed a go. There are many water sports available at the lake, too. Whale and wildlife watching is an attraction towards the more remote south.

Health and hygiene are of the highest standards. Accommodation is also of a high standard and relatively inexpensive – motels and small, medium-class hotels are the most common options.

South Pacific

The islands of the South Pacific are everything you would imagine; they are stunningly beautiful. The people are beautiful too. The only real downside is that everything is very expensive.

Before the arrival of the white man there was no malaria, tropical ulcers or bacterial infection. The people died either in accidents or of old age. Mutiny on the Bounty epitomises the sweeping beaches, the mass of coconut palms and the innocence of the people. The islands still offer ready smiles and happy welcomes.

November through to March the South Pacific can be subjected to tropical storms, hurricanes and cyclones, so is best avoided during this period. If you do choose to travel then, when the weather is cold and the rain pours down in buckets day after day, you will wish you had paid more attention to the weather forecast and booked in the dry season!

FIJI ★★★★

Flight time: 24-30 hours
Best time to visit: May-October

Fiji appears to have more attraction for the family than many of the other islands of the South Pacific. This is possibly a result of cost. It is generally less expensive to stay and eat in than French Polynesia, but has much of the same natural beauty. It is English speaking.

The food, health care and accommodation standards are good. The only deterrents from Europe are the distance, the jet lag and the cost.

The best time to visit is between May and October when the weather is cooler and a cyclone is unlikely to hit.

FRENCH POLYNESIA ★★★★

Flight time: 24-30 hours
Best time to visit: June-September

Tahiti and Bora Bora are everything you would imagine. The islands are surrounded by coral reefs which act as a barrier to the ocean, giving shallow, safe seas. The beaches are palm fringed and stunningly beautiful. The only blights on the islands are as a result of tourism. Papeete is safe but unattractive.

The major negatives are the high prices (you will need a budget of at least US $150 per day just for food and drink in the hotels for a family of four) and the distance – it takes up to forty-eight hours of solid travelling to get to Bora Bora from the UK.

KIRIBATI ★★

Flight time: 24-30 hours
Best time to visit: June-September

Kiribati is being developed to attract tourists but is still fairly inaccessible, with a limited flight service from Honolulu.

MARSHALL ISLANDS ★★

Flight time: 24-30 hours
Best time to visit: May-October

The attraction would be the unspoilt beaches, but there are few hotels or attractions for the family other than total escapism.

NAURU

There is little on Nauru to attract the family on holiday.

SOLOMON ISLANDS ★★

Flight time: 24-30 hours
Best time to visit: May-October

Distance, cost and sparse health care would redirect me to other islands in the South Pacific when travelling with my family.

TONGA ★★★

Flight time: 24-30 hours
Best time to visit: May-October

Tonga is still a little less commercialised and orientated towards tourism than some of the other South Pacific islands. It is beautiful and has a mass of tropical beaches over 170 islands. There are some modern health care facilities available on the islands.

TUVULU ★

Flight time: 24-30 hours
Best time to visit: May-October

Well off the beaten track, Tuvulu is not the ideal South Pacific paradise to aim for with a family. It is isolated and has only one 'real' hotel. Parasitic illnesses are common.

VANUATU ★

Flight time: 24-30 hours
Best time to visit: May-October

Vanuatu has been appearing on more South Pacific travel itineraries recently, and tourism is definitely growing. However, with children, especially when travelling from the UK, there are more accessible islands with the same to offer which, unlike Vanuata, are malaria free.

WESTERN SAMOA ★★★

Flight time: 24-30 hours
Best time to visit: May-October

Tourists are more often directed to American Samoa by accessibility, levels of health care and an overall better-developed tourist infrastructure.

There is concern about the impact of tourism, but somehow the Samoan people have retained their true Polynesian way of life, which is centred around the family and chiefs.

Unspoilt, lush and traditional, with very little to threaten the family it would make for a relaxed holiday with tales of cannibals and pirates.

What About the Weather?

Before booking your destination, think carefully about which season it will be when you are planning to arrive. Will it be especially rainy, hot, humid, cold, stormy, cloudy or windy? Assume nothing. Many advertised winter sun destinations are very cold from December to February, particularly in desert and mountainous regions, and many hotels and villas are not well heated. By October the evenings in Spain and Portugal can be very cold, and as the hours of sunlight decrease the swimming pool will be freezing unless it is heated. Obviously, water parks can be a very chilly experience outside the high summer season.

Children are more at risk from the cold than from the heat. Wherever and whenever you go, take at least one thick jumper, a warm coat and a blanket. Avoid monsoon seasons – not only to avoid heavy rainfall, but also malaria, dengue and other infectious illnesses, as mosquitoes proliferate in the wet and contagious fevers are much more common.

Checking the Weather

Reference and geography books are the most reliable means of judging what the weather will be like in your destination at the time of year you intend to travel. Travel agents may be unsure and holiday brochures may be biased. It is also important to realise that temperature in isolation is a poor indicator of how comfortable a climate will be. How hot or cold we will feel is a combination of temperature, humidity and the wind factor.

Make sure to check the hours of sunshine and the average rainfall, as these will also affect your enjoyment of the holiday.

Temperature

Note that while textbooks will usually give the average daily temperature, many holiday brochures will give the average daily *maximum* temperature. This makes a huge difference. For example, the average

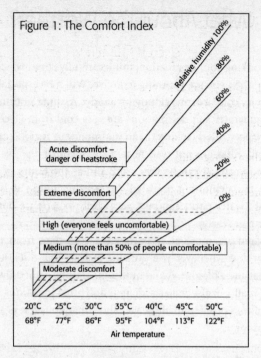

Figure 1: The Comfort Index

maximum daily temperature in June in Mauritius is 23°C, but the average daily temperature is 18°C. In Mauritius in June the temperature may reach 23°C for thirty minutes a day, but for the rest of the day it is much cooler and often windy.

Weather information can be obtained from the Meteorological Office (Overseas Enquiry Bureau) which is open twenty-four hours a day. Telephone 01344 420242.

Humidity

Humidity is a measure of the moisture content of the air. We can stand dry heat much better than damp heat, which makes us feel listless and lacking in energy. For example, at 27°C and low humidity we may feel comfortable, but if the humidity is high, we will feel hot and sticky. High humidity means that it is more difficult for our bodies to lose heat through sweating.

Choosing Your Destination:
a summary

- With young children, choose a destination where you will be confident. It is hard breaking new ground with babies and toddlers.

- Check that any vaccinations you may need are indicated for your children's age group.

- Is malaria a risk? If so, is it resistant – i.e. of the type that cannot be prevented by drug prophylaxis? Will you be able to cope with administering the tablets to your family? (see Chapter 5)

- Check the weather in geography books and independent guides, not just in travel agents and tour brochures.

- Avoid a country's peak season if possible. This is usually related to demand, and is the result of school holidays, not ideal weather conditions. The southern Mediterranean is much more pleasant in the spring than in the intense heat and high humidity of August.

- If your children are under school age, you must take advantage of offers outside school holidays while you can. Not only will it be a fraction of the price, there will be less noise, less crowding on beaches and relatively few childhood illnesses around.

- If you must holiday in the school holidays, broaden your horizons. The Caribbean has its low season when the Mediterranean has its peak. Prices are often comparable for a family, especially when you add on car hire, tour prices, competition for taxis and dining out.

- Don't rely totally on your travel agent. Don't be afraid to follow up and fax or email the hotel yourself with any special needs or requests for cots, room next to the pool, etc.

CHAPTER 5

Judging the Health Risks
of Your Destination
Immunisations, Malaria Tablets and Planning How to Avoid Illness Before You Travel

It is important to know which immunisations and malaria prophylaxis are recommended for the area you will be travelling to. You should contact your GP or local travel vaccination centre well in advance of the proposed travel date. Five to six weeks before is recommended, but you will need longer if your child is not up to date with the usual childhood vaccinations and booster jabs.

Most vaccines are safe for use with children. The malaria tablets you and your children will need will depend on the part of the world you are visiting. The order of the immunisations will be tailored to your needs and the time you have left before travel. Even if you have booked a last-minute trip, or left it within four weeks of departure, you will still be able to get cover for most high-risk illnesses before you travel.

Many health centres held in GP surgeries do not charge for children's vaccinations, except yellow fever. If you visit a private clinic, there will be a charge for each vaccine.

Figure 2 is a guide to which vaccines and anti-malarial drugs you are likely to require when travelling in each country of the world, but you should contact your GP or local travel clinic to confirm this information. The data is updated continuously and the guidelines, particularly for anti-malarial regimes, change constantly. The table also indicates the other illnesses that could be a danger to you and your children. The information below was correct at time of going to press. For the monthly updated information, telephone your local travel clinic or ask your GP.

Key to Figure 2

Malaria Regimes:

P   Proguanil

C   Chloroquine

PC   Proguanil plus Chloroquine

ME   Mefloquine (Larium). For children under one year or 15kg, the alternative regime would be Proguanil plus Chloroquine, which would not be as effective in areas of drug resistance.

Yellow Fever Vaccinations and Certificates:

A   Yellow fever vaccination certificate might be required if travellers pass through a country where yellow fever is present.

B   Yellow fever vaccination certificate might be required if travellers pass through a country where yellow fever is present, except for children under six months old.

C   Yellow fever vaccination certificate might be required if travellers pass through a country where yellow fever is present, except for children under one month old.

D   Vaccination is essential and requires a certificate.

E   Vaccination is essential and requires a certificate, except for children under six months old.

F   Vaccination is essential and requires a certificate, except for children under nine months old.

G   Vaccination is essential and requires a certificate, except for children under one year old.

H   Vaccination is recommended.

I   Vaccination is compulsory if transitting an area within six days.

J   Vaccination is compulsory if transitting an area within six days, unless under six months old.

K   Certificate might be required on leaving.

Other illnesses:

Leish   Leishmaniasis

Schist   Schistosomiasis (bilharzias)

Tryp   Trypanosomiasis (sleeping sickness – Africa, Chagas disease – Central and South America)

Figure 2: Vaccines and anti-malarial drugs required, by country

Country	Hepatitis A	Recommended malaria regime	Typhoid	Polio	Yellow fever	Meningitis A+C	Other illnesses
Afghanistan	YES	PC	YES	YES	A	–	Dysentery, TB, rabies, leish, worms
Albania	YES	–	YES	YES	C	–	–
Algeria	YES	–	YES	YES	C	–	–
Angola	YES	ME	YES	YES	A	–	Cholera, dysentery, plague, rabies, schist, filariasis, sleeping sickness
Antigua	YES	–	YES	YES	–	–	Dengue, schist, worms
Argentina	YES	C (in north-west)	YES	YES	–	–	Chagas, dysentery, rabies, worms, leish in north-east
Australia	–	–	–	–	G	–	Dengue in the north-west, dangerous sea and land animals (snakes and spiders)
Austria	–	–	–	–	–	–	Tick encephalitis
Azerbaijan	–	C (in south)	–	YES	–	–	–
Azores	–	–	–	–	C	–	–
Bahamas	YES	–	YES	YES	C	–	Dysentery, dengue
Bahrain	YES	–	YES	YES	C	–	Dysentery, rabies, leish
Bangladesh	YES	PC or ME (no risk Dhaka)	YES	YES	I	–	Cholera, dysentery, dengue, rabies, typhus, filariasis, worms, leish
Barbados	YES	–	YES	YES	C	–	Dysentery, dengue

Country					
Belgium	—	—	—	—	—
Belize	YES	C (rural areas)	YES	A	—	Dysentery, dengue, leish, filariasis, worms, Chagas
Belorussia	—	—	—	—	—	Dysentery
Benin	YES	ME	YES	G	YES	Cholera, dysentery, rabies, schist
Bermuda	—	—	—	—	—	—
Bhutan	YES	PC (in south)	YES	A	—	Dysentery, worms, rabies, TB
Bolivia	YES	PC or ME	YES	H+A	—	Cholera, leish, worms, Chagas
Bosnia and Herzogovena	—	—	—	—	—	Dysentery
Botswana	YES	PC (in north, Nov-June)	YES	G+B	—	Dysentery, rabies, cholera, worms
Brazil	YES	ME	YES	B+H	—	Cholera, amoebic dysentery, plague, leish, schist, worms, Chagas
Brunei	YES	—	YES	C	—	Typhus, worms
Bulgaria	—	—	—	—	—	Dysentery
Burkina Faso	YES	ME	YES	G	YES	Dysentery, cholera, rabies, sleeping sickness, worms
Burma	YES	ME	YES	A	—	Cholera, dysentery, dengue, rabies, worms, filariasis, plague
Burundi	YES	ME	YES	C	YES	Cholera, dysentery, typhus, sleeping sickness
Cambodia	YES	ME	YES	A	—	Cholera, dysentery, rabies, worms

Country	Hepatitis A	Recommended malaria regime	Typhoid	Polio	Yellow fever	Meningitis A+C	Other illnesses
Cameroon	YES	ME	YES	YES	G	YES	Cholera, dysentery, rabies, sleeping sickness, worms
Canada	–	–	–	–	–	–	–
Canary Islands	–	–	–	–	–	–	–
Cape Verde Islands	YES	–	YES	YES	C	–	Cholera, TB, rabies, typhus, schist, worms
Cayman Islands	YES	–	YES	YES	–	–	–
Central African Republic	YES	ME	YES	YES	G	YES	Cholera, TB, rabies, typhus, worms, sleeping sickness
Chad	YES	ME	YES	YES	G	YES	Cholera, TB, rabies, typhus, worms, sleeping sickness
Chile	YES	–	YES	YES	–	–	Cholera, worms, filariasis
China	YES	ME or C	YES	YES	A	–	Bact dysentery, rabies, schist, filariasis, leish, plague
Colombia	YES	ME	YES	YES	H+C	–	Cholera, dysentery, dengue, leish, worms, Chagas
Comoros	YES	ME	YES	YES	–	–	–
Congo	YES	ME	YES	YES	G	–	Cholera, TB, rabies, typhus, schist, worms, sleeping sickness
Cook Islands	YES	–	YES	YES	–	–	–
Costa Rica	YES	C	YES	YES	–	–	Dysentery, rabies, leish, filariasis, worms
Croatia	–	–	–	–	–	–	Dysentery

Country						
Cuba	YES	–	YES	YES	–	Dysentery, dengue
Cyprus	–	–	–	–	–	Typhus
Czechoslovakia	–	–	–	–	–	Dysentery, worms
Denmark	–	–	–	–	–	–
Djibouti	YES	ME	YES	C	–	Cholera, dysentery, rabies, typhus, sleeping sickness, schist, worms
Dominica	YES	–	YES	C	–	–
Dominican Rep	YES	C	YES	–	–	Dysentery, dengue, rabies, leish, schist
Ecuador	YES	PC	YES	H+A	–	Cholera, amoebic dysentery, leish, schist, worms, filariasis
Egypt	YES	C	YES	A	–	Schist
El Salvador	YES	C	YES	B	–	Dysentery, rabies, typhus, leish
Equatorial Guinea	YES	ME	YES	H+A	–	Cholera, dysentery, rabies, sleeping sickness
Estonia	–	ME	–	–	–	–
Ethiopia	YES	ME	YES	H+C	YES	Cholera, dysentery, rabies, typhus, sleeping sickness, schist, worms
Fiji	YES	–	YES	C	–	Dengue, filariasis, dysentery
Finland	–	–	–	–	–	Dysentery, Tick encephalitis
France	–	–	–	–	–	–
Gabon	YES	ME	YES	G	–	Cholera, dysentery, rabies, typhus, leish, sleeping sickness

Country	Hepatitis A	Recommended malaria regime	Typhoid	Polio	Yellow fever	Meningitis A+C	Other illnesses
Gambia	YES	ME	YES	YES	H+C	YES	Sleeping sickness, cholera, dysentery, TB, rabies, schist
Georgia	–	–	–	–	–	–	–
Germany	–	–	–	–	–	–	–
Ghana	YES	ME	YES	YES	D	–	Dysentery, cholera, rabies, typhus, sleeping sickness, schist, worms, TB
Gibraltar	–	–	–	–	–	–	–
Greece	–	–	–	–	–	–	Leish
Greenland	–	–	–	–	–	–	–
Grenada	YES	–	YES	YES	C	–	–
Guadeloupe	YES	–	YES	YES	C	–	Schist
Guam	YES	–	YES	YES	–	–	Dysentery, dengue, leish, worms, filariasis
Guatemala	YES	C	YES	YES	C	–	Dysentery, rabies, leish, worms, filariasis
Guiana, French	YES	ME	YES	YES	G	–	Cholera, dysentery, typhoid, leish
Guinea	YES	ME	YES	YES	H+C	YES	Cholera, dysentery, filariasis, schist
Guinea-Bissau	YES	ME	YES	YES	H+C	–	Cholera, dysentery, filariasis
Guyana	YES	ME	YES	YES	H+A	–	Cholera, bacterial dysentery, rabies, leish, tryp, schist, flukes

Country							
Haiti	YES	C	YES	YES	A	–	Dysentery, dengue, filariasis
Honduras	YES	C	YES	YES	A	–	Dysentery, dengue, rabies, leish, Chagas
Hong Kong	YES	–	YES	YES	–	–	Rabies
Hungary	–	–	–	–	–	–	Dysentery
Iceland	–	–	–	–	–	–	–
India	YES	PC	YES	YES	B	YES	Cholera, dysentery, rabies, leish, filariasis
Indonesia	YES	PC (not nec in Bali)	YES	YES	A	–	Dysentery, dengue, rabies, filariasis
Iran	YES	PC (March-Nov)	YES	YES	C	–	Dysentery, leish
Ireland	–	–	–	–	–	–	–
Israel	YES	–	YES	YES	–	–	Dysentery, rabies, leish
Italy	–	–	–	–	–	–	–
Ivory Coast	YES	ME	YES	YES	G	YES	Cholera, dysentery, sleeping sickness, schist
Jamaica	YES	–	YES	YES	C	–	Amoebic dysentery, dengue, worms
Japan	–	–	–	–	–	–	–
Jordan	YES	–	YES	YES	–	–	Dysentery
Kazakhstan	–	–	–	–	C	–	–
Kenya	YES	ME	YES	YES	H+C	YES	Cholera, typhus, leish, sleeping sickness

Country	Hepatitis A	Recommended malaria regime	Typhoid	Polio	Yellow fever	Meningitis A+C	Other illnesses
Korea	YES	–	YES	YES	–	–	Typhus
Kyrgyzstan	–	–	–	–	–	–	–
Laos	YES	ME	YES	YES	A	–	Amoebic dysentery, dengue, rabies
Latvia	–	–	–	–	–	–	–
Lebanon	YES	–	YES	YES	A	–	Cholera
Lesotho	YES	–	YES	YES	A	–	Cholera, TB, rabies
Liberia	YES	ME	YES	YES	G	YES	Cholera, dysentery, rabies
Libya	YES	–	YES	YES	C	–	Dysentery, rabies, TB, schist
Lithuania	–	–	–	–	–	–	–
Luxembourg	–	–	–	–	–	–	–
Madagascar	YES	ME	YES	YES	A	–	Cholera, dysentery, plague, rabies, typhus, sleeping sickness, filariasis
Madeira	–	–	–	–	C	–	–
Malawi	YES	ME	YES	YES	A	–	Cholera, dysentery, rabies, schist, filariasis
Malaysia	YES	–	YES	YES	C	–	Dengue, dysentery
Maldives	YES	–	YES	YES	A	–	–
Mali	YES	ME	YES	YES	G	YES	Cholera, dysentery, rabies, schist, filariasis
Malta	–	–	–	–	E	–	–

Country							
Mauritius	YES	C (rural areas)	YES	YES	C	–	Schist
Mexico	YES	C (rural areas)	YES	YES	B	–	Dysentery, dengue, rabies, leish, scorpions
Moldavia	–	–	–	–	–	–	Dysentery
Monaco	–	–	–	–	–	–	–
Mongolia	YES	–	YES	–	–	–	–
Morocco	YES	–	YES	–	–	–	Dysentery, TB, rabies
Mozambique	YES	ME	YES	YES	C	–	Cholera, dysentery, dengue, rabies, tryp, filariasis, plague
Namibia	YES	PC (in north, Nov–June)	YES	YES	C	–	Rabies, schist, dysentery, sleeping sickness
Nauru	YES	–	YES	YES	C	–	–
Nepal	YES	PC (no risk Kathmandu)	YES	YES	E+A	YES	Cholera, dysentery, rabies, worms, leish
Netherlands	–	–	–	–	–	–	–
New Caledonia	YES	–	YES	YES	C	–	Dysentery, worms
New Zealand	–	–	–	–	–	–	–
Nicaragua	YES	C	YES	YES	C	–	Dysentery, dengue, rabies, leish, worms
Niger	YES	ME	YES	YES	G	YES	Cholera, dysentery, rabies, sleeping sickness, schist, filariasis
Nigeria	YES	ME	YES	YES	H+C	YES	Cholera, dysentery, rabies, sleeping sickness, schist, filariasis

Country	Hepatitis A	Recommended malaria regime	Typhoid	Polio	Yellow fever	Meningitis A+C	Other Illnesses
Niue	YES	–	YES	YES	C	–	Dysentery, filariasis
Norway	–	–	–	–	–	–	
Oman	YES	PC	YES	YES	A	–	Rabies, typhus, leish, schist
Pakistan	YES	PC	YES	YES	B	–	Cholera, dysentery, rabies, typhus, leish, filariasis, dengue
Panama	YES	PC	YES	YES	H+C	–	Dysentery, dengue, rabies, leish, tryp, filariasis
Papua New Guinea	YES	Resistance is a problem	YES	YES	C	–	Dysentery, dengue, worms, filariasis
Paraguay	YES	C	YES	YES	K (rural areas)	–	Cholera, dysentery, rabies, leish, schist, worms
Peru	YES	PC	YES	YES	H+B (rural areas)	–	Cholera, dysentery, rabies, leish, flukes, worms
Phillipines	YES	PC (rural areas)	YES	YES	J (rural areas)	–	Dysentery, rabies, schist, flukes, worms
Pitcairn Islands	YES	–	YES	YES	C	–	–
Poland	–	–	–	–	–	–	–
Polynesia, French	YES	–	YES	YES	C	–	Dengue, dysentery, filariasis, worms
Portugal	–	–	–	–	–	–	–

Qatar	YES	–	YES	YES	C	Schist
Romania	–	–	–	–	–	Dysentery (bact), rabies
Russian Fed.	–	–	–	–	–	Tick encephalitis, TB, dysentery
Rwanda	YES	ME	YES	YES	G	–
Saint Helena	YES	–	YES	YES	–	–
Saint Lucia	YES	–	YES	YES	C	Dengue, schist
Saint Vincent and the Grenadines	YES	–	YES	YES	C	–
Samoa	YES	–	YES	YES	C	Dengue, worms
São Tomé and Principe	YES	ME	YES	YES	H+C	Cholera, dysentery, sleeping sickness, filariasis
Saudi Arabia	YES	PC (rural areas)	YES	YES	A	Amoebic dysentery, leish, schist
Senegal	YES	ME	YES	YES	G	Cholera, dysentery, TB
Seychelles	YES	–	YES	YES	A	Dengue, filariasis
Sierra Leone	YES	ME	YES	YES	H+C	Cholera, dysentery, TB, rabies, schist, filariasis
Singapore	YES	–	YES	YES	C	–
Slovenia	–	–	–	–	–	Dysentery
Solomon Islands	YES	Resistance is a problem	YES	YES	A	Dengue, worms
Somalia	YES	ME	YES	YES	H+C	Dysentery, cholera, rabies, TB

Country	Hepatitis A	Recommended malaria regime	Typhoid	Polio	Yellow fever	Meningitis A+C	Other illnesses
South Africa	YES	PC (rural areas and safari)	YES	YES	C	–	TB, schist, worms
Spain	–	–	–	–	–	–	Dysentery
Sri Lanka	YES	PC (except Colombo)	YES	YES	C	–	Amoebic dysentery, dengue, rabies. worms, filariasis
Sudan	YES	ME	YES	YES	–	YES	Cholera, dysentery, rabies, schist, filariasis, TB, leish
Surinam	YES	ME	YES	YES	H+C	–	Cholera, dysentery, leish, tryp, schist, worms, filariasis
Swaziland	YES	ME	YES	YES	A	–	Dysentery, dengue, rabies, schist
Sweden	–	–	–	–	–	–	Tick encephalitis
Switzerland	–	–	–	–	A	–	–
Syria	YES	C (in north, May–Oct)	YES	YES	–	–	Rabies, typhus, leish, schist
Taiwan	YES	–	YES	YES	–	–	Dysentery
Tajikistan	–	C (south border area)	–	–	–	–	Dysentery
Tanzania	YES	ME	YES	YES	H+C	YES	Cholera, dysentery, rabies, sleeping sickness, plague
Thailand	YES	Cam, Burm border	YES	YES	C	–	Cholera, dysentery, rabies, leish, dengue

Country							Diseases
Togo	YES	ME	YES	YES	G	YES	Cholera, dysentery, rabies, sleeping sickness, schist
Tonga	–	–	–	–	C	–	Dysentery, dengue
Trinidad and Tobago	YES	–	YES	YES	C	–	Worms
Tunisia	YES	–	YES	YES	–	–	Rabies
Turkey	YES	Rural areas March–Nov	YES	YES	–	–	Dysentery, rabies
Turkmenistan	–	–	–	–	A	–	Dysentery
Tuvulu	YES	–	YES	YES	C	–	Filariasis, dengue
Uganda	YES	ME	YES	YES	H+C	YES	Cholera, dysentery, rabies, schist, TB, plague, filariasis
Ukraine	–	–	–	–	–	–	–
United Arab Emirates	YES	PC (northern rural only)	YES	YES	–	–	Dysentery, rabies, schist
Uruguay	YES	–	YES	YES	–	–	Cholera, dysentery, rabies, leish, flukes, worms, chagas
Uzbekistan	–	–	–	–	–	–	Dysentery
Vanuatu	YES	Resistance is a problem	YES	YES	–	–	Dengue, filariasis
Venezuela	YES	PC or ME (rural areas)	YES	YES	H+C	–	Cholera, rabies, leish, schist, worms, Chagas, filariasis
Vietnam	YES	ME (rural areas)	YES	YES	C	–	Dysentery, dengue, rabies, leish, filariasis, plague

Country	Hepatitis A	Recommended malaria regime	Typhoid	Polio	Yellow fever	Meningitis A+C	Other Illnesses
Virgin Islands	YES	–	YES	YES	–	–	–
Yemen	YES	PC	YES	YES	C	–	Dysentery, rabies, typhus, leish, schist
Zaïre	YES	ME	YES	YES	G	–	Cholera, dysentery, rabies, typhus, sleeping sickness, filariasis, plague
Zambia	YES	ME	YES	YES	–	–	Cholera, dysentery, rabies, schist, filariasis, sleeping sickness
Zimbabwe	YES	ME	YES	YES	A	–	Cholera, schist, worms

The Safety of Modern Immunisations

You might be deterred from visiting a country because of the injections that are needed before you travel. You might have doubts or feelings of guilt about subjecting your child to the needle and the possible consequences of any complication or side effects caused by a vaccination. However, you must be aware and remember that all those available under licence in the UK are extensively researched, very well tolerated and extremely safe.

Side effects are very rare. A child who is healthy and well nourished will slip out of the health centre after a few pinpricks, primed to fight unseen enemies and enjoy their trip to the full. Very few will react to immunisations unpredictably, although if your child has any allergies you must tell the doctor. Some vaccines are derived from eggs, and others contain antibiotics, so an allergy to either constituent must be declared to avert a potentially serious allergic reaction. At the same time, discuss any concerns at all and take into account the particular vaccine and from what age it is recommended to be given.

There are still a few minor illnesses to be encountered abroad, and diseases such as dengue-fever, for which no vaccine is available. However, they are generally rare and do not have the same severity, likelihood of occurring, or risk of fertility as those for which there are vaccines on offer.

It is important to note that children who are already ill or feverish should not be vaccinated until they have recovered. Their immune defences will be concentrating on fighting the bug causing the illness and should not be compromised by loading more bugs into the body.

Except in the above circumstance, I adhere to the philosophy that the more bugs a child is exposed to when they are young and strong, the better. I always imagine the immune system as a muscle. The more exercise it gets, the bigger and stronger it becomes. Vaccinations help flex this 'muscle' without putting the child at risk from the disease.

A recent article in a respected sunday newspaper concluded that children who attend nursery schools at a very young age have much stronger immune systems later in life. Other studies suggest that a better-developed immune system will protect against problems such as asthma, and even cancer. There is some evidence that the incidence of leukaemia in children is much higher in middle-class children who have been kept at home and sheltered from common illnesses. Tumours may be the result of viral invasion. If your immune system is in good fighting order you are less likely to fall victim. This is readily illustrated in AIDS patients whose immune system is failing. Many will develop characteristic cancers such as Kaposi's sarcoma.

Therefore, unless you intend to keep your child at home in the UK for the rest of its life, I do believe that you are protecting them by immunisation.

Note that pregnant women should avoid live vaccines (which contain live organisms), such as polio or yellow fever.

Further Information

Most vaccines are low doses of the bacteria or virus that would normally cause the illness. The offending bug has usually been altered in some way (attenuated), or killed, so that it is incapable of causing the disease. Instead of becoming ill the body is given time to learn to recognise the particular bacteria or virus and develop antibodies that will be ready to attack the bug next time it is introduced into the body.

All manufacturers of vaccinations have a medical information department that is usually willing to help and advise patients, either over the telephone or in writing. They will be informed, up to date and the best possible source of data on their products. The employees working in the medical information section of any pharmaceutical company are either trained medics or qualified scientists whose knowledge in their field is excellent and unbiased. They are not salesmen and will often be more cautious about the details they give you than your own doctor. They may either reassure you or confirm your fears – either way they are likely to help you to make your decision.

Ask your doctor or nurse in the health clinic which vaccine they use and, if possible, the name of the manufacturer. Your local pharmacist will then be able to provide you with the manufacturer's address and telephone number. Don't be inhibited about contacting them by phone. Once through to the main switchboard, ask for the medical information department. When you are put through ask anything you want to know. Appropriate questions might be:

1. How long has the vaccine been available?
2. How many people have received the vaccine over the years?
3. What are the side effects?
4. Can it be given to toddlers?
5. Is a penicillin, egg, or any other allergy going to interfere with the vaccine?

Even if the voice on the other end of the phone asks you to hold while they check or look up the information, you should be confident that they are giving you good advice.

The Importance of Age

Children in the UK very rarely catch measles or chicken pox before they are twelve months old. This, to me, is amazing. It is possible that the immunity passes on from the mother and gradually wanes over the first year. Children suffer more with common illnesses the older they get, and teenagers in particular often present with much more severe symptoms than younger children presenting with the same infection.

I vividly remember catching chicken pox from my younger brother. He was about five years old and had thirteen spots in total. I was ten years old and developed over three hundred. They were everywhere, including my nose, my eyelids and inside my mouth. My son, Paris, caught chicken pox from nursery school when he was two years old, and didn't even seem to notice. Measles also struck me when I was thirteen, and I lay like a limp rag for two weeks while my youngest brother ran around me covered in spots. Measles and most other viruses are invariably far more aggressive in teenagers and young adults, who are usually society's fittest and strongest members. Measles and bacterial meningitis may kill a sixteen-year-old, but when the same measles virus or meningitis bacteria attacks a seven-year-old brother or sister, complications are far less likely to arise.

Also worthy of note is that although the triple vaccine (the MMR) is given from the age of one year old in the UK, it is not licensed for adults. So, although we may imagine that young children would be more vulnerable to a particular vaccine, provided the dosage administered has been tested by the manufacturers and is correct relative to the age and size of the child, we need not be unduly worried.

Figure 3: Minimum age and booster guide for the use of the principal travel vaccines

Travel vaccine	Minimum age children can safely be given the vaccine	When are booster doses necessary?
Diphtheria (usual childhood course)	2, 3 and 4 months (3 doses)	3 years old
Tetanus	2, 3 and 4 months (3 doses)	After 10 years
Pertussis (Whooping cough)	2, 3 and 4 months (3 doses)	
Polio	2, 3 and 4 months (3 doses)	School entry (5 years old) Booster should then be given 10 yearly
Yellow fever	9 months (single dose)	10 yearly
Meningococcal meningitis A&C	2 months (single dose) (May be less effective under 18 months)	3 yearly
Hepatitis A + B (Twinrix paed)	1 year (3 doses)	Hepatitis B booster after 5 years Hepatitis A booster after 10 years

Travel vaccine	Minimum age children can safely be given the vaccine	When are booster doses necessary?
Hepatitis A Immunoglobalin	No minimum age (single dose)	Protection lasts just 2-6 months
Hepatitis A Havrix junior	1 year (single dose)	Booster given 6-12 months after initial injection. Gives protection for up to 10 years
Hepatitis B	No minimum age (3 doses)	Every 3-5 years
Rabies	No minimum age given (3 doses)	Every 2-3 years
Japanese encephalitis	Vaccine is available for children only if requested for specific named cases (3 doses)	After 2-4 years
Tick-borne encephalitis	No minimum age given (3 doses)	After 1 year
Typhoid injection	18 months (single injection)	Every 3 years
Typhoid given orally	6 years (3 oral doses of one capsule)	Protection lasts 1 year
BCG (Tuberculosis)	Usually given at 6 weeks old	Booster may be required after 15 years
MMR (measles mumps and rubella)	1 year	
Hib Meningitis	2, 3 and 4 months	

Prophylactic Antimalarial Drugs for Children

Malaria has killed more people than any other disease in the history of mankind. Although some parasites attack in purges, malaria is unabating, and is always present in many parts of the world. If malaria is a risk in the country you will be travelling to, you must ensure that your child is protected with the correct dosage of the recommended drugs. Two million people worldwide die each year from the disease, and those most at risk are pregnant women and children under five years of age.

In the UK, around two thousand cases of malaria are diagnosed each year. Of those, few are fatal, but death has been known to occur within twenty-four hours of symptoms developing.

Unfortunately, antimalarial drugs do not give complete protection, and symptoms may develop up to a year after your holiday. This is confusing and may go undiagnosed by your doctor. It is likely that he will never have seen a case of malaria before and, because so much time has elapsed between your holiday and the illness, you may neglect to mention that you visited a region where it was a problem. It has been suggested that malaria is the most misdiagnosed illness in the UK, because many patients are considered to have flu.

When you arrive at your destination, you must be aware of the risk and concentrate on reducing the number of mosquito bites received. Getting a child to comply with the dosages below is not easy, but is very important. If you are travelling to a country where malaria is drug resistant and it may not be easy to seek medical help, it is advisable to carry the anti-malarials quinine and Fasidine for self-treatment in an emergency. Larium may also be used in a one-off, high dose. Dosages should be discussed with your doctor or travel clinic before you set off on your travels.

Malaria, its drug treatment and signs and symptoms, are detailed in Chapter 12.

Figure 4: Anti-malarial drug dosage guide

Age	0–5 weeks	6 weeks–11 months	1–5 years
Weight			10–19 kg
Chloroquine Weekly dose	37.5 mg or 3.75 ml syrup	75 mg or 7.5 ml syrup	150 mg (1 tablet) or 15 ml syrup
Proguanil Daily dose	25 mg (¼ tablet)	50 mg (½ tablet)	100 mg (1 tablet)
Mefloquine Weekly dose	Not recommended (N/R)		N/R <15 kg 2–5 years ¼ tablet (62.5 mg)

Conclusion

Before travelling, make sure that you do the following:

1. Confirm that you do actually need the vaccine by checking with a travel clinic. Note that you may only need a particular vaccine if you are visiting a certain region of the country or travelling outside the cities.
2. Discuss allergies and any other issues that concern you, either with your own doctor or a nurse at a travel clinic.
3. Check that the vaccination, which you are considering, is licensed and recommended for your child's age group.
4. It is essential that your child is well when the vaccinations are given.

If you have decided to take advantage of the protection offered by immunisation, you should feel confident and guiltless. It may even be that in future years you will find that you have benefited your child in other ways by keeping his immune system 'on its toes' and protecting against other problems. Also, consider that even if your child has a minor reaction to the relatively innocuous vaccination, it is nothing compared to how she would have suffered if she had come in to con-

6–11 years	>12 years
20–39 kg	>40 kg
225 mg (1½ tablets) or 22.5 ml syrup	300 mg (2 tablets)
150 mg (1½ tablets)	200 mg (2 tablets)
6–8 years ½ tablet (125 mg) 9–11 years ¾ tablet (187.5 mg)	250 mg (1 tablet)

N.B. The most important guage for dosage is weight. An underweight child must be treated as a younger one, or they might overdose. An overweight child must be treated as an older child, otherwise they might not receive a theraputic dose.

tact with the real thing. It may have meant death. The immunisations that have received the worse press are the diphtheria, pertussis and tetanus vaccines, together with the measles, mumps and rubella injections. I thought long and hard about immunising both of my boys and both times decided to let them have the vaccine, as none of the findings which have received so much press attention have been duplicated or proven. I also justified it to myself by thinking that if they reacted badly to the vaccination how on earth would their little bodies cope with the full-blown disease?

Note

The diseases for which vaccinations have been developed can all cause serious risk to human life without treatment. Thankfully, many diseases which have been catastrophic can now be prevented and contained with the benefits of modern medicine. However, even when protected by all the available vaccines, common sense is still your most powerful weapon against similar and related illnesses:

1. You must pay stringent attention to what and where you eat and drink (Chapter 11)
2. Avoid being bitten by mosquitoes and other biting insects and creatures
3. Beware of stray and wild animals, including bats, which can carry rabies
4. Avoid being bitten, scratched or even licked

If you pay careful attention to the above guidelines you will avoid many other transmittable diseases for which there are no available vaccines.

Diseases Preventable by Vaccination

The following facts on preventable diseases and their vaccinations has been compiled to help you to make informed choices about protecting yourselves and your children from contracting major life-threatening illnesses while travelling abroad.

Cholera

Cholera is caused by a toxin-producing bacteria that lives in the intestines of infected humans. The illness is acquired from contaminated water or food. Although unsanitary water plays the main role in the transmission of the disease, shellfish can harbour the responsible bacteria in high concentrations, and food – even fresh fruit and vegetables – which has been in direct contact with infected excreta or contaminated water can pass on the infection. Regions prone to cholera outbreaks are the Indian subcontinent, Africa, South-East Asia and South America.

Symptoms

Sudden onset of painless, profuse, odourless diarrhoea. The volume of diarrhoea is enormous and predominantly water with flecks of mucous, similar in appearance to rice water. After the diarrhoea begins, vomiting usually follows that is characteristically effortless and productive of a rice-watery liquid.

This drastic loss of fluids causes severe, life-threatening dehydration with associated muscle cramps and extreme weakness.

Prevention and Treatment

Cholera outbreaks often make news headlines, so you should be able to avoid taking your children into areas of danger.

Unfortunately the cholera vaccination is no longer very effective, and is estimated only to give protection levels of around 50 per cent. This, combined with the fact that the disease is relatively uncommon among travellers, has led to a decreased level of demand for the vaccine. It is no longer widely recommended and no country now requires the immunisation as an official condition of entry, unless the border staff are trying to extort a bribe.

Even if you do opt to have your family vaccinated against cholera you must be scrupulously careful what you eat and drink. Vigilance in this area will help to avoid a whole plethora of other contagious illnesses and food poisoning while you are travelling (see Chapter 11).

If you are visiting endemic areas, such as Bangladesh, go prepared. Buy commercially available sachets or tablets of sugars and salts to take with you. These include Rehydrat and Dioralyte, which are both available to buy over the counter in most pharmacies (see page 237).When added to clean water these provide effective oral replacement of vital electrolytes (e.g. salt) and fluids, so if there is any delay getting a doctor you may be able to prevent your child getting so drastically dehydrated that they will need intravenous fluid replacement.

With adequate oral and, in more severe cases, intravenous fluid and electrolyte replacement, recovery from the symptoms of cholera is remarkably rapid and there is a very low associated death rate in children and adults.

While fluid replacement is the most important aspect of treatment, the required volume of fluid may be enormous and an effectively administered antibiotic will dramatically reduce the duration and volume of diarrhoea by inducing rapid eradication of the causal bacteria.

The recommended antibiotic treatment is tetracycline. Recommended dose 10–12.5mg/kg, every six hours, for forty-eight hours.

This drug should not be used in pregnant women or generally in children under eight years old because it causes discolouration of the teeth and is laid down within the structure of growing bone. However, because dosing is only for forty-eight hours, such a short treatment should have no adverse effect.

An alternative to pack is Co-trimoxazole (Bactrim or Septrin). This antibiotic has a variety of uses and is indicated for children as young as six weeks old.

Diphtheria

Diphtheria is a very serious, highly contagious illness caused by a toxin-producing bacteria. It is very rare in developed countries due to the extensive immunisation programmes in very young babies.

However, in many poorer countries, diphtheria is still a common and tragic illness. It can still be contracted in many parts of the world, but survival rates are much higher in the West.

Diphtheria can progress to a life-threatening illness within a day of the appearance of the first symptoms. It is easily transmissible by dust or coughing and sneezing.

Symptoms

Fever, sore throat, difficulty in swallowing and enlarged lymph glands in the neck. The toxin released by the bacteria causes destruction of the upper airway's tissue cells and the formation of a greyish-yellow membrane which can obstruct the upper air passages, causing asphyxiation (choking). The toxin also enters the bloodstream where it can cause serious, permanent damage to the heart, nervous system or kidneys.

Prevention

The vaccine is an important, standard, childhood immunisation. It is highly effective, long lasting and a very important defence against a potentially tragic condition.

The usual course is three injections given to infants between three and six months old along with the tetanus and pertussis (whooping cough) vaccines. If you have followed advice it is more than likely that your children will have been protected as babies, but if you have any doubt and your doctor or health visitor has no records, you should ensure that your children are vaccinated before travelling. In many parts of the world diphtheria is still a killer.

Treatment

Treatment of the actual disease is with the administration of the anti-toxin, which needs to be administered before the toxin is able to cause its damage. An antibiotic – e.g. penicillin – should also be given. If your child is allergic to penicillin, erythromycin is the next best option.

It is important to note that even with good medical treatment there is a one-in-ten chance that diphtheria will be fatal. In places with low standards of health care the incidence of death will be much higher.

Keep up to date with boosters (see page 162).

Hepatitis

Hepatitis is a serious infection of the liver by one of a number of viruses, most commonly hepatitis A or hepatitis B.

Symptoms

Jaundice, fever, lethargy, chills, headache, digestive problems, fatigue, feelings of weakness, aches, pains, loss of appetite, nausea, vomiting, abdominal pain, dark urine, light-coloured faeces, yellow skin and, in severe cases, the whites of the eyes may turn yellow.

Hepatitis A

Hepatitis A is the most commonly acquired travel illness and is endemic in many areas of the world from Turkey to Mexico.

Many viruses infect the human liver and may produce severe hepatitis, but hepatitis A is the greatest threat to children as it is so easily transmitted. As a result, they may be at risk if you choose not to vaccinate them at all. Even in its most severe form it is unlikely to be deadly, but it is a serious illness that can incapacitate its victims for several weeks.

The major concern is that the incubation period of hepatitis A is between three and five weeks, during which time large amounts of viruses are shed in the faeces, which means that there is a good chance it will be passed on to another member of the family before any symptoms show.

Hepatitis A spreads from the intestines of an infected host by contaminated water and food. Outbreaks can often be traced to uncooked food or food handled after cooking. Raw and inadequately cooked shellfish are associated with a high risk of hepatitis A infections. All age groups are at risk.

In tropical climates most cases occur during the rainy season, with low incidence during the dry periods.

Prevention

Spread is reduced by hygienic measures and extreme care with food and water intake.

Immunisation against the hepatitis A virus is readily available either by injection with human immunoglobulin or the recently developed Havrix (see below). Twinrix protects against hepatitis A and has the added protection against hepatitis B.

a) Immunoglobulin

This was once used widely, successfully controlling the outbreak of hepatitis A in, for example, nursery schools. It would only be recommended today if you have left it too late to have the Havrix vaccine (see page 172).

Immunoglobulin acts by boosting the host's entire immune system, so would theoretically help defend against many other bugs and viruses that a child may encounter on holiday, including measles and rubella. It is used for pregnant women who have come into contact with rubella to prevent them from catching the illness which would damage the developing foetus.

The positive for immunoglobulin is that it gives immediate immunity. It can therefore be given the day before you travel, so even if you book a last-minute trip you will still be able to get protection from the hepatitis A virus. However, a concern voiced by some is that because immunoglobulin is derived from pooled human blood products, there is a tiny risk of some as-yet-undiscovered disease not being detected during the screening process, which may be passed on – as was the case with HIV. Another negative is that it is thick and viscous, so must be given through a wide-gauge needle. The injection is therefore painful and it stings. You may be well advised to ask for the jab in your child's bottom, which is less tender than a skinny little arm.

I recall a particularly painful immunoglobulin injection during which the doctor had to withdraw the needle and change it because the solution proved to be too thick to pass down its gauge. He changed it for a much wider one which really hurt. (Incidentally that doctor was my dad!)

Immunoglobulin should be given after all the travel vaccines have had their chance to work. If not, some of the effect of the immunisation programme will be lost.

b) Havrix

Junior monodose may be given to children over one year old. It must be given approximately three weeks before departure to allow the immunity to build up. Havrix is administered as a single dose that will be effective for twelve months. If a booster vaccine is given within three years, immunity will be extended to last for up to ten years.

The vaccine contains attentuated (weakened) hepatitis A virus. Once the injection is given the body learns to recognise the hepatitis A virus and produce antibodies that are specifically designed to attract and destroy it. Thus the body is protected, and because the hepatitis A virus is attenuated it cannot attack our liver in the same way as the intact virus could. Our body therefore learns to fight the virus the next time it meets it without being at risk.

The side effects are that there may be a little discomfort or redness around the injection sites and a child may have very mild symptoms of the actual disease – such as slight fever, malaise, fatigue, nausea and loss of appetite – but these symptoms are a fraction of the severity of the full-blown disease.

Treatment

If any member of the family were to contract hepatitis A in general there is not much that you can actively do. You must wait for the healing process, which can take many weeks.

Liver has amazing powers of rejuvenation, but if yours is preoccupied with fighting infection it can't mop up all the toxin from your blood efficiently and the patient will feel terrible.

Fatty foods, processed foods, all alcohol and some medications should be avoided. The best treatment is rest, eat plenty of fresh food and drink plenty of fresh, boiled water.

Hepatitis B

Hepatitis B is a serious illness, and although the symptoms are similar to those of hepatitis A, hepatitis B is a chronic recurring illness that can cause serious liver damage, which may progress to liver cancer.

Hepatitis B usually develops 60-180 days after injection of human blood or plasma, or use of inadequately sterilised syringes or needles. It can also be sexually transmitted.

Because of the mode of transmission of hepatitis B, your child will be unlikely to catch it under normal circumstances. The only real threat would be if your child were to need hospital treatment, particularly a blood transfusion. In this instance you are very likely to have a great deal more to worry about, but you should be aware of the risks in many parts of the world where the screening of all blood and blood products is economically impossible. (See page 316 for blood transfusions.)

Prevention and Treatment

If you intend to travel abroad for a long time (more than six months), or live in a country that does not share Western health care and screening standards, you should have your child immunised against hepatitis B. In some parts of the world there is a 15-20 per cent incidence of hepatitis B in the local population, so if you are living among them your family should be protected.

Twinrix paediatric gives protection against hepatitis A and hepatitis B.

Hepatitis C, D and E (Non-A, Non-B Hepatitis)

New strains of the virus responsible for causing hepatitis in humans are steadily being uncovered. It is possible that others already exist or may develop in the future. Research is ongoing.

Hepatitis C, like hepatitis B, is transferred by blood and blood products, so prevention measures are the same. A vaccine is currently being developed.

Hepatitis D has been classified relatively recently. Hepatitis D is transmitted in blood and blood products, so prevention measures are the same as for hepatitis B and C. Immunisation against hepatitis B does afford some immunity.

Hepatitis E is transmitted by the same mechanisms as hepatitis A – by infected food and water intake. The greatest danger is to pregnant women. Prevention is by careful attention to hygiene and great care with food and water ingested.

None of the above pose a great risk to the traveller of any age at present.

Typhoid

Typhoid is a widespread and potentially fatal infection caused by the ingestion of the bacteria *Salmonella typhi*. The infection is passed on via contaminated food and water and may be spread by human hands, flies and other insects. It can also survive freezing and drying, and so may be carried onto food and into drink from the water supply, sewage, dust, ice and shellfish.

Although no age group is exempt, typhoid is generally a disease of older children and young adults. Children under two years old rarely present with the illness. It is even more unlikely in those under one year.

Symptoms

Headache is the most common symptom in children, which is unusual and clinically distinctive because the severe frontal headache seen in children with typhoid fever is relatively rare in paediatric medicine. There may be a high fever but the heart rate will be slow which, again, is unusual. Cough, diarrhoea and abdominal pain are frequent symptoms and vomiting can occur.

A rash often appears on day seven to ten of the illness. It is characteristically a variable number of rose-coloured spots which are usually first noticed on the abdomen and disappear with pressure. Sometimes each spot is capped with a small blister. After two to three days the spots may disappear, leaving brownish stains which are much harder to notice on darker skins.

Untreated typhoid lasts for approximately four weeks. The most serious consequence of the illness is destruction of the gut tissue, which can lead to haemorrhage and perforation. This does not usually happen in the early stages of the illness, but treatment needs to be sought before this stage has chance to develop.

There is also the potential for renal, cardiac and liver complication, and increased risk of abortion in pregnancy.

Treatment and Prevention

The typhoid vaccine was at one time a monster after which you were left feeling sore, disorientated, weak and drained for days. The availability of a relatively new oral vaccine may be the preferred choice for those put off a repeat of the injected vaccination experience, although an improved vaccine has since been developed with fewer side effects.

Oral protection against typhoid is a series of three capsules that must be given separately over five days, specifically on days one, three and five. The immunisation must be repeated each year and is not recommended for children under six years of age. The side effect may be a mild tummy upset.

Protection by injection lasts for three years and is available for children older than eighteen months. The side effects may be local irritation and discomfort at the injection site or mild symptoms of the illness including headache, fever and malaise.

Immunisation should be given ten to fourteen days before departure. It is important to realise that immunisation does not protect a child from massive doses of ingested bacteria. The vaccination is only effective about 60 per cent of the time, so careful attention must still be directed towards avoiding ingestion of this aggressive bacteria.

If your child is feverish and you suspect that he has typhoid, you must seek medical attention. There are a number of antibiotics that are useful in treating the illness, but the more effective ones have a number of side effects that should be monitored in children.

If you cannot get medical assistance, sulphamethazole with trimethoprim, chloramphenicol, amoxycillin and the 'strong' option of ciprofloxin are effective.

Also ensure that the child does not become dehydrated and that their temperature does not reach dangerously high levels.

Paratyphoid

Paratyphoid is similar to, but milder than, typhoid and is caused by a different strain of the same bacteria, *Salmonella paratyphi A, B* & *C*.

Strain B is most common. Paratyphoid runs a shorter and gentler course than typhoid, with relatively little toxicity.

Japanese Encephalitis

This is a rare infection causing inflammation of the brain. It occurs primarily in rural Asia, especially during the rainy season. The disease is caused by a virus that is mainly transmitted by the bite of rice-field breeding mosquitoes. It can be fatal.

Symptoms
Fever, headache and vomiting. Convulsions in children may be the first sign. Lethargy is common and there may be confusion and delerium that progresses into coma. The duration of the illness is very variable, but recovery is long and young children are the most prone to complications, including mental impairment and personality changes.

Prevention
Because Japanese encephalitis is rare, the vaccination available is only recommended for those going off the beaten track for long periods of time. There are no guarantees about its effectiveness, and the vaccine is not licensed in the UK for general use. It is only available in specialist health clinics or by special request to the manufacturers from your doctor. The vaccine is indicated for children, but for the

majority of travellers the first line of protection is to avoid being bitten by mosquitoes as far as is possible. (See page 281.)

Treatment
There is no specific treatment recommended.

Measles

Measles is a highly infectious and potentially very serious viral disease. It is caught by inhaling infected droplets and is rare in children under six months old due to the passive immunity passed on from the mother. Most children who are not immunised would be most likely to develop measles in their second year of life.

Symptoms
The incubation period is seven to twelve days and the child is infectious from a few days before the rash appears until five days after it goes.

The symptoms are fever, a sore throat, cough, headache, runny nose, red eyes, general misery and an irregular, red, mottled, raised rash which starts behind the ears, spreads, lasts for about a week and then fades. White spots in the mouth (Koplik spots) are a sign that doctors look for to confirm measles. Vomiting and diarrhoea are not uncommon and complications include ear and chest infections, which must be treated to avoid long-term damage. There is a slight risk of encephalitis.

Prevention
The controversy about the MMR vaccine has led to an increase in the potential for widespread outbreaks. All the medical evidence continues to point to the vaccine being completely safe. The link between autism and MMR, despite exertive efforts, is still unproven.

The fact that the symptoms of autism affect children at about eighteen months, just after the time the vaccine is usually given, is confusing for parents, but the incidence of autism is the same in vaccinated and non-vaccinated children which strongly suggests that the link cannot be MMR.

The vaccine is usually given in the UK at about twelve months of age along with mumps and rubella. The side effects of the vaccine are generally mild symptoms of the illness, local and allergic reactions.

Measles can be caught worldwide. In the tropics, children may catch the virus at a slightly younger age (between six and twelve months) but the outcome and incidence of complications follow similar patterns. The vaccine is effective after two to three weeks and gives long-lasting protection.

You may prefer not to go abroad until your child is twelve to thirteen months old and has been vaccinated, yet despite the fact that children in the tropics do catch measles at a slightly younger age, most well-nourished children born in the Western world will catch measles between their first and second birthday and are unlikely to be at any more risk abroad than at home before this time.

It is not advisable to go abroad immediately following the vaccination just in case there are any adverse reactions. Also remember that immunisation will not be effective for two to three weeks.

It is important to note that the measles, mumps and rubella vaccine may interact with some travel injections and should not be given within one month of any other live vaccine (e.g. polio) or within three months of immunoglobulins. Severe allergies to eggs are a contraindication for the vaccine.

Treatment

If you decide not to vaccinate your child and your child contracts the illness, it is advisable to seek a doctor, then concentrate on keeping the child comfortable and resting with plenty to drink. Paracetamol will ease discomfort and lower the temperature. Wash crustiness away from the eyes with clean warm water. If the temperature remains high after the fever has begun to subside your child may have developed a secondary infection, possibly in his ears or chest, and will therefore need antibiotics to prevent any lasting damage which could occur if left untreated.

Meningitis

Meningitis is the inflammation of the membranes that cover the brain and spinal cord. Children are particularly susceptible and, as we know, the disease, which may be caused by a virus or bacteria and transmitted by contact with an infected carrier, can be fatal.

Viral meningitis is usually the less-severe form and, although the symptoms are similar to those seen with the more aggressive bacterial infections, most children make a complete recovery.

Bacterial meningitis is more serious and life threatening. The strain that is most common in the UK is caused by the *Haemophilis influenza* type B bacteria. This strain is quite different from meningococcal bacteria *(Neisseria meningitidis* types A and C) which cause epidemics in sub-saharan Africa and Asia.

In Africa and Asia the age group most at risk are five- to fifteen-year-olds. Compare this with the UK, where those most at risk are under five years old.

Symptoms

Severe headache, confusion, drowsiness, fever, rising temperature, stiff neck, nausea, vomiting and photophobia (sensitivity to light). Convulsions may occur in young children. Babies have a characteristic high-pitched cry and the fontanelle (soft spot) may bulge outwards and feel tense.

A rash of red spots may occur which does not disappear when pressure is applied to it. For example, if you were to press a drinking glass on to the spots on a child's skin and the rash is still visible, it could have been caused by the toxins produced by the meningococcal bacteria, which can interfere with the blood-clotting process.

Prevention and Treatment

The meningitis 'Hib' vaccine is widely used in the UK to combat type B meningitis, so it is more than likely that your children were immunised as babies. Infants are given three separate vaccinations between two and twelve months old. Check your vaccination records or confirm with your doctor or health visitor. This vaccine, however, is different from the one required for protection in Africa or Asia from group A and C meningitis.

A safe and effective vaccine against group A and C is available, but is not normally required unless travelling to an area of a current epidemic. Long-stay visitors (especially backpackers or those living/working with local people, particularly in schools, hospitals or orphanages) and those undergoing rural travel should also consider being protected.

It is worth noting that visitors to Saudi Arabia on Hajj (the annual Muslim pilgrimage) are required to receive the vaccination.

The vaccine is safe from the age of two months, but children under eighteen months have a reduced duration of protection. Over eighteen months, cover lasts for three to five years.

If the vaccinations are not given and either strain of the disease is contracted, a child may become gravely ill within hours and may pass rapidly into a coma. It is crucial to get urgent medical attention without delay.

Children treated in time with antibiotics – which may be administered by injection or orally – nearly always recover from bacterial meningitis. In sub-saharan Africa and certain parts of Asia it is advisable to carry your own needles, then if anything were to happen you must insist upon their use. The economy in this area does not allow for blood screening and good sterilisation techniques. HIV and AIDS are rife.

Your child will need hospital treatment, but if there is going to be a delay in getting your child there, you should seek out any doctor, nurse, midwife, pharmacist or even vet to give your child an injection of benzylpenicillin.

The recommended doses of benzylpenicillin to be given by injection into a muscle are as follows:

Children under one year:	300mg (dissolved in a few ml of pure boiled water)
One to nine years:	600mg (dissolved in a few ml of pure boiled water)
Over ten years:	1200mg (dissolved in a few ml of pure boiled water)

Injectable amoxycillin is an alternative if benzylpenicillin is unavailable. If your child is allergic to penicillin, injectable co-tri-moxazole or erythromycin would be advisable.

If you are outside the realms of medical help and injectable antibiotics are not available, you should give high doses of more than one oral antibiotic. The best would be a combination amoxycillin and co-trimoxazole. Your child is far more at risk from the infection than from antibiotic overdose, and aggressive treatment is necessary.

Mumps

Mumps is a viral infection, most commonly affecting children, that causes fever and a characteristic swelling of the main pair of salivary glands, to such an extent that the child has a hamster-like appearance.

The disease is spread by sneezing and coughing. It is rarely serious in children, who may not even feel particularly unwell.

Symptoms
The incubation period is approximately two to three weeks. The symptoms are fever, headache and tender, swollen glands below the ears and beneath the chin. There will be difficulty swallowing and chewing, but the illness is invariably mild. A less-common symptom is painful testes in boys. Very occasionally meningitis, encephalitis and pancreatitis are complications.

Prevention and Treatment
The vaccine is usually given in the UK at about twelve months of age, along with the measles and rubella vaccines. The side effects are generally fever, malaise, local and allergic reactions.

Due to the mildness of the illness, it need not be a major concern on holiday if a child has not been vaccinated beforehand. If, however, a child does catch mumps abroad, or presents with the symptoms while you are on holiday having caught it at home before you left, you should concentrate on making him or her comfortable. Give them plenty to drink, ease pain and fever with paracetamol and, if possible, liquidise or mash their food to make it easier for them to swallow.

Pertussis (Whooping Cough)

This is a highly infectious bacterial disease occurring almost exclusively in children under five years old. It is easily spread by coughing and sneezing and can be fatal. The infection clogs the airways with mucus, making it difficult for the child to breathe. If not fatal, the illness can produce lasting lung damage.

Symptoms

The incubation period for the disease is between seven and nine days. Then, after one or two weeks of cold-like symptoms, a characteristic severe cough with a distinctive sound develops and lasts for several weeks. A whooping sound is produced when the child desperately sucks breath into their lungs after a coughing fit, but this may not occur in babies or very young children. The coughing can be so racking that the child may turn blue due to lack of oxygen and vomiting often occurs when the coughing ceases. Attacks are more common at night. The whole illness is exhausting for the child and those caring for it.

There are a number of complications associated with the illness including lung collapse, hernias, pneumonia and convulsions or, more severely, brain damage resulting from the lack of oxygen in the blood reaching the brain.

Prevention and Treatment

Children who have received all the usual childhood vaccinations will have been immunised as babies. The pertussis vaccine is given along with diphtheria and tetanus, in the triple vaccine of three injections, four weeks apart, between the ages of two and four months of age. The first vaccine alone offers a massive protection against the diseases, so if travel is planned for the very early stages of a baby's life, even the first vaccine alone would give a lot of immunity, although it is best to get all three done. UK practices try and get the vaccinations done as soon as possible anyway, so do contact them if you are planning to travel, and see if it is possible to get all three done in reasonable time.

The vaccination should be considered if travelling abroad with children under five years old who have not been immunised, particularly babies and infants. Children over five years old are not at great risk.

If you have opted not to have the full protection of the vaccine, you should keep your children, as far as is possible, away from infected children – even those who just seem to have a cold.

If the illness is contracted your child will need effective antibiotic therapy, and may need treatment for dehydration if the vomiting has been severe. Cough medicines are of no value. The bacteria responsible for the illness is sensitive to a range of antibiotics, including erythromycin and tetracycline, but only during the early stages. If the antibiotic is not started before the severe coughing stage it will not be effective.

Poliomyelitis (Polio)

Poliomyelitis is a viral infection that can cause untreatable meningitis and paralysis. Until the relatively recent advent of the vaccine, the illness was a serious epidemic world health problem and the most common cause of paralysis in children. It was also a common cause of death.

The virus responsible inhabits the intestine and is passed in the stools in large numbers for up to six weeks after the start of the illness. It is spread by the faecal contamination of food and water, even in swimming pools. It can also be transmitted by coughing.

Symptoms
The patient is anxious, irritable, feverish and complains of stiffness and pains in their neck, trunk and limbs, with severe headache. Paralysis usually occurs during the fever, rarely afterwards, and may be the first distinct sign of poliomyelitis in infants or very young children. Death may occur from paralysis of the muscles used for breathing.

Prevention and Treatment

The oral polio vaccine is a safe, effective and painless means for preventing the tragedy of childhood paralysis and death. If you have followed the advice of your doctor and health visitor your child will have been immunised as a baby, but if you neglected to take your children to be vaccinated when they were very young you should seriously consider protecting them before you take them outside Western Europe, the US, Australia or New Zealand.

The vaccine is usually given by mouth at two, three and four months of age or in older children similarly as three doses, four weeks apart. A booster should be given at the age of five which lasts for approximately ten years. It is very safe. It is important to note that the polio vaccine takes eight weeks to be effective, so the course should be given well before you intend to travel. Also, the vaccine interacts with the typhoid vaccine, so you should ensure that they are given well apart. If you opt not to take the safe option of protection by immunisation, you should adopt very high standards of personal hygiene and pay scrupulous attention to what your children eat and drink. Be very careful where they swim and even who they play or have contact with abroad. Naturally, avoid other sick children. Once the infection progresses it cannot be effectively treated.

Rabies

Rabies is endemic in most parts of the world. There are only a few countries that remain rabies free, and these include the UK, New Zealand, Australia, Taiwan, Japan, Hawaii, Western Malaysia and Antarctica.

Rabies is a viral infection that is spread by an animal bite or scratch. If the skin is broken, even a lick from the infected animal can result in the infection being passed on.

The animal carrier can be wild or domestic and apparently tame. Foxes, wolves, raccoon, mongooses, skunks and bats all transmit the virus but in 90 per cent of cases in man worldwide, rabies is caught from a domestic cat or dog. Rabies is an infection of the nervous system and is usually fatal if not treated before symptoms develop.

Symptoms

The incubation period following the bite ranges from four days to many years but is usually between twenty and ninety days. It tends to be shorter after bites to the face than after those on the limbs, after which symptoms develop at around day thirty to thirty-five.

The illness usually starts without specific symptoms over the first few days. Fever, chills, weakness, tiredness, photophobia (sensitivity to light), muscle pain and mood change then occur. The victim may become anxious, irritable and depressed. There is also likely to be pain in the area of the healed bite. Most patients then develop furious rabies which is distinguishable by the characteristic fear of water and, as the illness progresses, terror, even at the mention of water. Patients with furious rabies produce excess saliva and have painful muscle spasms in the throat, and therefore do actually foam at the mouth. There are many other severe and distressing mental signs, including delirium, hallucinations, raging and convulsions.

The virus is passed on in milk, so following a bite do not breast-feed.

Prevention and Treatment

The rabies vaccination is only deemed necessary for those travelling into remote areas at some distance from medical treatment, or for those who may be exposed to an unusual risk of infection. It is a series of three injections given over a month, and after thirty days it is effective for up to three years. It is often injected into the stomach muscles where it can cause some local pain. Other side effects include fever and malaise.

Please note that even if your children have been immunised you must still seek urgent medical attention if they were to be bitten by an infected animal. In addition to the risk of rabies, there are many other infections that can be passed on by a bite from a mammal, including tetanus.

Once bitten by an infected animal, the infection is transmitted and the virus takes time to multiply in the bite area. After days, or even weeks, the virus gets into the nerves. It then travels up the nerves and into the brain and spinal cord where it multiplies further.

Because of the delay before the virus begins to attack the nerve system, you should have time to get to a hospital. While in Nepal, a friend of mine was bitten by an animal she never saw. One of the guides took her straight back to the city to get treatment, even though it was three days walk for them, alone.

If you or one of your children are bitten you should wash the wound immediately. Wound cleaning is an effective way of killing or removing the virus from infected wounds and is therefore very important. Wash the wound for at least five minutes with soap or detergent and water. Your child may cry but at least they will survive. Remove any foreign material and rinse with plenty of clean, plain water. If possible, apply alcohol (at least 40 per cent) or tincture of iodine, both of which will kill the virus. Then get medical attention fast. It will be too late once the symptoms develop. You should be given the course of rabies vaccinations which should be started as soon as possible. (Request the human diploid vaccine.)

If the animal was not wild or a stray, try to identify the owner and note their name, address and telephone number. The animal should be kept under observation to detect any changes in its behaviour. If it does remain healthy for five days you are unlikely to contract rabies. However, the animal should be checked for two weeks.

If the animal does become ill or dies you must complete the course of vaccinations and should, in addition, be given a serum that will further protect you. If you were bitten by a wild, stray or domestic animal that is unavailable for observation the same applies, especially if the bite was on the face, neck, head or finger.

Children must be warned not to play with or touch any animals while on holiday unless you enter a farm, zoo or conservation programme site and are invited to by the animals' handler. All wild animals should be kept at a distance, even those that gather at feeding areas around tourist spots and look perfectly healthy.

Avoid any animal that is acting strangely and remember that 90 per cent of rabies infections in man worldwide are as a result of a cat or dog bite.

Rubella (German Measles)

Rubella is a viral infection that causes a rash. The illness is usually mild in children.

Symptoms

The incubation period is usually two to three weeks. Small red spots first appear behind the ears, then spread to the face and all over the body. The child will have a mild fever and the lymph nodes at the back of the neck will be enlarged. There is a slight risk of encephalitis. The child will be infectious one week before and at least four days after the rash first appears. The greatest danger of rubella is to pregnant women, as the virus can cause birth defects.

Prevention and Treatment

The vaccine is usually given in the UK at about twelve months of age along with the mumps and measles vaccines. The side effects of the vaccine are generally mild symptoms of the illness, local and allergic reactions.

Children with rubella usually don't even feel ill, so you need not worry about travelling abroad before immunisation. But if you suspect that your child has contracted the disease you must keep him or her away from anyone who may be pregnant.

Any pregnant woman who has had contact with rubella and who is not up to date with her vaccines should seek medical advice. She should be given an injection of immunoglobulin, which will help protect the foetus.

Tetanus

Tetanus is a dangerous disease caused by a bacterial infection of the nervous system. The bacteria produces a toxin that causes violent, painful muscle spasms.

It is caught by the introduction of spores into the body through even a slight wound. The spores are found in soil and faeces, even in dust or the air, all over the world and so anybody – and everybody – is at risk, everywhere. Deep wounds are a greater concern because the bacteria likes to live in an environment without much oxygen. However, even a minor trauma should not be dismissed – for example, a prick from a thorn might introduce soil into the skin and could be deadly.

Symptoms

Early signs are spasms in the chewing muscles, and difficulty in opening the mouth. There is difficulty swallowing and an infant would be unable to suckle. Fever and severe stiffness progress into increasingly regular violent muscle contractions, which increase in severity over a week.

A baby's cry would be stifled by the face wrinkling up at the same time. An older child's face would have an altered expression caused by contraction of the facial muscles, often described as a sardonic smile. Their body would have a stiff, ramrod appearance.

Death is from exhaustion or asphyxia during convulsions.

Prevention and Treatment

Children who have received all the usual childhood vaccinations will have been immunised as babies against tetanus, along with diphtheria and whooping cough in the triple vaccine. They will have received three injections four weeks apart, between the ages of three and six months. Protection then lasts for ten years. Children of ten and over will need a booster before travelling if they have not had one since infancy. The only side effects that are likely are tenderness around the injection site and/or a slight fever.

Immunisation is a very important protection against the tetanus bacterial organism in every country of the world, and it is sensible to ensure that your child is protected from this terrifying, deadly disease. Even if you decided not to vaccinate your child as a baby it is a good idea to consider it before travelling abroad, especially if good medical treatment is not readily available. Children are constantly cutting and scraping themselves on road surfaces and mucky sticks, so they are at real risk.

At the very least, and if travelling to a country with good health care standards, ensure your child is taken to hospital and given a protective dose of the vaccine if they are cut, bitten or injured.

The incubation period is just ten days, and if your child falls ill while you are away they will need injections of antitoxin, large doses of antibiotics and good hospital care.

Tuberculosis

Tuberculosis is increasing worldwide, although in the UK extensive immunisation has brought the disease under control. In industrial Britain tuberculosis, known then as consumption, was a killer, weakening its victims – including the Brontë sisters – over months or even years.

It is a highly contagious bacterial infection which most commonly affects the lungs, but if left untreated will also affect the kidneys, brain membranes and joints.

The mode of transmission is usually by inhalation or ingestion of the infected droplets produced when a sufferer sneezes or coughs.

Symptoms
Early signs include a dry cough, fever, night sweats, reduced appetite and a child's failure to thrive.

If young children who are infected are left untreated – particularly infants or under-fives – the symptoms will become more severe and complications will develop, including pleural effusion, blood in the sputum and meningitis. Although this may not be until months after the early signs began, the disease is then likely to be fatal or cause long-term damage.

Treatment and Prevention
Most young children born in the UK over recent years are vaccinated at six weeks old with BCG to protect against tuberculosis. Check with your doctor or your own records to confirm whether or not your children have been immunised. You may remember it as a single

injection given separately, possibly at the hospital, which developed into a small blister at the site of the needle puncture.

Although tuberculosis is widespread, the infection does not pose a major risk to the traveller unless staying for more than a month in Asia, Africa, Central or South America. However, if you and your children are likely to be staying with local people or to be in close contact with them – including close family – it is advisable to be protected.

Even if your children did not have the vaccine as babies they may have acquired some immunity. A simple test called the Heaf test is carried out to determine whether or not this is the case. It uses a multiple-puncture technique but is completely painless. This should be done well before your departure date because if the Heaf test determines that your children do need the vaccination, it should be given eight weeks in advance. Teenagers over fifteen years old who are travelling with you should also be tested as the BCG vaccine given to babies may not always give lifetime immunity.

If your child were to become infected with tuberculosis, the illness takes time to develop and does not present as a medical emergency in the early stages. You will have time to get them home where they will usually be admitted to hospital – mainly to prevent the spread of infection – and treatment will be given in the form of a combination of antibiotics which need long-term administration for up to a year.

Yellow Fever

Yellow fever is a disease caused by a virus that is transmitted by the bite of a particular species of mosquito. It is active in several African, South and Central American countries. In about 5 per cent of cases the illness is fatal, usually as a result of liver or kidney failure.

Symptoms

After a three- to six-day incubation period, the symptoms begin as headache, backache and fever, progressing into nausea and vomiting. The victim has a flushed, swollen face and a bright-red tongue. They then begin to show a tendency for bleeding – the gums begin to bleed, the patient produces black, blood-filled vomit and the stools are full of blood. The disease may progress into a form of lethal hepatitis affecting the liver, although most victims actually recover. It is during the recovery phase that the patient may become jaundiced, giving the skin the yellow tinge that has given the fever its name.

Prevention

Infection can be prevented by a safe and highly effective vaccine that gives protection for ten years.

A number of countries require proof of immunisation if you have passed through endemic countries. You must present your vaccination certificate, which is valid for ten days after the injection.

The vaccine can be given to children over nine months old at specialist yellow-fever centres. It produces few side effects, although many countries which stipulate that travellers must have their certificate state that children under one year are exempt.

The only hitch is the expense. The yellow fever vaccine costs approximately £45.

It is also important to note that children or adults who have an allergy to eggs or chicken protein should not be given the vaccine.

The vaccine is live and so should not be given to pregnant women.

Treatment

Treatment is largely confined to controlling the symptoms by replacing fluid and electrolytes in the patient. Blood transfusion is sometimes required to correct blood loss following haemorrhage.

CHAPTER 6

How to Get There

Travelling by Air

The Risk of Cot Death

There has been some speculation that flying can contribute to the tragedy of cot death, but the evidence is inconclusive. The research was carried out in 1992 although not published until 1999. It noted that babies placed in a room with reduced oxygen supply may have a reduced oxygen content in their blood. However, it is thought that provided we remain vigilant and take all the usual precautions, babies are at no greater risk from cot death after flying than they would be on the ground.

It is, however, important to avoid flying in or near the smoking section of the aircraft, and to keep the baby cool during the flight. After landing, *always* place your baby on his back to sleep. Don't smoke around your baby and avoid smoky places. Keep your baby cool, but don't let paranoia ruin your holiday – don't forget that millions of babies born in the tropics survive.

When my son was first born, I was powerfully anxious about the risks of cot death. An Indian midwife tucked my baby against me one night when he was just three days old. It was 4.30 a.m. and he was absolutely refusing to go to sleep. I was close to tears. She tenderly assured me that he would be fine. 'You will never roll on to him,' she promised. 'You are his mother.' I must have looked doubtful. 'We don't have cot death in India,' she continued. 'A new baby always sleeps next to its mother where it belongs.'

That night I enjoyed the best night's sleep.

An Indian doctor later gave the same advice. Provided that she has not drunk too much alcohol or taken any sedative drugs, a mother will not roll on to her baby. I found this wonderfully reassuring and my son slept in my arms for the first five months of his life. After this time he seemed much stronger. He could kick off his blankets if he was too hot, and I began to sleep easier. I then did the same with my second son who was born in 2001, and I would do the same again.

If you are travelling into very high temperatures with a very young baby, consider sleeping next to him. You will be much more aware of his temperature, breathing levels and any threatening mosquitoes.

Pre-booking Seats

Many airlines will pre-book your seats for you, but it is a matter of deciding where you will be most comfortable. In my opinion, when travelling with an infant the bulkhead seats are not as ideal as most people imagine. These seats are right next to the emergency exits and have a partition directly in front of them. On an aeroplane with a central run of seats, the in-flight movie screen is often attached to this partition, and the fixings to secure a kind of suspended travel cot sit just below the screen. This has the disadvantage that you may be constantly fighting your child in an attempt to stop them from standing up in the cot to touch the flickering lights of the movie screen above. Also, you will make enemies up and down the length of the plane, as they want to watch the movie, not your child doing a balancing act.

With a very young baby the cot may be an advantage, but if you manage instead to get other seats with a little more leg room your baby may be more comfortable in his familiar car-carrying seat on the floor.

On a jumbo, you also have the added problem with the middle row of bulkhead seats. There are five seats in the middle row, so if you book as a couple with an infant there will be three occupied seats next to you. Unfortunately the wall fixings for the travel cot are over the middle seat, so your baby will be in someone else's lap if you have booked two seats at one end – this will be awkward for you and them!

The final big disadvantage of the bulkhead seats is that the arm-rests are fixed. This means that if you are travelling with an older child who may not be able to sleep upright, you cannot lift up the arm rests and allow them to lie flat across you and/or your partner.

So what are the best options? The key to pre-booking is to ask for seats with extra leg room. Then there is room for bags, books, toys and sleeping arrangements. The seats with extra leg room vary from plane to plane, so ask when pre-booking or checking in.

A few airlines provide 'cots' that fit on the floor in-between the seats under your feet. They are little more than human-shaped card-board boxes with a thin mattress, but they keep your child off the floor and I have seen many infants settle in one then sleep for an entire eight- or ten-hour flight, curled up with an airline blanket and pillow. However, be aware that these floor cots are only available on certain aircraft. Jumbos often have them, but you do find that even the airlines who claim to have them on board often don't carry them. If you pick an airline specially for this, it will be very frustrating when the steward shrugs and apologises because the ground crew forgot to load the floor cot (this is fairly common).

As long as the seatbelt sign is not on, older and longer children often sleep well if laid out on the floor on a mattress of pillows. Most airlines will not recommend this, but they won't prevent it either. The only reason for concern would be if the aircraft were suddenly to hit turbulence without the pilot having received any warning.

If you decide to take your chances, or aren't able to pre-book your seats, find out how busy your flight is when you arrive at the airport. If it is quiet, ask check-in to reserve you the seats at either end of a row. It is a slight gamble, but if you are only paying for two seats and you request the window and the aisle seat in a row it is very unlikely that the check-in will land a lone passenger between you if it's quiet.

On a jumbo, if you book the two aisle seats at either end of a row of five, you are likely to find that the middle three will be left empty. Even if you find this is not the case, you can virtually guarantee that one of the three sandwiched between the two of you and your infants will be more than happy to swap their place for one of the aisle seats, and you will still end up sitting together.

I have tried this several times, twice while pregnant, then a number of times since on very long flights. It has worked every time. Obviously if the flight is heavily or fully booked, this strategy won't work.

Pre-booking a Travel Cot

This is tricky. No matter how firmly your travel agent promises you a travel cot, check with the airline. Many aircraft don't carry cardboard cots and some airlines do not allow infants in the bulkhead seats because they may obstruct the emergency exits. These airlines do not carry wall-mounted cots either. Up until your baby is nine months old it is likely that he will sleep more comfortably in his car-carrying seat or on your knee anyway. At twelve months old you can arrange him on the floor with airline pillows and blankets.

Relaxation and Aiding Sleep

You will be amazed at how comfortably – and long – your baby will sleep on an aircraft. On night flights children will invariably sleep through the entire journey. Even in the day the gentle hum of the engines seems to lull babies and children in the same way as a car journey.

Take it for granted that your child will sleep and they will. It is only if you get anxious and expect trouble that they absorb your concerns and therefore deliver. If they do start to create trouble, I have always found that even from a young age I could persuade children to wear seat belts and sit down by convincing them that I was on their side, but that the stewardess would be really cross if they didn't do as they were told. They couldn't care less if I went purple with rage but a few mock stern words or a frown from the stewardess usually does the trick.

It isn't always easy to pick the timings of your flights but for long haul, given the choice, I would depart early evening and fly overnight every time. Night flights are ideal for a child of any age. Ten hours in daylight is much harder, but the positive aspect is that they seem to pass in a blur when I am preoccupied with trying to feed, entertain and cope with children. By contrast, when I am alone and free to do as I please, I often find such long journeys torturous.

Babies and toddlers will often fall to sleep more readily on a plane than they do at home. Slightly older children may be excited and need time to settle. Once this has passed, brush their teeth, change them into their night clothes and read them their favourite story. They will soon be snoozing for hours.

If your baby is slightly unwell, a dose of Calpol or Disprol can be relied upon for a good night's sleep. For children over two years of age, a dose of an antihistamine, such as promethazine (Phenergan), will calm excitement and act as a sedative. When I was a child, my doctor father would dose us all up with Phenergan every Christmas Eve. It is a drug that has been used safely for many years, and an added bonus is that antihistamines prevent motion sickness. I have never yet been driven to use them, but even the security of having them as a back up may be a good idea for anxious parents who can relax in the knowledge that it is there, just in case they can't cope.

Short haul is better tackled in daylight. You arrive at your destination relatively fresh and organised, so you will be able to negotiate which room you are about to be checked into, get a meal, and deal with all the hazards in your room. Others may disagree, but when I am checking in for a two-hour flight exhausted, in the early hours of the morning, I can't even find which pocket my passport is in.

If you are a nervous flyer, try as hard as you can not to let your child sense it. Statistics state that even if you flew every day for the next 26,000 years you would never be involved in an air crash, so don't forget that you are in far more danger driving to work than you are flying, and that you have more chance of winning the lottery than being killed in an aeroplane.

If your child is attached to a soother or comforter, don't forget it.

When Paris was eight months old, I took my dad on a trip on Concorde. As infants are free I thought it would be nice to take my baby along, too. The idea was that, in years to come, I would be able to show him the photos and tell him about our adventure at Mach 2.

Somehow, when we were all busy taking photographs of each other under Concorde's nose, the pushchair was whisked away along with a precious satin-edged comfort blanket. By the time I realised, it was too late. The hold was closed and it was time to board the plane. Soon after take-off Paris noticed that it was missing and the trouble started. Before long he was screaming inconsolably, and this continued for most of the duration of the flight. He bellowed with fury and threw a bread roll in my champagne. It certainly didn't turn out to be my trip of a lifetime.

In-flight Feeding

Invariably, you will need to make a special request for a children's meal at the time of booking, but don't rely on in-flight meals, especially with young children. They are often served at irregular times, particularly on long-distance flights and when travelling through time zones.

The chances are that your child won't eat the meal anyway. It is amazing how, no matter how hungry a child is, if they don't like the look of something they won't let a grain of it past their lips.

There is also the concern regarding differing levels of hygiene. Most airlines adhere to strict guidelines, however when flying between third-world countries the meal and ice or water served may not be safe. A friend of mine actually contracted dysentery on a flight to Pakistan.

Take back-up snacks such as bananas, raisins, bread rolls and crisps, and, if you are in any doubt about the water available on the plane, take plenty of bottled water to prevent dehydration.

On most flights there are safe drinking-water dispensers and paper cups around the toilet areas. If you prefer, ask the stewardess for bottled water or fruit juice. Don't be embarrassed when she frowns at you as you ask for your tenth soft drink. It is important for the comfort of you and your children.

For babies, take on board jars of baby food and ask your stewardess to heat them for you. They will happily provide boiling water for warming bottles and food, but it isn't such a good idea juggling with it in your seat.

Plan carefully for your baby's meals and have a few extra at hand. A packet or two of powdered baby rice or chicken casserole in your hand luggage will be light as a feather and provide several back-up meals in the event of your flight, or the rest of your luggage, being delayed. For bottle-fed babies, pack extra formula milk for the same reasons.

In-flight Entertainment

For babies and younger children, you are it. It is unlikely that the film will be particularly suitable for children. More and more airlines, such as Virgin, British Midland and United Arab Emirates, have the fantastic advantage of a mini screen for every passenger, with changeable channels and even user-friendly video games.

To a large degree, older children will entertain themselves. They will read, play with the head sets or hand-held computer games. These games are not to be used during take off and landing, but are often sold on the aircraft reasonably cheaply and are permissible once the flight is underway.

On a long journey, it may be a good time for you to catch up on listening to them read. Choose a book you wish you had read as a child, or one you enjoyed that will bring back memories. There will be little or no distractions and your child will benefit from your input and interest. It may also be an opportunity to find out mathematics principles or any other topics they are struggling with. If you can't help them there and then, write it down and look it up when you get home.

Babies love to be read to as well. From the age of five months old, books entranced both my sons. The only time Paris would keep still was when sitting on my knee gazing at the brightly coloured pages. On a trip to Iceland when he was twelve months old, he sat on my knee for the entire two-and-a-half hour daytime flight, there and back, reading book after book and pleading with me, 'Again, again.' My husband and I took turns and we had a very enjoyable, stress-free journey. It was a bit repetitive and boring, but when everyone around commented on what a perfectly behaved child he was, I smiled with relief.

You will be given a few puzzles and crayons on board which will occupy young children for a short time. However, take extra paper, pencils and possibly a colouring book in your own luggage.

On my first trips, I bought small jigsaws, games, plastic animals and all manner of tiny toys which I spent most of the flight clambering around on the floor to retrieve. The only things I will pack into hand luggage now are books, comics, paper, pencils and one new little surprise.

Nappies

Don't forget them as the airlines will not provide them.

Change your baby's nappy last thing before getting on the plane. Take a handful in your hand luggage and then a reserve stock just in case your luggage is delayed. We arrived in China with an eighteen-month-old Paris to find all our cases were still in Heathrow, and that we were down to our last nappy.

Discomfort During Take-Off and Landing

Your baby may have an inconsolable crying fit during take-off or landing. This is probably because of the pressure build-up in their ears, which causes pain. On my first-ever plane journey from London to Tobago with a young baby, Paris was as good as gold for eight hours. We had to land in Barbados en route, at which point he woke up and began to cry. We took off again and he became hysterical. The Caribbean stewardesses barked at me, instructing me that he was hungry and that I must feed him. Although I knew he wasn't, I tried to persuade him to take a bottle of milk. The stewardesses watched me with irritation and finally confiscated him to try and console him between them. As we began to descend again into Tobago they brought him back still screaming and shrugged. A toddler in the next row looked on with amusement while sucking gently at her dummy. I was helpless – there was nothing I could do to soothe him. Then I saw the toddler drop her dummy and begin to cry while tugging at her ears. It was only then that it dawned on me that my poor five-month-old child was screaming in pain.

From then on I would always save some of his feed or give him a lolly at take-off and landing. Sucking equalises the pressure in the ear and relieves the discomfort.

If your baby is breast-feeding or has a comforter there will be no problem. If not, save a bit of their bottle or give them a treat to avoid their pain and you being deafened.

An alternative is a product called 'Children's ear planes'. These are ridged, disposable ear plugs that claim to regulate the rate of change in ear pressure and so ease the discomfort and pain often experienced while flying. They are suitable for children aged one to eleven and cost around £3.99. I am quite sure my children would abjectly refuse to have anything placed in their ears, but if you can persuade yours to keep them in place they may prove worthwhile.

Travelling by Car

I consider travelling in your own car – either around Great Britain and Ireland, or into Europe – to be one of the ultimate freedom holidays. You can stuff your boot with things you might just need, stop where and when you want, and even follow the weather. If you arrive in Normandy and it is pouring down, you could be basking in the sunshine in the South of France later the same day. Fly-drives are also incredibly flexible and so relaxing. You are free to stop and tend to your children's needs whenever you choose, you can go as near or as far as you decide on the day, and need not stop until you find somewhere that satisfies the whole family.

Fly-drives are hugely popular in the US, but many countries as far flung as Costa Rica and Malaysia now offer similar holiday packages. Often in such countries the roads are good and the cars are of a comfortable standard with air-conditioning. However, with or without children, it is important to remember that the roads abroad are a very real, and potentially fatal, danger. There are more tourists and expatriates killed on the roads each year than by any of the diseases we protect ourselves against with such care.

Driving in a strange country, with strange road etiquette, not to mention the signs in a foreign language and driving on the wrong side of the road, all amount to a recipe for disaster, so make sure that foreign roads are treated with the greatest of respect.

Teenagers are at very real risk, especially if they have the means to hire a car themselves. I lost a school friend to the roads in Spain. Some years later a friend's son was killed in Majorca at the tender age of eighteen. It happens all summer. The most deathly road in Europe is reputed to be that between Faro airport and the Algarve. Tourists jump off a plane into an unfamiliar hire car, often driving on the wrong side of the road. They are trying to find their way, switch gears with the wrong hand and make sense of the Portuguese road signs in the heat. This, combined with a tourist-hating, hot-blooded local in a hurry, spells trouble.

Naturally some countries are far worse than others. You can usually judge by the state of the local cars how bad the local people are at driving them. Italy has one of the highest death rates on the roads in Europe. A walk round Rome, counting the number of dinted cars, is a good illustration of this. Another hint is the cost of local insurance. In some places such as Jamaica, you have to put down a US$1,000 deposit which is non-refundable if you have an accident, whether it is your fault or not.

Any travel book will advise you about cost savings with vulnerable children as cargo. The three most important factors are Safety, Safety and Safety.

Portugal and Spain are very dangerous places to drive. France, too, has many more deaths per one thousand of the population per year than the UK. Naturally, countries where drink-driving laws are strict are much safer places to travel by road.

If you do decide to hire a car, check that it has seat belts in the back and take your own children's car seats. They may be bulky, but if you are planning to travel any distance on foreign roads they will be an invaluable asset and could save lives.

- When you get your hire car, check your insurance and which petrol the car takes. Find your lights, horn and hazard lights before you set off.
- If the children start fighting or screaming, stop the car. There is enough to cope with on strange roads without the added stress and confusion coming from the back.
- Drive defensively at all times and avoid getting lost at night in strange cities.

Driving through Naples at night a few years ago, we were forced to stop at traffic lights where we were accosted by a window washer. It was an oppressive area and we were too frightened to wind down the window even if we had wanted to give the washer some money. As the lights changed we sped off and the guy tried to smash our windscreen with his metal-backed sponge.

Always take the greatest care and adapt to the country you are driving in. Decide where and by which route you will travel when you arrive and judge the quantity of traffic, the local driving ability and the weather. Motorways may not be so scenic but they are often a country's safest road system.

It is a good idea to avoid the roads altogether in hot countries during very heavy rains. Often the road drainage systems are very poor or non-existent, and they can quickly become flooded.

Despite all this, I have covered many tens of thousands of miles on foreign roads in complete safety. Be careful and be lucky.

Some Tips to Help Make Your Journey Easier

- If you take a trip by car with young babies, don't forget a window blind. We spent an entire week driving around France with a towel trapped in the window. It was November but it was warm and sunny and our son squawked until we assembled a makeshift screen to shield him. If the weather is hot, a blind will be essential. Even then beware of heat stroke.

- In intolerably hot weather, make sure you have an air-conditioned car or travel out of the heat of the day, otherwise your journey will be a totally miserable and potentially dangerous experience.

- If you don't have air-conditioning, stop the car regularly and try to cool your baby down by taking him into an air-conditioned room. If this is impossible, buy chilled mineral water, even if only to put the bottle against his forehead and the back of his neck (make sure it is not too cold!). Fan your baby too, again particularly around his face and the back of his neck.

- If you can stand them, children's tapes always keep things quiet in the back. The repetition sends my husband mad, but it is far more tolerable than a bored and protesting toddler.

- Have the essentials ever ready, including nappies, baby wipes, tissues, snacks and drinks.

- If your child suffers from motion sickness, avoid positioning them so they face backwards, and don't let them read when the car is moving. If your child has complained in car journeys at home, depending on frequency or the severity of their symptoms, it is a good idea to give them an anti-motion sickness drug which will also help your child relax and sleep. Remember to give the drug well before you intend to set off so it has time to take effect.

- Don't allow older children to read on twisty roads, and avoid giving them greasy meals. On long, straight roads such as motorways, most children will be fine reading, but warn them of the symptoms and tell them if they feel queasy to put down their book immediately.

- Reassure them that if they need you to stop at any time they must simply tell you. With younger children, keep an eye on them and if they go pale and quiet, stop anyway and let them run around.
- Talk to your children and sing with them. Encourage them to invent their own games and distract them by suggesting car games you played yourself as a child:
  - Ask them to watch out for car-registration letters or numbers. Counting in this way from one to ninety-nine will keep them quiet for hours
  - You may find 'I Spy' crushingly boring, but the children will be far more enthusiastic about a game that you join in with
  - If travelling in a foreign country, guess what the words on road signs and adverts mean, or let your child test you from a phrase book. Encourage them to give you clues which will make them think about it themselves, and sow the first seeds of a new language in their little brains
  - Teach them all the capital cities of the world
  - Encourage them to make up and tell you a story; it will help develop their imagination and creative skills
  - Practise times tables or spellings and concepts.

Travelling by Local Transport

Short treks are no problem, but travelling across country in many parts of the world that are unfamiliar to you is destined to be hard work. It is hard enough without children, so planning a huge journey across mountain and savannah should not be taken lightly.

Buses can be smoky, sweltering, stink of diesel, and have unpredictable drivers. We were once on a bus from the south of Turkey to Istanbul when our driver got off and had a fight in the street with another road user. He re-embarked covered with blood and just carried on driving.

Getting pushchairs, children and luggage on trains is also hard work. Be aware of people rushing to help you – for example, the kind old man who helped you board so concernedly might have actually picked your pocket, leaving the whole family without passport, tickets or money.

Organised tours are sometimes expensive and may make you feel that you are missing out on real travel experience. The balance is that they will often be more relaxing and a much, much easier means of exploring and seeing the sights with children in tow.

If you do decide to go it alone, in many countries of the world, by the time you have been cheated you don't save that much money, and after being hassled and confused into getting on to the wrong local bus crammed with chickens and a driver with a death wish, you may wish you had paid up for the tour, whatever the cost.

Tour guides usually have a grasp of local politics and geography, and can save you from being duped by the most popular local frauds. In Rome, the guide warned us that crooks were rushing up to confused tourists, flashing badges and shouting, 'Police – we need to see your passports and your currency,' then disappearing with the lot. In the US Virgin Islands, we were warned not to let ourselves or our children to be photographed with one of the locals' donkeys. The owners would encourage the snap, then charge you US$15. In South American countries it is important to check that any change you are given is still legal tender. Many vendors will try to give you currency that is no longer in circulation and therefore useless.

A good intermediate between tour bus and local transport is to hire a private taxi. This will often be a much more relaxing way of exploring a foreign country for the whole family than hiring a car and driving yourself, but don't forget that swindling is the international inclination of almost every taxi driver on earth. Negotiate the price hard and fast before you set off for the day, and refuse to pay a penny more when you return at night. Often a tip is deserved, but if having been your best friend all day, your driver turns around and tries to fleece you, with children or without, don't be a bit surprised.

One worldwide favourite con is agreeing a price with you, then, when you come to settle up, telling you that they didn't mean sixty kroner, sols or rupees, they meant sixty US dollars. Don't give in, you are battling for all the tourists that come after you, too.

The driver of a cycle-powered taxi in Beijing became quite hostile when I firmly dismissed his claim that the price he quoted me in local currency equating to £8 had suddenly jumped up to £50. He argued that he had quoted me in US$ not Yuan. I got more annoyed than him and threatened to call the police. With this he disappeared with my change. As the average wage in China is £250 per month, there was no way to justify a £50 fare for a 45-minute bike ride. Plus, because of the strictly controlled one-child policy, he would only have had one mouth to feed, so he was just being greedy.

Travelling by Boat

The experiences I have had on short ferry rides with a rowdy toddler who refused to be contained as I trailed after him, were absolutely petrifying. Any second he could have lurched overboard and disappeared down among the waves for ever. This put me off cruising too soon, but when my elder son was three, we set off on a trip around Western Africa and the Indian Ocean. His quote of the holiday, when all the other passengers were in bed with seasickness and he staggered from one side of a narrow corridor to another as the ship yawed was, 'It's a bit wobbly on this boat.'!

The fact that a child of any age can fall off a boat means that you can never really relax with them out of sight. If you are considering a cruise, choose a ship that sails mostly at night and docks most days. It is then just like any other holiday, with plenty of variety and activities on shore. Being confined on a ship for days at sea can be very tedious even without a child. The ship's pool gets steadily more filthy as the days wear on, and aside from golf lessons and afternoon tea, there is nothing much else to do but get drunk! Not a good idea when in charge of children on the open sea.

Older children will probably enjoy a cruise more, but prepare for seasickness and remember that long, elaborate dinners will be crushingly boring for them. Also, appreciate that the captain's cocktail party is hardly ideal children's entertainment, but they will enjoy the fuss, the bingo, and the evening entertainment. They will also always be first on the dance floor in the disco.

By contrast, ferry rides are often only a short part of a holiday. As such, they are bearable with a toddler and pleasant with older children.

Hiring your own boat or an organised day trip out to sea will be great fun. On the whole, children seem to keep still in smaller boats.

Beware of sunburn, which can be much more severe on the water due to the reflection of the sun's rays off the water's surface. You will all burn much more quickly and deeply, so hats and factor 30 are imperative.

Travel Sickness

The terms 'motion sickness' and 'travel sickness' apply to sea, car, air or even a swing. It is a thoroughly miserable condition which has ruined many expensive cruise holidays, when those prone to seasickness find themselves bedridden for a day.

Aircraft can fly above adverse conditions. The only problems that usually arise are when air traffic control insist that planes are held in areas of high turbulence for operational reasons. I once spent an hour circling above Lisbon in a violent storm. I rarely suffer from motion sickness, but people vomiting and turning green all around me was torture.

You will usually have had signs if your child suffers from car sickness and, if they do, you can almost guarantee they will suffer if you hit turbulence, so prepare yourself.

Symptoms

The condition is typical of headache and nausea followed by vomiting, pallor, and cold sweating of the face and hands. Increased salivation and light-headedness occur. They will also feel apathetic, miserable, depressed and be unable to get up from their seat or bunk.

Motion sickness can be life threatening because, in some cases, the sufferer becomes so dejected they can lose their will to live and make uncalculated decisions. Small children will be very quiet and pale with sweaty palms. If they complain of tummy ache, get ready.

Avoiding Travel Sickness

The exact cause of seasickness is still unclear, but it is known to be linked to the balancing system in the ear. Because it can last for several days, it needs to be carefully considered and prepared for before travel. Once you are all on board and feeling horribly sick it is often too late to resolve the problem. The eyes also play a definite role in easing or worsening the feelings of sickness. This can be manipulated by asking the child to fix on the horizon or the seat in front, so that the brain has something on which to focus. Reading and playing computer games often bring on motion sickness in children who do not normally suffer the symptoms.

Deter children from watching oncoming traffic, or waves if at sea. Also worthy of note is that some people suffer more if travelling backwards on a train or coach.

I also believe that travel sickness is closely linked to fear. Seasickness is certainly more severe if you are afraid of drowning. There also seems to be an element of genetic inheritance.

Sleep eliminates sickness, so if you have left it too late to take the tablet, encourage your child to close their eyes and listen to a story that you can distract them with. Sucking a sweet may also help.

Limit the amount your children eat before a trip. Eat light, fat-free meals. Choose your seats carefully – it can make a difference:

- On an aeroplane the seats between the wings are the most stable
- The front of the car or bus gives good visibility and less likelihood of travel sickness
- On a boat, stay on deck and watch the horizon or, if you have no option other than to go below deck, stay away from the smell of petrol, and the diesel fumes of the engine. Choose a seat near a window so that you can still see the horizon. Midship is usually

the best place to be, but on some small craft the back may sit low in the water and buffet around least.

- Ask the crew

Treatment

Several treatments are available over the counter. They are effective, but you must remember to take them the prescribed number of hours before you travel.

1. *Cinnarzine* is apparently used by the navy. It is effective, but should not be given to children under five years old.

    Between five and twelve years the dose is one 15mg tablet to be taken approximately two hours before travelling. The dose should be repeated every eight hours until you have time to find your sea legs.

    Over twelve years to adult the dose is two tablets(30mg) three times per day.

2. *Dramamine* (dimenhydinate) can be given to children over one year of age:

    One to six years: $\frac{1}{4} - \frac{1}{2}$ (50mg) tablet

    Seven to twelve years: $\frac{1}{2} - 1$ tablet

    Daily dosage 2–3 times per day.

3. *Phenergan* (promethazine) can be given to children over two years of age:

    Two to five years: 5mg

    Six to ten years: 10mg

    Eleven years to adult: 25mg

The dose should be taken the night before travel and repeated every eight hours. Phenergan comes in liquid form and is also useful for treating allergies (a double dose once a day), and as a sedative to aid sleep.

PART TWO

Preparation

CHAPTER 7

Essential Papers and Insurance

Children's Passports

If you are applying for a British passport for your child for the first time, they will not be added to your passport as they were allowed to be before 1999. Now even a one-week-old baby will need its own passport with a photograph, unless the child is already on your passport or your partner's. The child will still be able to travel on your passport, but only if it is already named on it, either

a) until your passport expires or
b) until you apply for the child's own passport, at which time your child must be taken *off* your passport.

Applying for a Child's Passport After October 1998

1. Request a passport form for a child under sixteen years of age at your main post office. (Smaller post offices do not carry the form.)
2. Complete the form, which must be countersigned by a professional who has known *you* for at least two years.
3. The form should then be sent off with the child's birth certificate and two passport-sized photographs, both signed on the back by the professional who has countersigned the application form.

4. The post office offers a service which guarantees that your passport will be returned to you within 10 working days (two weeks). It costs just £4 extra. The cost of a child's British passport is £16. The £4 service is very reliable, and has the added bonus of being checked by a post office employee, who will not accept the completed application if there are any mistakes or missing documents.

A child's passport lasts five years, but the photograph should be updated. The guideline is that you should change the photo if you suspect that you will have problems with passport control not recognising your child from its photo. If you have left it to within ten working days before you travel to apply, then you will need to go to your local passport office. You must make an appointment and they will process your application and post it to you within one week. This is called the Fast Track service.

If your child has had its own passport before, you can use the Premium same-day service, but it is expensive at £70 per passport. This service is not available for first-time applications or for children who have been previously included in a passport. To make an appointment call the Passport Advice line: 0870 521 0410.

- Make it a habit to check the expiry date of each member of the family's passport – when you updated your married name or added a child to your passport, even if you were sent a brand new passport, it may have been back-dated to expire on the same date as your old passport, so so do check it
- Many destinations demand that you have six months left on your passport before expiry on the date of travel

Visas

Visas are a frustrating, hopelessly bureaucratic anomaly. Requirements change constantly. Sometimes you can get visas at the borders, often you can't. It is better to apply before you go.

Contacting the embassy concerned is the best way of finding out whether or not your family need visas to enter a country. Unfortunately, if you try to do this by phone, it will often cost 50p per minute for a recorded message which might not answer all your questions.

When applying for my family's Chinese visas, I spent around £10 listening to all the information and still didn't find out what I wanted to know. Did I need a separate visa for my child on my passport and, as I had booked the trip so near to my departure date, did I have to travel to London to get it? I wrote off to the embassy asking both these questions and received three visa forms back without any covering letter or even a note. Running out of time and to be safe, we all travelled to London. The Chinese Embassy only accepts visa applications between nine and twelve o'clock, so we were obliged to stay in London overnight to be certain of arriving on time.

At 9.05 a.m., after queuing for a short time, I presented the three completed forms. A Chinese woman stamped everything about six times then told me to return in three days. I explained that I couldn't and that I had travelled down from Manchester. She barked back at me, 'Unless you travel today you not get visa today.' I stared at her. 'But I wrote to you and asked you whether I could apply in Manchester and you didn't reply and now I've come all this way and I need my visas.' She looked at me blankly and told me that I could have applied in Manchester anyway. I could have screamed. I felt like jumping over the counter and throwing all her papers into the air and inconveniencing her as much as she had inconvenienced me. A simple scribbled line would have avoided a 500-mile round trip and a £120 hotel bill. However, I was helpless in the face of bureaucracy and was forced to leave empty handed.

We finally got our visas three days before we were scheduled to travel. Paris did in fact require his own visa, although he was on my passport at the time.

Important points

1. Printed travel brochures giving visa information are usually accurate

2. Some larger travel agents have dedicated visa information sections that are kept up to date. If they are unsure, they will provide you with the addresses and telephone numbers of the relevant embassy
3. Apply in good time, if you are applying by post
4. If you are short on time, consider using a passport and visa agency. They will take your application to the embassy and pick it up for you as soon as possible. The cost is approximately £20 – 25 per visa
5. You can apply in person in London, but be prepared for a return trip a few days later
6. Some embassies have a branch outside London where you can apply in person. If you have no luck finding out this information, telephone the overseas student department in your local university. If they don't know they should be able to tell you who does
7. Some countries do not require a separate visa for children travelling on your passport, but many do. This information will only be reliable from the embassy itself. If in doubt and short of time, apply for a separate visa anyway. Although the price of a child's visa is the same as an adult's – it may cost between £10 and £35 – it is a small price to pay relative to a cancelled trip.

Travel Insurance

You will often find that you will get free travel insurance for infants – and even older children up to the age of twelve – on your own policy. This indicates to me how low the risk of a child's illness or injury abroad requiring medical attention actually is. Insurers never give something for nothing and by their nature would demand a high premium if there was a high probability of a claim.

Even if you don't normally get insurance for yourself, consider getting it for your children. Medical treatment abroad can be very costly and run into tens, even hundreds, of thousands of pounds.

If you have private health insurance this may cover trips abroad, but check it carefully and compare the terms and conditions with that of a specialised travel insurance policy.

You must be covered for repatriation – an emergency flight home. From European resorts and cities you may have the option of an air ambulance, but from farther-flung destinations you may need a combination of a helicopter and the entire section of an aircraft with a full medical team in attendance. Someone has to pay for all this.

If you are well insured it may be advisable to have your child treated abroad immediately, but in many third-world countries your child may be more at risk from a visit to the hospital than the illness or accident. In addition, in many underdeveloped countries the cost of screening blood is prohibitive, so if your child needs an operation or blood transfusion they would be at serious risk from HIV and hepatitis B. In such instances get them home.

There should be a twenty-four hour emergency service included on your policy with a free, or collect call, telephone number you can ring for advice and assessment of your situation. This would be of invaluable help if you were to run into problems. Carry a note of it on you at all times.

The other main advantage of travel insurance is that the family will be covered for cancellation. Paris presented with full-blown chicken pox three days before a trip to Disneyland Paris. The holiday would have been a total waste of time. Children have a habit of doing this and it is advisable to avoid travelling when your child is ill. A simple cough or cold isn't a problem, but anything more serious is likely to mean that you would all have a miserable time. A child with a serious ear infection should not fly.

In my experience, travel insurance companies do pay up. I have made a few small claims over the years and they have all been settled satisfactorily through the post.

NB: If your belongings are stolen while you are away, it is absolutely imperative that you get a theft report from the police or your holiday rep and retain all the receipts for purchases. If you, or a member of your family, has an accident, retain all receipts for the medication or treatment. You will need to present documentation to the insurance company on your return as proof.

Also, check the small print of your policy. Some insurance policies do not cover water sports, diving, skiing, or even car hire.

The E111

In countries within the European Economic Area (EEA) – which consists of the fifteen member states of the European Union (Austria, Belgium, Denmark, Finland, France, Germany, Greece, Ireland, Italy, Luxembourg, Netherlands, Portugal, Spain, Sweden and the UK) plus Iceland, Norway and Liechtenstein – production of a valid E111 will entitle you to free or reduced-cost medical emergency treatment. Cover is not as comprehensive as that offered by travel insurance policies and might be complicated. For example, in Germany you have to locate specific, listed doctors to receive free treatment.

To obtain an E111, you must go to the post office, where it will be stamped and signed and returned to you. It will only be validated in this way.

Reciprocal Healthcare Agreements

Outside the EEA, some countries have a reciprocal healthcare agreement with the UK. These countries include Anguilla, Australia, Barbados, British Virgin Islands, Bulgaria, Czech Republic, Falkland Islands, Hungary, Malta, New Zealand, Poland, Romania, Slovakia, St Helena and Turks and Caicos Islands. However, cover is often limited to hospital treatment, not that in doctors' surgeries.

Details of which countries accept E111s or have reciprocal agreements with the UK can be found in the leaflet 'Health advice for travellers', produced by the Department of Health. To order a copy telephone the Health Literature Line on 0800 555 777.

CHAPTER 8

Planning and Packing

Once you have decided where to go, where to stay and how to get there, you will need to prepare for your trip. Before you had children, you may have booked at the very last minute, packed in seconds and taken off at a moment's notice. With children, everything changes. Detailed organisation and planning is crucial.

Travelling with children takes about ten times more preparation than travelling without. They will need immunisations, a passport, travel insurance, their own visas (if applicable) and ten times more luggage.

Provided all the groundwork is done, you can relax and look forward to your holiday. You should be able to avoid any major inconveniences and mishaps and have a thoroughly relaxing time. Minor illnesses and traumas are not unlikely, but if you are well prepared with knowledge and a well-packed medical kit, they should never ruin your holiday. Holidaying with children is often a challenge, if not an adventure, but the chances are good that sensible pre-planning will prevent your trip from being a complete disaster, even without experience.

Try to pack sensibly, although I know first hand that this is virtually impossible when you take a young child away for the first time. Before having a baby I had become a master at packing and would travel around the world for three weeks with one tiny rucksack small enough to carry as hand luggage.

At the airport, on our first trip abroad with a child, I found myself with three large suitcases, six pieces of hand luggage, a camcorder, a car seat and a push chair. We were only going for a week.

With a baby under six months you will need a lot of luggage to ensure a comfortable holiday. The best way to keep your luggage to a minimum is to pack long before you need to. After a few days repack, then again after another week, and remove all the items you will be able to survive without. Resist the urge to add anything extra, unless it is absolutely essential.

If you want to use or wear items in-between times, writing a check-list will ensure you don't forget them and that you don't grab everything in sight, 'just in case', before you close your suitcase for the last time.

The most essential things to remember are the following. As long as you have them you will survive:

Essentials
- Passports and visas
- Tickets and hotel reservations
- Insurance
- Credit cards, cash and/or travellers' cheques
- Baby food, bottles, formula milk, sterilising equipment
- Medical kit
- The things money can't buy – such as comforters or your child's favourite toy

Plus, if you are taking your family on a driving holiday or picking up a hire car, don't forget your driving licence. We once arrived in southern Ireland on a Sunday and tried to pick up a rental car. Unfortunately, neither I nor my husband had brought our driving licence and, plead as we did, no licence meant no car. We had to go and stay overnight in Dublin, then return to the airport on Monday morning when the DVLC was open and the rental company could check our details. This, thankfully, they did, and handed over the keys as soon as they received fax confirmation from Swansea.

Bulky Items

Pushchair or Baby Buggy?

You may not be able to decide whether or not to take a baby's pushchair or buggy with you, but for the under threes it will be invaluable in most instances. Even for slightly older children it may be useful in the airport, on train stations, waiting at bus stops or while walking out at night. Your child can sleep (theoretically) while you go shopping after dark or eat in restaurants.

It will be an asset in the airport, especially if you have a night flight. You will be able to transport your sleeping child right up to the point of embarkation, where the crew will take the buggy from you and put it in the hold. At bus stops and train stations your child will be secure and unable to lurch out into the road or on to the tracks.

It may be advisable to take a sling, too. Walks on the beach, up mountains, across rough terrain and on pavements in poor condition are impossible with a buggy.

Many countries have only narrow, rough tracks by the roadside and use of a pushchair will be dangerous. Latin, Caribbean and other hot-blooded drivers are often maniacs and you will frequently find yourself jumping off the path into a surrounding field as a car screeches around a sharp bend. This is impossible with a buggy.

If you think that your best, warm pushchair may be more of a hindrance than a help, buy an old, second-hand buggy from a car-boot sale. It will probably only cost you a few pounds, so give it a good clean and take it with you. You can use it in the airport and if you find it cumbersome when you arrive at your destination, just abandon it. Even if you are trekking it is likely that you will have a base where you will be able to leave the buggy, and if it only cost you £4 it doesn't matter if it disappears.

There are three-wheeled strollers on the market which are suitable for use on any terrain, but they are very expensive at around £300.

Travel Cot

Even if you imagine that your baby will not sleep in any cot other than his own, he will. Older babies may take a short time to adjust but it won't take long. If you are tense your clever baby will play up to this just as they would in any other situation, but within a few days they should settle just as happily in a strange cot as they would at home.

Take a few familiar toys, books and blankets, and don't forget any comforters your child is attached to. It may even be worth buying and taking a back up. A familiar music box or mobile may be awkward to pack, but this would often be a more practical solution.

For most babies, taking a heavy and cumbersome travel cot halfway around the world is totally unnecessary. It is important to prearrange a cot in your hotel room or apartment before you go. Eighty per cent of the time when you arrive at your hotel, even though the receptionist assures you your cot is already in your room, it is not. However, they usually arrive fairly swiftly. This minor inconvenience is repeated the world over and is surely an international ploy of housekeeping to secure more tips!

If you intend to stay in real budget hotels, you are unlikely to acquire a cot or, if you plan to move around, prearranging cots in a series of different hotels will be impossible. In these instances you must either be prepared to sleep with your baby or improvise.

A friend of mine brought up in Ireland with eight brothers and sisters once told me that the youngest baby of the family always slept in a large drawer. This has a rather romantic tinge about it and a practical sense too, especially if you are not finding it easy to sleep with your wriggling progeny. If you're desperate, try it.

Travel Car Seats

If your baby is younger than nine months old she will probably still fit in her baby-carrying car seat. If so, it is definitely worth taking it with you. It will be useful on the plane if you don't get an aircot, it will be essential for feeding them on the move, plus you can jump in a taxi with your baby and go to a restaurant in the evening with them strapped in their seat. The theory is that they will fall asleep in the taxi and not wake up again when you all get out. Instead they will remain as good as gold, sleeping peacefully in their familiar seat while you enjoy a nice meal and a good bottle of wine.

We found that this does happen a lot of the time and is far superior to juggling with trolleys. Babies are guaranteed to wake up when shifted from taxi to pushchair, and it is a matter of luck whether or not they go back to sleep. For toddlers and older children, it is only worth taking their bigger car seats if you are hiring a car at the other end.

When prearranging your car hire from the UK, remember to request one that does have rear seat belts as your car seats will be useless without them. Developed countries do offer the option of children's car seats. Ask if they guarantee this option at the time of booking and check that they are well padded and clean.

Feeding Arrangements

Many hotel dining rooms will not have high chairs. Even if they do, they may be occupied by the time you make it to dinner, or even be unsafe.

The carrying car seat is great for children under nine months old. For older babies, a portable feeding chair that fixes on to any table edge with screw contraptions may be useful. (Unless the tables are all glass, as happened to us once.)

Fabric pouches and booster seats that rely on a certain chair structure are of limited value. You have no way of knowing whether or not they will fix to the hotel dining room's chairs. With older babies and toddlers the best bet is likely to be feeding them sitting in the buggy.

Baby Walkers

Don't bother.

They are treacherous contraptions at the best of times. There are thousands of accidents every year when babies fall out of them into fires, down stairs and on to stone floors or sharp objects. You don't want to see your baby sinking in to the swimming pool in hers.

Baby Bath

No way. Take a sponge.

Potty

Holidays may be a good time to begin potty training. You are all more relaxed and accidents on a tiled floor are better than on your carpet.

Buy the cheapest one you can find and then you don't need to bring it home if it proves useless.

Electrical Items

When taking electrical items abroad, don't forget your travel adapter. However, just as importantly be aware that most of the electrical items made for use in Britain with our voltge of 240V are useless in countries where the electricity supply is 110/120V (such as the US) even with an adapter, which just changes the shape of the plug.

To change between 240V and 110/120V you will need a transformer, too. Our 240V hairdryers will do nothing more than puff air and kettles will never boil on a 110V supply, so when travelling abroad check your appliance for suitability in your destination before you pack it.

Practically all specially designated 'travel' appliances will work off both 110/120V and 240V supplies, usually automatically. However, if you arrive and your travel kettle, hairdryer or other appliance doesn't work, check for a hidden switch that changes the voltage manually.

Travel Kettle

A travel kettle is one of your most essential travel companions when going away with a baby. Even with older children an emergency pot noodle may be a godsend. You can't rely on hotel staff in the kitchen having the same hygiene standards as you, and in some countries water needs to be boiled for five minutes (three or four times in your kettle). If you are absolutely certain your room or apartment will have one then you needn't bother, but otherwise don't forget yours. If you are relying on the hotel kettle it may be scummy, so it is a good idea to boil it filled with sterilising fluid before you use it for making up your baby's feeds.

As mentioned above, before buying a travel kettle make sure it will boil at 110/120V and not just 240V. Test that it works before you leave home. If you then arrive and it doesn't boil, be patient. You may need to flick a switch to make it respond to a lower voltage or it may just be that it takes longer to boil. My travel kettle takes about fifteen minutes to boil in the Caribbean off the 110V supply, and around seven minutes at home in the UK.

Baby Listener

I was once at a New Year's Eve party in an exclusive hotel. Everyone was dressed in all their finery and sipping champagne while one over-zealous mother danced around a baby listener she had plugged in next to the dance floor.

I never actually got on with my baby listener, so never really tested its range in hotels. But judging by that mother's response to the flashing light on hers, it was working perfectly, despite her baby being four floors away.

If your room is close to the pool, a battery-operated listener may be useful when your baby is having their afternoon nap, or when you're in the restaurant at night – but if your hotel room is at risk from intruders don't leave your baby sleeping there alone.

If you do use a listener it will be at its most useful abroad if you are in your own apartment or villa. Here it will be just as useful as it is at home, and if you don't take it you might miss it.

Don't rely on the plug-in adapters unless you are travelling to a 220/240V country. Take a battery-operated listener, as it will work anywhere.

Camcorder Battery Chargers

Remember your plug adapter and it should work whatever the voltage.

Bottle Warmers and Sterilising Systems

You should be able to cope without your bottle warmer for a fortnight, and you might even find that your child prefers cool milk on a hot night. It is unlikely that you will want to take your bulky plug-in steamer-steriliser on your travels, but if you are used to this method and can't imagine any other there are compact travel steam sterilisers available that fit two bottles. However, I have only seen them for use with a 220V supply, so they can't be used in the US, the Caribbean, etc.

If you normally use sterilising solution, take everything with you. Even if you don't, consider it while abroad as an alternative to the steam method. However, do practise it once or twice at home before you leave.

If you are no longer breast-feeding, you will already have all the feeding bottles, teats and bottle brushes you need. You won't need to buy a new sterilising system, just some sterilising tablets or fluid and a reasonable-sized plastic container with a lid. The sterilising fluid or tablets dissolved in a small amount of water have the added benefit that they can be used to wipe down the bathroom, kitchen surfaces and floor areas. This will keep the bug level down in your accommodation at least.

It is easier to travel with sterilising tablets rather than fluid. They are lighter, less bulky and you need have no fear of them leaking. Fluids such as Milton do bleach clothes, so it is not a good idea to pack it in your suitcase. If you do take fluid, carry it in your hand luggage wrapped in a plastic bag.

When using a foreign water source, boil all the water you use even though you are adding sterilising tablets. Each sterilising tablet then needs to be dissolved in a set volume of water as marked on the packet. If you use bottled water **check the seal is intact**. It may still be a good idea to boil bought water as a precaution. Note that even in the UK bought bottled water must still be boiled before it is given to babies in any form.

You can use the feeding bottles to measure the volume of water needed to make up the sterilising fluid. Don't forget they have fluid-ounces and millilitre measurements marked on them. If you prefer, measure the set volume per tablet (and per two tablets) in a measuring jug at home, then, with a waterproof pen, mark the level this reaches on the plastic container you'll take with you. You'll then know where to fill the container up to each time.

If you are camping, simply boil all your bottle-feeding equipment in a large covered pan for at least twenty-five minutes.

Presterilised bottle kits are available to buy. They are basically a system of sterile plastic bags, but may be useful as a back up.

Food and Nutrition

UNDER ONE YEAR

Breast-feeding

If you have established breast-feeding and are very comfortable with it, then you can travel anywhere in the world easily. Although I would never be deterred from travelling with a bottle-fed baby, there is little doubt that it is easier to travel farther and wider and to more remote places with a baby who is breast-feeding. Do be sensitive about the other culture's modesty and follow the lead of local mothers. Carry a shawl for privacy and warmth as you feed.

Breast-feeding is well recognised to be better for babies, and when travelling it offers significant advantages. Many potent anti-bacterial and anti-rotavirus antibodies are secreted in maternal milk. These will protect your baby from stomach upsets, diarrhoea and other illnesses while travelling. It is also very convenient. Preparing bottles without a reliable electricity supply, although possible, is very hard work.

I struggled with breast-feeding, but persevered for five months. When I booked a trip to Tobago, I decided to stop because I didn't want to risk suffering from the complications (mastitis, etc.) while on holiday. A couple of times I did regret having stopped. The first time was during the plane's descent, when my baby was screaming from the discomfort in his ears. I knew that he would have suckled at the breast, despite not being hungry, which would have eased the pressure in his ears and so relieved his pain. The second time was when I arrived at the hotel late at night and had to start boiling kettles and mixing feeds when all I wanted to do was throw myself into bed.

There are few disadvantages to breast-feeding, the only significant one being if the mother was to fall ill. Some food-poisoning bacteria can be passed on in maternal milk. If the mother were to become dehydrated the milk supply would be compromised. For this reason a back up supply of milk feed, a bottle, a teat and some sterilising tablets should be packed for an emergency. The bottle would also be invaluable if your baby were to fall ill and need re-hydration therapy.

In desperation, a baby can be fed from a spoon but it is a long, laborious process. While breast-feeding in hot, humid climates you may develop thrush on your nipples that can transfer to the baby's mouth. If this happens, you must both be treated with an anti-fungal agent or re-infection will occur.

Bottle Feeding

Ideally, you will need a reliable electricity supply. A refrigerator is a great asset but a kettle is essential. If not, bottle feeding is possible, but much more difficult.

To be prepared you will need to pack all the formula milk your baby is likely to drink over the duration of the holiday. You will probably be able to buy a brand of formula milk abroad but, as they all taste different to your baby, you may find it is a battle to make him adapt to the unfamiliar taste, which will be stressful when you should be relaxing and enjoying your time together.

You are the best judge of what quantity your baby will get through in a time period. Calculate what you will need then take extra, especially if travelling to a hot climate, as your baby will be thirstier and need more to drink.

Appetites of any age group tend to diminish in high temperatures and at least if your baby is getting plenty of milk over the duration of your travels, he will stay healthy.

If your child will tolerate ready-made cartons of baby milk it may be a good idea to take a few with you. They are about the right size for a bottle on the plane or beach in an emergency. If you arrive late at night at your destination, they will be a much easier alternative to boiling up kettles and mixing powder scoops.

Unfortunately my first son would never drink them but, fortunately, I bought and tried them before we travelled. They are bulky and heavy but are a convenience.

Although we stop sterilising our babies' bottles at around six months in the UK, it is advisable to continue doing so abroad if you cannot guarantee a good quality of tap water. If you are away from your accommodation for long periods of time, do not pre-mix the bottle feeds as the milk can spoil. Instead take bottles of fresh boiled water and the formula milk separately. Mix each bottle fresh as you need them.

Solid Feeds

If your baby is fussy it is a good idea to take a full supply of jars, cans and packets with you. Foreign supermarkets may only stock a few ageing, familiar branded cans. In many European or Caribbean resorts, Australia, America and other countries of Western standards, you will be able to buy baby food easily, but it is unlikely that you will be able to buy your baby's favourite. It is a safer option to go prepared. Jars can smash easily in your luggage, so packets of powdered food or cans are easier to transport. Rusks are a light option to pack, too. Supplement your child's diet with local fruit. Banana is easily transported, mashed and prepared. Mango, papaya, guava and other tropical fruits are easy to squash to baby food consistency with a fork.

It is important to buy fruit whole and prepare it yourself. Even on the breakfast table fruit may have been handled or washed in local water, which will contaminate it. You should peel the fruit yourself and take care not to contaminate the flesh of the fruit when you handle it.

TODDLERS

Milk Feeds

Although, after twelve months, you will be giving your child fresh cows' milk at home, in many countries of the world this is not recommended as, if milk is unpasteurised, it can harbour bacteria and pass on many illnesses. If your toddler will still drink formula milk for the holiday, your life will be relatively easy.

My two boys would happily switch from fresh cows' milk at home to formula milk on holiday. I also found one-litre cartons of long-life milk useful while travelling. They are very heavy, but buy you time to hunt out where you can purchase pasteurised milk.

In most places we found we could get branded tetra-packs, even in China, but a few times we were obliged to leave milk out of the diet. With toddlers and children, don't be too concerned about the lack of milk intake on holiday. Even in the worst-case scenario, a two-week diet of chips and Coke won't do any lasting damage.

Powdered skimmed milk from the supermarkets is not recommended for feeding children under one year old, but above this age you can try it. Most toddlers don't like it, but if yours does, it is a useful, lightweight back up to mix with boiled water for the first few days of the trip.

Solid Feeds

Feeding a toddler abroad can be a doddle or a nightmare, but don't get stressed. You may find that they have a drastically reduced appetite in the heat, which is natural, as their bodies aren't burning up calories as fuel to keep themselves warm.

It is a good idea to apportion part of your suitcase to snack and emergency meals for your toddler. I always packed dry, instant noodles, small pasta shells (if you sit them in boiling water for five minutes they soften to an edible level), raisins, crisps, cereal, bread sticks, cheese biscuits, pretzels and glucose sweets for an instant sugar burst.

Supplemented by milk and local fruits this stock gives plenty of carbohydrates and fats, plus the sugar and salt that are important in the heat. These were not, perhaps, in their most desirable form, but we always survive for a week or two with a pacifying snack to hand wherever we are.

Persuading the hotel staff to prepare a meal before the restaurant opens can be a stressful and costly business. You are much better with a kettle and a few pasta shells in your room. Many toddlers will eat pasta alone. They like bland foods and don't worry that there is no tomato or meat sauce on it. If your child refuses plain pasta, try a little instant soup on it. This will transform it into, for example, tomato or chicken flavour etc. Otherwise try the instant flavoured noodles.

SMALL CHILDREN

If you are staying in a hotel, just pack supplementary snacks. Small children may demand a bowl of instant noodles before the hotel restaurant opens, but you are less of a slave to their stomachs than you are to a baby's or toddler's. If you are self catering, then pack a few back-up favourites and snacks for emergencies. Cereal is handy but remember, in many countries you won't be able to get the milk to put on it. If you can't, you can always pour yoghurt or flavoured, sterilised milk drink over the cereal and hope the children like the novelty of it.

You may decline into a holiday of crisps, chocolate and Coke, but the worst of that is the battle you have when you get home and the child wants to know why they can't continue the same diet. (See page 262, feeding children local food.)

OLDER CHILDREN

Hopefully they will be able to pick from a restaurant menu. If they are being faddy, don't make mealtimes an issue. Help them avoid choosing high-risk foods. (See page 265.)

Nappy Changing

Nappies and Wet Wipes

In many countries of the world, disposable nappies are not available. In others they are prohibitively expensive. In Beijing, Western-branded nappies are approximately £20 per pack of thirty-two. It is therefore advisable to take your disposable nappies with you. They may be bulky but they are light and will leave a gap in your luggage by the end of the holiday for any souvenirs.

If you do use them abroad be sensitive when disposing of them. Putting them down the toilet could have catastrophic results. Take nappy sacks with you. A soiled nappy is a potential breeding ground for disease when abandoned.

Refastenable nappies are preferable. You can then put them on or take them off in between dips in the sea or pool.

A pair or two of padded washable training pants are a good back up. It is important to save some nappies for the plane journey home, so if you begin to run out of them use the training pants instead for the last few days on the beach.

If you consider baby wipes to be too expensive, take plenty of tissues, cotton wool and baby lotion.

A wipeable changing mat would be useful, although not essential. A hotel towel will suffice. Pocket size, padded and waterproof changing mats are available.

Swimming Aids

Inflatable Baby Seats

Inflatable baby seats which float are very popular, but are not ideal because they provide little stability, giving the baby virtually no independence in the water at all. They do not build confidence as they set the baby above water level, which removes the sense of being in the water. They are really just a little boat with the legs cut out. The bobbing sensation is a pleasure for the babies but most will only spend a few minutes in the seat before trying to lunge sideways.

Arm Bands

For very young babies, arm bands are of little use. Babies are unable to support their heads enough to keep them out of the water even though their bodies will be kept afloat.

Arm bands do help build confidence, and if you do intend to use them to help teach your child to swim it is a good idea to get them used to wearing them in the water while they are very young.

Rubber Rings and Floats

From around eighteen months your child will be able to enjoy independence in the water with the aid of correct-sized rubber rings. These are useful aids to improve the confidence and swimming strength of small children.

Special Buoyant Swimwear

There is a whole host of swimsuits available that provide buoyancy in the water. They use either inflatable air pockets or polystyrene floats that are actually sewn into the swimsuits. These are excellent. They allow a child to move their arms freely, the suits are much more comfortable than arm bands, and they allow enough stability and support for children as young as eighteen months to be completely independent. There is also the huge added benefit that, as your child becomes more confident in the water, you can gradually reduce the buoyancy in line with their swimming ability.

Checklist of Essentials

For babies

1. (a) Bottle-feeding equipment:
   - A bottle brush (if you forget to pack one, use your tooth-brush)
   - Three to four bottles
   - Three to four teats
   - Sterilising tablets or fluid (tablets are better for travelling)
   - A plastic container for sterilising in
   - More formula than you think you will need
   - A few cartons of ready-made formula, heavy but useful in an emergency

   or

   (b) Breast-feeding equipment:
   - Breast pads
   - Standby bottle-feeding equipment: two bottles, two teats, sterilising tablets, a bottle brush, and a small pack of formula milk
2. All your baby's solid food:
   - Jars, cans, powdered foods and rusks
   - Snack foods, raisins, breadsticks, dry biscuits, cereals
   - A plastic bowl and spoon, or two
   - Feeding cups
   - Bibs (especially important if you are travelling to cold conditions, to prevent your baby from being damp).
   - Tissues
3. Travel kettle (check that it works from a 110 and 220V supply)
4. Wet wipes for every occasion
5. A sponge and flannel

6. Baby shampoo and soap
7. Disposable nappies, cream and nappy sacks
8. Fabric nappies, pins, plastic pants etc. Even if you use disposables, a few fabric nappies as a back up may be useful if you run out.
9. Training pants. Ideal on the beach or when swimming, and washable.
10. Pushchair or baby buggy (sun parasol and/or rain cover)
11. Carrying sling or backpack
12. Carrying car seat (insect net to fit)
13. Favourite toys, books and blankets
14. Comforter (it may be advisable to take a spare)
15. Insect repellent
16. Swimming aids
17. Clothing
    - Warm clothing
    - Swimwear
    - Pyjamas to protect from insect bites at night
    - Sun hat
    - Cotton T-shirts
    - Shorts
    - Socks
    - Beach shoes
    - Soft shoes
    - Cotton sleep suits, long-sleeved and long-legged
    - Long-legged trousers and long-sleeved tops in light natural fabrics to help avoid insect bites after dusk
18. Liquid clothes wash
19. Sterilising surface cleaner
20. Small bottle of washing-up liquid to wash bottles and bowls, etc.
21. Highest factor sun block you can get suitable for baby's skin. Water-resistant rather than waterproof.
22. Shawls and blankets

Non-essentials

1. Baby listener
2. Travel cot

3. Music boxes or mobile
4. Bouncy chair

Additional Needs for Toddlers

1. Milk feeds:
   - Formula milk, UHT cartons of milk or powdered semi-skimmed milk
2. Solid feeds:
   - Favourite snacks
   - Raisins
   - Cereals
   - Dry instant noodles
   - Small pasta shells (if you sit them in a cup of boiling water for five minutes, they will become soft enough to eat)
   - Crisps
   - Breadsticks
   - Cheese and sweet biscuits
   - Pretzels
   - Glucose energy sweets
   - Long-life/'stay fresh' bread (will last up to fourteen days)
   - Drinking cups
   - Portable feeding chair
   - Reins, wrist attachment, audible distance alarm
   - Potty (useful for camping)

For All Age Groups

1. Documentation: passport, visa, E111 or health insurance details, vaccination certificates
2. Insect repellent containing DEET (Diethyl tolumide)
3. Plug-in mosquito killer (or coils) and nets
4. Camera and spare camera film and batteries
5. Camcorder, blank camcorder tapes and battery recharger
6. Beach shoes or old pumps
7. Comfortable shoes that your child can easily walk in

8. Swimwear and swimming aids
9. Sun hat – essential when travelling on water
10. Toothbrush and paste
11. High-factor sun block. If your children will be spending a lot of time in the water choose a waterproof cream that does not sting the eyes if it is rubbed in, as invariably does happen.
12. Towels
13. Phrase book with a list of medical symptoms
14. Sunglasses
15. Prescription glasses if necessary
16. Plug adapter

Older Children

Their own little bag for them to pack and carry.

The Medical Kit

Everything mentioned below is available over the counter in your local chemist, except the antibiotics which you may have to ask for on a private prescription. However, once you have them they won't expire for a few years, so you will be able to take them on subsequent holidays.

Essentials

1. Sachets of oral replacement salts – e.g. Rehydrat or Dioralyte
2. Paracetamol syrup – e.g. Calpol or Disprol. Will provide pain relief, alleviate fever and reduce inflammation.
3. Malaria prophylaxis tablets
4. If travelling into a malarial region outside the reach of medical help, drugs to treat malaria should be carried, such as quinine combined with Fansidar.
5. Antiseptic powder spray – e.g. Betadine or Savlon (povodine iodine)

6. Antibiotic treatments:

(a) Antibiotic oral tablets. Check dose for your child's age group when you pick up the prescription. Carry at least one but preferably two (one as a back up).

- Naladixic acid is useful for gastro-intestinal and urinary infections
- Co-trimoxazole is useful for many bacterial infections, including stomach upsets, urinary-tract infections and general respiratory infections
- Amoxycillin and Augmentin are useful for many bacterial infections, including general respiratory-tract and skin infections
- Metronidazole or Tinidazole for amoebic dysentery and giardiasis

(b) Antibiotic eye drops/lotions

- Fucithalmic is effective and non toxic. Allergic reactions are quickly limited by discontinuing use.

(c) Antibiotic powder is better in the humid tropics for skin infections (e.g. impetigo). Cream is very efficient for skin infections in temperate climates.

(d) Eardrops are effective for infections in the outer ear

(e) If your child is prone to middle ear infections or tonsillitis, consider taking specific antibiotics with you to treat flare ups.

(f) If your child has an existing medical condition, pack enough routine medication to last the duration of the trip. Keep a written record of the generic (not trade) name of the drug, so that if you need to buy the drug abroad, you will be able to.

7. When travelling with a young baby, you may be advised to take an electronic thermometer with you. Dummies with a built-in thermometer are claimed by the manufacturers to be accurate within 0.1°C.

8. Caneston cream for superficial fungal infections

9. Motion-sickness tablets (Dramine, Phenergan or Stugeron, depending on the child's age)

10. Sudocrem antiseptic, good for nappy rash, sunburn and bites

11. Calamine for sunburn, prickly heat and itchy bites
12. Phenergan for motion sickness, sedation, bites and allergic reactions to antihistamines
13. Water sterilisation tablets
14. Water purification tablets (iodine) for emergencies, if you anticipate travelling to where you will be unable to buy bottled water, or boil your own supply

The First Aid Kit

- Packet of absorbent cotton wool
- Sterile gauze squares in various sizes
- Plasters
- Bandages
- Triangular bandage
- Adhesive surgical tape
- Safety pins
- Tweezers and scissors
- Swiss army knife
- Two 5ml syringes
- Five needles (preferably two different sizes)
- One dental needle
- One intravenous cannula
- One skin suture with needle
- Once packet of steri-strips or other skin closure mechanism
- Alcohol swabs for cleaning skin

Additional items, such as an intravenous blood-giving set and blood substitute solution may be worthwhile additions to the luggage if travelling to remote, rural areas. Discuss with your doctor.

NB: Keep what you will need for the first night at the top of your suitcase, and remember infants (children under two years) often have no weight allowance on the plane.

PART THREE

While You Are Away

CHAPTER 9

Settling In

On Arrival

Transfer

If you don't have transport included in your package, your first trial is the journey from the airport to your accommodation.

Unfortunately, taxi drivers the world over cannot be trusted:

- Before leaving arrivals, you should always ask someone inside the airport terminal what the approximate cost of the fare to your destination should be
- Always negotiate your fare before getting into a taxi or insist a visible meter is switched on
- Confirm the currency or you may get to the end of your journey and the driver will claim that he meant US$20 not $20 Hong Kong
- Try to have the right change so he does not try to extort more money
- Don't follow anyone to a 'taxi' outside a designated taxi pick-up zone. The taxi is then likely to be unlicensed, uninsured and the state of the car unreliable.

Arriving At Your Accommodation

Room Allocation

In a resort hotel with babies and young children, try to secure a room on the ground floor. Lifts and balconies are both treacherous with toddlers. Stairs are wearying after a long day, especially with buggies and a car seat to carry. If your hotel has rooms backing on to the pool, try to get one. You can sit in the sun and pop your baby in the room for a sleep. Younger children can play out of the heat of the sun while you enjoy it.

The main disadvantages of the ground-floor rooms are intruders and insects. No matter how clean a hotel is they are constantly battling to keep crawling insects out. Mosquitoes also find their way easily into rooms on the lower floors. With older children, rooms or apartments on higher floors mean that you will be able to keep your windows open at night with less fear of intruders and mosquitoes, but with younger children the windows must be locked.

If your child is unlikely to sleep in a strange cot or bed alone, request a king- sized bed. A big bed often means a big room, too.

If you are having to prepare milk feeds, a room with a fridge or minibar (to use as a fridge) is a distinct advantage. Many hotels do not have this facility, but check with reception if this is an option before your room is allocated.

Comfort And Safety In Your Room

On arrival, do a safety checklist. Most mothers will do this instinctively, but if you are tired and jet lagged, you might crave the child-free days.

- Double lock the door with a bolt, chain or key so that it is impossible for your toddler or child to get out of the room while you are still asleep. Paris was eighteen months when he worked out how to escape from our hotel room in China. When he was three he decoded a series of locks, with a few random fiddles, to escape on to a stone staircase in Spain.

- If the windows don't lock properly you must insist on a room change
- Shield all electrical points behind furniture. In many parts of the world these are positioned just at fiddling height and are of a lower standard than those at home. Don't be afraid of rearranging the room to improve safety.
- Remove all unstable furniture with sharp edges, projecting nails or thin glass tops. Ask housekeeping to remove anything you feel is a danger to your child. At worst, stick it out on the balcony or in the bathroom or wardrobe.
- Remove all breakable objects
- Put all complimentary matches and glass ashtrays out of reach
- Move the toilet brush. You don't want to get up one morning to find your toddler using it to clean her teeth.
- Take up mats that slide on tiled floors. Don't allow your child to run around on tiled floors wearing just socks.
- If there are any heavy doors in your room, wedge them so they cannot crush a child's fingers
- If there are any glass doors that your child may run into, they should be marked with visible warning stickers. If not, mark them in some way yourself, either with draped fabric, washable paints, children's stickers or even squiggles of toothpaste on the far side.
- Move any unfamiliar flowers or plants from inside the room
- Check the safety and stability of the balcony
- Look under the beds and in the cupboard for poisonous substances including rat or insect traps
- Store medicine, razors and scissors out of reach

Jet Lag

If you have had a long journey across several time zones, children are likely to suffer from jet lag. The body is used to a regular daily pattern. After long periods in the air in a pressurised cabin, sleep patterns, digestion and circulation will be affected.

There is a lot of advice about how to avoid jet lag, but I never manage to do it. The guidelines are to avoid fatty foods, alcohol, coffee and tea the day before you leave and during the flight. Drink plenty of water to combat tiredness, dehydration and headaches. Wear loose-fitting clothes of natural fibres. Walk around the plane to stretch the muscles.

It is generally accepted that jet lag is worst going east. Eastbound, your watch must be put forward (+ hours). Travelling westbound it must be put back (− hours). It is much easier to stay up past your bedtime and sleep well than go to bed hours earlier than normal and try to get to sleep.

To minimise jet lag:

- Travelling west, if it doesn't interfere with school, try to keep the children up later and let them lie-in longer for a few days before your trip
- On arrival westwards, keep the children up and awake as long as you can. Don't let them go to bed at 4 p.m. or they will be up and ready to go at 3 a.m.
- Going east, allow them to gradually adjust. It is inevitable they will be up late the first few nights, but ensure they don't lie-in too late.
- Children may suffer from loss of appetite on arrival, or want to eat at irregular times. Give them regular healthy snacks and tidbits.

Foreign Roads

There are more tourists killed on foreign roads than by any of the tropical diseases, parasites or dangerous animals. (See travelling by car, page 200.) It is difficult to drive on foreign roads on the opposite side, but it is equally difficult to remember which way to look as a pedestrian. Instead of looking right, then left, we need to look left, then right, but years of conditioning mean we instinctively always look right first. I once almost stepped in front of a silently approaching tram in Amsterdam a few hours after arriving. Simon grabbed me back just in time.

- Practise looking both ways until you are sure the road is clear on both sides
- Beware that roads may not even look like roads; tracks can be used by vehicles

Tell Your Child What To Do If They Are Separated From You

- Protect your child from getting lost – bright clothes really do help and keeping toddlers on reins, wrist straps or safe in their buggies is best
- If your child understands, arrange a place to go to immediately if you become separated. If they are lost suggest that they go into a shop and approach a female assistant to help them find you. This will get them off the streets and they will be safe until you find them.
- Teach your child the hotel name and room number as soon as possible
- If your child is too young, put the address of your accommodation on a luggage label around their wrist or in their pocket

If you do lose your child, don't panic. In most countries of the world children are treasured and you need have no fear that any harm will come to them.

CHAPTER 10

Acclimatising to the Elements and Change of Environment

Arriving in the Heat

The Effects of Heat on the Body

In a hot environment, if the heat lost by the body by sweating and flushing of blood to the skin's surface is insufficient, there will be a rise in body temperature that will lead to rapid breathing, irritability and confusion. If the temperature continues to rise, the body gives up and can even stop sweating. The temperature will continue to rise dangerously. If it rises above 41°C, in effect the body begins to cook.

The brain is affected first, followed by the liver and kidneys, then muscle cells. As the body's internal temperature rises further, the damage caused is likely to be irreversible. If the internal body temperature reaches 50°C for just a couple of minutes, cells in every organ of the body will be destroyed. Death will follow.

Heatstroke

Heatstroke refers to the overheating of the body's inner core, not just the skin which can suffer prolonged exposure to intense heat with the only major damage being blisters and superficial burns.

Babies are unable to sweat efficiently, and can suffer dangerous increases in internal body temperature very quickly. As a result, they are particularly susceptible to heatstroke.

Children sweat more in hot climates but are generally more active and less able to judge when they are getting dangerously hot. Heatstroke is therefore relatively common when unacclimatised children go on holiday to the intense heat and strong sun of a Meditteranean or Caribbean summer.

Humidity is also an important factor. High humidity interferes with the body's ability to sweat and cool down. Even adults who aren't exercising may suffer heatstroke if the air temperature and humidity are both high. Children suffer more.

Most children will get too hot at times on holiday, either by overdoing the running about, spending too long in a hot car, or walking in the midday sun. The danger is when the child becomes so hot that the body effectively gives up trying to cool itself. If the child is not cooled down quickly it will lead to a medical emergency.

Symptoms

The skin will look and feel hot but will be dry as a result of the lack of sweat. In the early stages your child will become extremely irritable, confused and might complain of a headache. Babies will cry inconsolably until you make attempts to cool them. If this stage goes unrecognised, babies and children will become drowsy, lethargic and might have a rapid pulse rate. Their temperature may rise to 40°C. In severe cases, your child might become confused, have epileptic-like seizures, begin to lose consciousness and even stop breathing.

Heatstroke in the Shade

When I took Paris to Tobago for the first time, he was five months old. At midday, we sat down for lunch in the shade and left him asleep plastered in waterproof sunscreen. We enjoyed a relaxing forty-five minutes before he woke up and began complaining. We left the restaurant and placed Paris in his pushchair under a parasol as we enjoyed the sunshine. At around 3 p.m. we judged that the sun was weaker, so allowed Paris to roll around on a towel in the sun, plastered with more sunscreen. At 4 p.m., he began to complain gently, so I moved him back into the shade. Soon after he began to cry louder and louder and louder. We tried to soothe him but there was nothing we could do. We eventually left the poolside, very embarrassed by all the fuss we had created. Paris continued to cry inconsolably for over an hour. Eventually I collapsed next to him on the bed and began to blow over his back and the nape of his neck. He stopped crying. I stopped blowing and he began howling. I blew cool air all over him. He became quiet again and after ten minutes of sobbing fell in to a deep sleep. Simon and I both fell asleep exhausted, and it was not until the morning that it clicked in my mind that Paris had been suffering from a mild case of heatstroke. Clearly a baby is at risk even if they have been in the shade for most of the day.

Prevention

- When you arrive at your destination, allow time for acclimatisation
- Children will actually acclimatise more quickly than adults, but are more susceptible in the interim. They are therefore most at risk in the first day or two.
- Keep children out of the sun during the hottest part of the day. This might not be at midday as humidity rises in the afternoon. Keep babies and young children in the shade for as much of the day as you can.
- Do not apply waterproof sunscreen too thickly. It acts as a layer of fat and hinders sweating and heat loss.
- Ensure that your child rests and cools down with a cold drink at intervals. While in the early stages of your holiday, discourage them from running about in the sun too much.
- Encourage them to take regular dips in the sea or swimming pool to cool
- Don't travel in a car at the hottest time of the day without air-conditioning
- Ensure that babies and children wear hats, preferably ones that cover the nape of their necks. Strong, direct sun on the nape of

the neck will interfere with the temperature regulatory centres in the brain.

Treatment

Act immediately to cool your child. Get out of the sun and into an air-conditioned room and remove all their clothes. Sponge them down from top to toe with cool water. If you don't have a fan, blow all over their skin, particularly on the back of their neck. If you can, get an ice pack or anything cold – even a chilled canned drink or an ice lolly in its wrapper. Make up an ice pack by tying ice into a cotton T-shirt.

Monitor pulse rate and if you have packed a thermometer, measure their temperature. Give cool drinks and check the temperature continuously until it lowers to 37.5 - 38°C. You should then stop cooling, as you may risk your child becoming too cold.

If their temperature has reached more than 40°C and you feel that your child needs medical attention, don't mess about, call a doctor.

If your child begins to lose consciousness, place him in the recovery position (see page 337) and check breathing. If breathing stops, begin artificial respiration (see page 332) and get help urgently.

In milder cases, Calpol will lower temperature and relieve headache.

Heat Exhaustion

Unacclimatised children will lose a lot of salt in their sweat and can become salt depleted during the first few days of their holiday. This can then lead to salt-depleted exhaustion. Even following acclimatisation, 'water depleted' heat exhaustion may occur if your child does not have plenty to drink.

Symptoms

Fatigue, weakness, headache, nausea and sometimes vomiting. Muscle cramps are a distinct sign that the body is salt depleted. Excessive thirst and dehydration clearly indicate that your child needs to drink fluids.

Prevention
- Don't prevent children adding salt to their food. Allow them to eat crisps, pretzels and other salted snacks.
- They must also be given adequate water to drink to balance the salt intake. Ensure your child has plenty to drink throughout the day.
- Never embark on long walks or trips without fresh water
- Be aware that children will lose more fluids in less humid environments and at high altitude.

Treatment
If your child shows symptoms of salt depletion – headache, fatigue, muscle weakness – treat them with oral rehydration salts (see page 276). Mask the flavour with juice. Give plenty of bottled or boiled water.

Prickly Heat (Heat Rash)

On my very first trip abroad, I suffered agony with prickly heat. I was in northern France, in moderate temperatures, but it was the first time my pale skin had seen much sun and I burned slightly. This pain settled quickly but was replaced by tiny, raised lumps and an agonising prickly itchiness all over my chest and shins that literally forced me to tear off the top layers of skin with my nails. It kept me awake and miserable for two nights before it settled.

It happened again, two years later, when I was in Greece. This time I recognised the signs and instead of scratching, splashed my chest and legs with cold water, which stopped the agony from developing. I later realised I had been suffering from prickly heat.

- If your child presents with a 'heat rash' of tiny, raised pimples, do everything you can to prevent them from scratching. It will make it much worse.
- Splash the area with cold water and pat dry. Do not rub the area.
- Dab with calamine to stop the itching

- If symptoms are severe, a product containing camphor and anti-histamines will provide relief

Sunburn

Severe sun damage, due to overexposure to the sun, may predispose to skin cancer in later life. You must pay overzealous attention to protecting your child from burning.

- Burning is more severe around midday, when the sun is directly overhead and at its most intense
- The sun is more intense closer to the equator in the tropics and can burn the skin in minutes
- Reflected sunlight from water, sand and snow can burn, even if a child remains in the shade
- When skiing, reflected sunrays can burn the inside of the nose
- Be aware that sun penetrates clouds
- Sensitive skin can burn through light clothing

Prevention
- Cover babies and children in sunscreen whenever they are exposed to the sun. Do not expose infants to direct sunlight for any length of time.
- Use parasols or shades, even for short walks, when the sun is high
- Use the highest factor sunscreen available and reapply regularly, but do not apply too thickly. Sunscreens have a high fat content and when applied too thickly act as an insulator and so interfere with heat loss and temperature regulation. This increases the risk of heatstroke.
- Protect a baby's head with a hat or sun-cream. A child will burn on their scalp and their parting and through thin hair.
- Protect the soles of the feet – they burn, too
- Apply sunscreen to the top of the ears. They burn easily and are a very common position for skin cancer.
- Keep T-shirts on children, even when swimming

Treatment

Resting, drinking plenty of water and Calpol for the pain will relieve mild sunburn. Soothing antiseptics with zinc oxide (e.g. Sudocrem) will help. Products containing camphor have a cooling effect, and calamine lotion is soothing. Antihistamines may help and, if the pain and irritation is preventing sleep, a dose of Phenergan (promethazine) will be of great benefit.

In more severe cases

Leave blisters alone. They may become infected if they burst. If burns are very severe, a doctor may suggest the use of steroid cream with an antibacterial action.

Arriving in the Cold

Newborn babies cannot shiver and so are very vulnerable to the cold. Infants are prone to hypothermia in cool surroundings that would not pose a threat to an adult. Children too, are very susceptible to the cold. They lose heat more rapidly because of their shape and the fact that they have relatively low levels of insulating fat under their skin. In fact, cold is more dangerous to children than heat and, possibly, more difficult for an adult to judge. We might not feel particularly chilly, so assume our children are comfortable, when they might feel as if they are freezing.

Toddlers and small children will often rely on you to provide the right environment and do not have the understanding or the vocabulary to express how cold they are. Even six years olds may not turn around to you and say, 'I'm cold.' It is left for you to guess.

When Paris was three years old, we spent Christmas in Munich and Salzburg. In Salzburg the mountain air was dry and very cold. Although we kept him wrapped up, he was immobile in his trolley. He kept crying and insisting that he either walk or be carried. Because at the time he had an obsession about shoes, and was still insisting that he wear his summer shoes, crying hysterically if we tried to make him try on anything else, we allowed him to wear the light shoes, but this meant he could not walk in the snow. Paris was very quiet and sat in his buggy miserably. We kept asking him over and over again if he was cold and he would only complain about his hands which we would then warm up. His face was flushed and he looked very warm.

When we arrived back at the hotel, Paris flopped on the bed. As I undressed him, his body turned from pale to bright red and a raging fever began. The skin all over his bottom was chapped and mottled where it had been sitting against the cold plastic of the buggy. On hindsight, the poor little thing must have been freezing. We should have known because he was so uncharacteristically quiet, but I had stupidly relied on him to tell us when he felt cold.

He was very ill that night and I hardly slept. He had picked up an infection, too – the intense cold must have lowered his defences. I still get pangs of guilt when I remember him lying limp on the hotel bed, his little chapped bottom where the blood must have stagnated against the cold buggy broke my heart.

Hypothermia

If your child becomes very cold, they may become hypothermic. Hypothermia is very serious because it slows down the functioning of all the body's organs. If the body temperature drops low enough, the organs will stop working and this will be fatal. Hypothermia is clinically defined as a deep body temperature below 35°C.

Wet and windy conditions are when you are most at risk but, as I learned from experience, even when you feel warm, your child may be losing heat fast. Hypothermia can develop in children even after what we consider to be mild exposure to the cold.

Symptoms

The symptoms that a child has hypothermia are usually obvious – they are likely to be shivering, pale and blue. They will be listless, lethargic, confused and quiet.

By contrast, babies who cannot shiver, and small children, are harder to judge because their faces may be bright red and they will look warm. They will not complain of the cold but will be quiet, list-less and lethargic. The only real way of confirming hypothermia is by taking a child's temperature. Breathing may be slow and, in severe cases, your child may start to lose consciousness.

Prevention

- The temperature on earth falls by approximately 1°C for every 150m rise above sea level. If you are planning an excursion into mountains, you must take warm clothing. No matter how hot it is at sea level, it will be several degrees colder at altitude.
- Inactivity in the cold makes a child more susceptible to cold because active muscles give off heat. If your child pleads with you to let them walk, don't make the same mistake I did. This will also help keep the blood supply to their extremities. An active child is much better able to keep warm.
- Take a warm coat or jumper with you everywhere, especially at night or out on a boat
- In the cold, a lot of heat is lost from the head. A hat will prevent this.
- A waterproof raincoat or change of clothing is essential if rain is even a remote possibility
- Good shoes are another essential
- Never forget that even if you feel warm, your child is at risk from hypothermia

Treatment

Get your child out of the cold even if it means knocking on a stranger's door. An obviously sick child will break the barriers of language and race wherever you are in the world.

Warm your child by wrapping him in dry clothing or blankets. Older children may be given warm drinks and a warm bath.

Skin temperature is a good indicator that your child is recovering, but if possible continue to take his or her temperature.

Allow your child to rest in a warm bed but don't allow them to sleep until you are certain their body temperature has risen and they are more alert and breathing properly.

Arriving at High Altitude – Skiing or Trekking

At high altitude the air becomes thin, cold and dry. The lack of oxygen in the thin atmosphere does affect most people to some degree and can lead to Acute Mountain Sickness.

Acute Mountain Sickness (AMS)

Approximately half the people who ascend to altitudes of 3,500m and above suffer from Acute Mountain Sickness (AMS). As age increases, the risk of AMS decreases, which unfortunately means that your children are at greater risk than you are.

Symptoms

Symptoms rarely begin immediately on arrival, but generally develop after a day or two. In the majority of people, AMS may be a miserable condition but is trivial and passes quickly. Children acclimatise and adjust more quickly than adults.

On arrival the sufferer might feel light headed, weak, and notice a change of breathing pattern, but otherwise feel totally fit. Lethargy begins after a few days and sleep is disturbed. Irregular breathing is noticeable during the night. On waking, there is a headache which is not helped by painkillers. Standing causes dizziness and even vomiting.

After rest the symptoms disappear. If not, you must descend by at least 500m. Dangerous symptoms include a significant increase in breathing, breathlessness at rest, and frothy sputum. These are signs of pulmonary oedema (fluid on the lungs) and there is some evidence children are particularly susceptible to this. Confusion, drowsiness, unsteady walking and personality changes are all signs of cerebral oedema (fluid on the brain).

Children are difficult to diagnose because many of the symptoms could be confused with naughtiness. Watch out for irritability, apathy, loss of appetite without a high temperature and increased breathing.

Prevention
- Strenuous exercise should be avoided if there are any signs of mountain sickness
- Regular rest is important
- Meals should be light

Treatment
- If the symptoms are minor, take it easy and your body will adjust naturally. Gradually your blood will increase its oxygen-carrying capacity by an increased production of red blood cells.
- In South America, the whole family will be offered coca tea. Coca tea contains tiny amounts of cocaine, which acts as a stimulant and so helps to mask the fatigue some people feel on arrival at altitude, as well as easing the nausea.
- If the symptoms persist, you must descend

Other Concerns at High Altitude

Radiation
With altitude, radiation levels increase. You must pay strict attention to applying sunscreen and be aware that snow, like water, reflects the sun's rays, so the intensity is greater. Burning can be severe, even in cold conditions.

Dryness
Ensure that you all drink plenty of fluids. At altitude, the dry conditions mean that you lose moisture as you breathe, despite the cold. You should therefore ensure that dehydration does not occur. This would be more likely to occur if complicated with vomiting due to AMS.

If the symptoms persist you must descend.

Swimming Abroad

The Risks of Picking Up Illness

Wading, bathing and even showering can cause infection. Many diseases are transmittable in pools, which are not sufficiently chlorinated or cleaned. As mentioned earlier in the book, President Roosevelt contracted polio from his own swimming pool and was crippled for life.

African lakes harbour parasitic illness and many civilisations in the developing world use the local river for all their ablutions, polluting them with raw sewage.

Even the vast oceans are a risk to the swimmer. Many beaches in the world are heavily polluted, particularly in Europe. The last major outbreak of cholera in Lima, Peru, is thought to have come from the Pacific Ocean. Along heavily populated coastlines, the quantity of sewage pumped out into the sea means that the sea is contaminated with infective illnesses. This is true in the UK, too. I have watched seagulls at low tide off the west shore in Llandudno, gathering and feasting around the sewage pipe outlet off shore. As kids we were ill whenever we went into the sea off Abersoch. Along the hundreds of miles of Spanish coast, which is a mass of tourist resorts, the sea is potentially polluted.

- Many doctors advise us not to take our babies swimming before the triple vaccine. It is advisable to stick to this guideline abroad.
- Keep babies with their heads above the water to ensure they don't swallow anything
- Clean their hands with wet wipes when they get out
- Always tell children to keep their mouths tightly closed while swimming
- If you can see any sun-cream floating on the top of the water, or if you cannot smell chlorine in a pool, it is possible that the filter or chlorinating system is faulty. (It does happen – the baby pool in a hotel we were staying at in Margueurita was closed two days after we noticed it wasn't perfectly clean.)

The Danger of Drowning

- Make your child understand that they must not swim unsupervised
- Tell them that if they get into difficulty, they must call out to the nearest person for help – they mustn't risk going unnoticed while struggling and swallowing water
- Listen to the locals and ask them where they take their own children to swim
- Look for beaches with families on them, not just windsurfers
- Find out about currents and tides if you are straying off the usual tourist beaches
- Warn children of the dangers of cramp. Cramp occurs when our muscles become tired, and is more of a risk in chilly water.
- Discourage children from diving. Each year, a number of people break their necks diving into swimming pools in the UK. This can cause irreversible paralysis. In the sea, rivers and lakes, unseen rocks can do untold damage. Locals know where these rocks are and can avoid them. You will not and may dive in at exactly the same spot, but end up in hospital.
- If you allow your children to jump into swimming pools, ensure they jump as far away from the edge as possible. This will avoid them hitting the back of their head on the tiles as they hit the water.

Sea Creatures

- Ask the locals if there are any dangerous sea creatures to be wary of. These may include a high population of jellyfish in the Mediterranean, or sea urchins in the Caribbean, which usually cause pain rather than danger.
- Coral cuts can be nasty and easily infected.
- It is advisable that your children wear something on their feet in the water, such as pumps, jellies, or the rubber-soled diving shoes that are now available cheaply, even in baby sizes, in the high street.
- Tell your children to shuffle clumsily as they wade into the sea. This will warn any fish to move.

CHAPTER 11

Nutrition and Hygiene

Children will often suffer a loss of appetite on arrival in a strange environment. Jet lag, excitement, heat and unfamiliar food all contribute. You should never worry, as they won't allow themselves to starve. Usually, children are most at risk of being ill with diarrhoea in between weaning on to solids and three years old. But, when eating abroad, everyone is at risk.

It is estimated that roughly half of travellers every year suffer from a bout of diarrhoea, although most cases are mild to moderate. Try to ensure that your children are not amongst them.

Always carry a snack and a drink of fresh water for your children so that you are never tempted to take risks if stuck on a remote train or bus station at mealtime. Raisins, bread sticks, crisps, chocolate, glucose tablets or sweets will take the emergency out of a child's appetite.

Feeding Babies Abroad

I have always found feeding abroad no more difficult than at home – you will still need to sterilise bottles and boil water to mix with the milk or powdered food. If you have to prepare milk feeds, a room with a refrigerator is a distinct advantage. A minibar is a useful substitute. Budge up the beers and move in the bottles.

If you have forgotten your travel kettle, try to persuade reception to lend you one. If not, go and buy one with a local plug on it, as it will be worth the money to save the hassle of having to ask for boiled water constantly.

- In the heat, it is too risky to travel far from the hotel with ready made-up milk. Travel with the boiled water and powdered milk, pre-measured, in a small container or bag. Mix fresh as needed.
- If you need boiled water, ask in any hotel or restaurant that sells coffee or tea
- Always carry a jar of sweet baby food rather than savoury, as your baby will be more likely to eat it cold, if necessary

From about eight months you will be able to find food in restaurants to feed your baby. Most good restaurants will be able to supply one of the following even if it is not on the menu:

- Local bread – pitta, naan, ciabatta, etc.
- Eggs, prepared fresh to order. Omelette or boiled are safest.
- Chips
- Fresh rice. (NB: In Asia you may be offered honey sauce to pour over your baby's rice. It is delicious, but the present guidelines advise that babies under one year old should not be given honey because of a slight risk of botulism poisoning.)
- Noodles or pasta with butter or a tomato sauce
- Fresh whole fruit for you to peel yourself. Always clean the fruit with a baby wipe first to avoid contaminating the flesh while peeling. Pre-prepared fruit may have been handled with unclean hands or washed in local water, so avoid your child eating it.

Feeding Children Local Food

Children who are introduced to foods early on develop a much broader range of taste than those who are not.

Japanese children are not born liking sushi, nor are Indian children born liking curry. What they grow up liking depends on parental influences, available foods and, possibly, what their mothers ate while they were in the womb or while breast-feeding.

You will need to be careful, but try to encourage your child to try different things. Be wary of the high-risk foods highlighted below, but enjoy the fun of discovering new cuisines together. If you are in a local restaurant and cannot read the menu, call over a waitress, shrug and point at the children; she will soon get the message. If there is not a language barrier, ask them what they would pick for their children.

A phrase book is pretty essential when travelling with children, just in case you need to explain symptoms of an illness to a doctor. It is useful in restaurants, too, but it is amazing how many restaurants in far-reaching places around the world have menus in English, although often you will need to ask for them.

Wherever in the world you are, you will be able to find something for your child to eat. Paris is so fussy that at nursery they gave up trying to feed him. When he started school, despite my objections, he was constantly made to sit on his own on a 'naughty' chair in the dining room for refusing to eat or even try his lunch. He still won't eat most things, but when he is hungry enough he surprises me by eating satay with peanut sauce, chilli, or black tiger-prawn tempura off my plate.

- Deep-fried foods freshly cooked through and eaten piping hot are invariably safe, including, chips, spring rolls, fish, meat or vegetables in batter or breadcrumbs. Hot oil reaches temperatures of 180°C, well above that needed to kill any living organisms.
- Small pieces of marinated meat or fish, cooked on a hot grill or barbecue, will be safe if they are well cooked all the way through. Make sure the food is actually being cooked, not reheated. (The meat will be dryer and tougher when reheated.)
- Local bread, pancakes, tortillas or dry patties made from wheat or corn flour, will be filling and nutritious
- Children will usually eat wheat or rice-flour noodles
- In many countries of the world, fresh fish is an important part of the local diet. Freshly cooked, this will invariably be safe.

- Yoghurt is usually OK because it is full of harmless bacteria that inhibit the growth of food-poisoning bacteria
- Local fruits, peeled by you
- Fresh rice or pasta with a tomato sauce
- Eggs, prepared fresh to order. Omelette or boiled are safest.

The Role of Food and Drink in Spreading Illness

Certain foods are deemed high risk because of the likelihood that they will harbour the bacteria that cause illness. Even if your child has been vaccinated against typhoid and hepatitis, it is still important for them to avoid eating these foods and for you to pay rigorous attention to what they drink. Most of these foods are well known, but it may be difficult to convince your screaming child that the delicious-looking ice cream could make them severely ill.

Remember that most foods have the potential to cause illness if they have been contaminated by handling, run under unboiled water, or if they have been left uncovered and open to the air, dust and flies. Bacteria need food, warmth, water and time to grow. Once they land on warm, moist food, bacteria multiply every fifteen-twenty minutes so that each individual bacterium has the potential to become 1,048,576 in five hours.

In contrast, food which has been thoroughly cooked through, at a high enough temperature for long enough, then served fresh and eaten piping hot, is virtually guaranteed to be safe. While travelling you won't have control over the cooking methods and hygiene standards, so you must choose your restaurant carefully and select prudently from the menu.

If you are uncomfortable about the standard or temperature of the food, send it back. This can be difficult, especially for the polite British, but otherwise, don't eat it.

The number of stars a hotel has for luxury and facilities is no measure of the kitchen's cleanliness. The British cricket team visiting India were forced to postpone a game after all going down with serious food poisoning in their hotel.

Even five-star hotels need to depend on local suppliers and staff, who may have low hygiene standards. It only takes one trainee food handler who did not wash his hands properly to contaminate an entire batch of meals and cause catastrophe.

The sneaky thing about all the bugs pathogenic to man is that they never give themselves away until they are inside your stomach. There is no smell or change in the appearance or taste of the food. This is how they have remained so successful in spreading themselves. Food-poisoning bacteria – for example, *Salmonella spp.* and *E. coli* – are very different from the food-spoilage bacteria that alter the smell, colour and texture of foods and make them taste rotten. Food will still taste delicious even when teeming with virulent sickness- and diarrhoea-inducing organisms.

Spices and chilli can hide the flavours of rotting meat, but they will not defend you against illness. Chilli itself can be an irritant and cause diarrhoea, but this is distinguishable from early infection by its burning sensation.

Don't become paranoid; eating local food is one of the pleasures of every holiday. Just be informed and be careful.

High-risk Foods

Unpasteurised (Unboiled) Milk
Unpasteurised milk, and the cheese made from it, can transmit diarrhoeal illness, tuberculosis, listeriosis and brucellosis. It should therefore be avoided. This includes milk and cheese from cows, sheep, goats or even more exotic animals, such as yaks.

Ice Cream
Ice cream is often made from unpasteurised milk or contains some local water. Freezing does not kill the bugs that cause illness, and in some parts of the world – including exotic islands – frequent power cuts happen. When the electricity supply is cut off the ice cream melts and bugs can multiply. The ice cream will re-freeze, but will be even more potentially dangerous than before.

Cream

Like milk and ice cream, cream can harbour bacteria if it is not pasteurised and kept sufficiently cold. Even in the UK, fresh cream cakes are often responsible for causing food poisoning, which is why school fêtes no longer accept cream cakes on their stalls.

Salads, Vegetables and Fruit

All are potential sources of infection as there is a good chance they will have been washed in local water before they got to the table. Even before preparation, they could have been contaminated during transport, storage or even while growing. In some parts of the world, human faeces are used as fertiliser for growing crops, including the innocent strawberry. Unless the product is carefully washed in purified water, illness is a certain consequence for the unlucky consumer.

Seafood

Shellfish are renowned for their disease-harbouring qualities. The method in which they feed – by filtering vast amounts of seawater – ensures that if there are any nasty bugs floating around in the water, they are likely to collect in the shellfish and even proliferate, drawing their own nutrition from the filth filtered by their host. Shellfish often thrive near open sewers and in water contaminated with human excrement. Lobsters also collect on the seabed around the effluence and feed on the debris. Severe illness, including cholera and hepatitis, plus many other diarrhoeal illnesses, are spread in this way. Steaming seafood is not sufficient. The only defence is thorough cooking.

Seafood and fish harvested during a red tide can result in poisoning. A red tide occurs when there is so much plankton in the sea it appears red. The fish eat the plankton and the toxin accumulates in their livers and flesh.

Eggs

Raw or lightly cooked eggs and the products made from them – e.g. custard, mousse and mayonnaise – can cause food poisoning. The American love of coleslaw means that a dollop is often present in many parts of the world – be aware that coleslaw and potato salads made from fresh mayonnaise are a risk.

Sauces
Many fancy sauces contain cream, lightly cooked eggs and reheated meat or chicken stock. The low temperatures required to cook a sauce for a short time will not kill bacteria.

Chicken
Salmonella is not just a problem on the surface of cooked chicken; the bacteria can penetrate the flesh while the poultry is still alive. It is therefore important only to eat chicken that is freshly cooked and piping hot.

Meats
The bacteria that thrive and multiply in meat do so mainly on the surface. However, pork and beef should be cooked thoroughly to avoid tapeworm infestation. Mince, beef burgers and sausages may be contaminated in their core and should be well charred inside and out.

Rice
Rice is a potential hazard. Freshly cooked rice is not a problem, but rice that has been left sitting at room temperature may harbour the bacteria *Bacillus cereus*. *Bacillus cereus* is of serious concern to environmental health in the UK. Despite this, most people are not aware that rice is just as likely as chicken or seafood to poison them.

High-risk Drinks

Local Water
Most travellers now accept that it is foolish to drink local water and, as a result, diarrhoea and sickness are mainly contracted from food. However, you must be vigilant and ensure that contaminated water does not pass your child's lips.

- Never give in and let your child drink unboiled local water, no matter how thirsty they are
- Do not use local water for brushing teeth. I once travelled to Peru with a group. Just two of us did not suffer from any stomach upset. We had all eaten in the same restaurants but I discovered that only two of us had used bottle water for brushing our teeth. I am sure this made the difference.
- Local water must be boiled to 100°C for several minutes before drinking
- Chemical sterilisation is not as effective as boiling, and gives water an unpleasant taste. It is only useful as a back up and can cause damage to an unborn foetus, so should be given only in an emergency and, with care, to young children.

Ice

Ice is often made from local water and is as hazardous as drinking a cup of water from a tap in the street. If unsure, you must avoid ice religiously. Many countries recognise the problem and buy their ice from manufacturers that only use purified water. Around the world, many good hotels will do the same.

Bottled Mineral Water

I will never forget the vision of a small boy in India filling used mineral water bottles that he had collected from a tap in the street. He then carried off the bottles to be sold to the unsuspecting. This is not uncommon in poor countries, where people desperate to make money will sell you anything. Always check that the seal is intact. If you have a choice in a local shop or supermarket, buy the most popular brand. They have a reputation to protect.

Fruit Juices and Cocktails

Both may be diluted with local water or contain crushed ice.

Alcohol

Excesses of alcohol can cause dehydration. In addition it may be diluted with local water. This is interestingly prevented in Kenya by serving gin from sachets, as if it were ketchup.

Choosing Where and What to Eat

Hotel Buffets and Displayed Cooked Foods

If food is cooked well, served and eaten immediately, the chances of infection are minimised.

A hotel buffet supplies food, water, warmth and time – the optimum conditions for bacterial multiplication.

- Contamination can be caused by other guests handling, coughing and sneezing on food
- Flies carry a multitude of bacteria on their hairy legs
- Dust and dirt carrying contaminants can float on to food

Select the hottest, freshest, least-handled covered food on offer. You will easily be able to judge the turnover of food on the buffet. If it is too slow, ask for an omelette and fresh chips – most hotels will oblige.

Choosing a Restaurant

Generally, a busy restaurant has a high turnover of food. Theoretically the food should then be fresher, although this will depend on the care and skills of the chef at rotating stock and avoiding contamination during preparation and storing.

Restaurants busy with locals are not always a good choice, because the local stomach will have a higher resistance to local bugs. I was once chaperoned around India by a friend's brother. He made great efforts to ensure I never drank the local water, although he did so himself without any ill effect. He told me how children who have grown up in India but emigrated must drink bottled water when they return as their stomachs have become 'soft'.

- Ask your hotel desk or tour guide where to eat
- Ask other tourists where they have eaten that they would recommend
- Try to avoid restaurants that reheat food. This is a risk the world over. If you want to check whether or not a dish is precooked and

so reheated, ask the waiter if you can have it without e.g. onion or garlic. If the answer is yes, it is more likely that the food is being cooked fresh to order.

- A second indicator of how fresh food is, is how long it takes to arrive. Generally the longer it takes, the fresher it is.
- If a dish comes to your table lukewarm, don't eat it.
- International chains are usually predictable throughout the world. When I was a university student, I worked in McDonalds, and know that the systems are virtually idiot proof.

Buying Food and Drink on the Move

Most local grocers will have something, even if it just local bread and banana to make a sandwich.

You will often find familiar brands of tinned tuna, peanut butter, cheese, crisps and Delmonte fruit juice between the Coca Cola fridge and the Kodak film.

Always wipe hands and fruit that has been touched with a wet wipe.

- Make sure the packaging is intact and unpunctured
- If the product is fresh, can you peel it?
- Street stalls often smell delicious, but feeding children from them is not recommended
- Never eat food sold at train stations
- Check any seal is intact
- Avoid buying drinks with flip-top bottles and corks which can be replaced. Sealed cans and bottles of sparkling branded drinks are the safest option.
- Check that crockery and utensils used are clean and dry. I once witnessed a street vendor in Thailand doing his washing up in a puddle.

Barbecues

Beach and boat barbecues are a popular part of many day tours. If you attend one, choose the food from the barbecue yourself. Insist on the hottest and the freshest. Don't allow the chef to give your child the burger on the edge of the grill that has been sitting there for a while.

Always check that food has been cooked all the way through and is piping hot in the middle.

CHAPTER 12

Avoiding Diarrhoea and Sickness

Prevention is Better Than Cure

Remember that in most cases diarrhoea and sickness are avoidable. There is no reason for you to consider a bout of diarrhoea to be an acceptable part of your holiday, or refrain from travelling abroad for fear of it. Understanding how the illnesses are spread is vital, and knowledge of how to cope with your child if he becomes dehydrated may save his life.

Diarrhoea is often caused by infection, but not always. It can be the result of a change of diet, over-excitement, over-indulgence, an excess of fatty foods, or a high-mineral content in the local water. In these cases, the symptoms will usually pass quickly and there will be no temperature rise.

When the symptoms are caused by infection, the responsible organism will most commonly be a virus or bacteria (e.g. salmonella). Occasionally in the tropics, more persistent diarrhoea is caused by single-celled animals called protozoa (e.g. giardiasis and amoebic dysentery).

Most of the organisms responsible for causing diarrhoea and sickness are predictable in that they must be swallowed to do their worst, and many of them need to be swallowed in significant numbers. If you pay careful attention to personal hygiene, what your child eats and drinks, and where he swims and bathes, throughout your time abroad you should have no problems.

It is estimated that 30 per cent of travellers' diarrhoea is caused by a virus called rotavirus. This bug is also known as the 'infantile gastro-enteritis virus' and exists all over the world. It is also common in the UK.

Avoiding Diarrhoea and Sickness

- Always carry a snack and a drink of fresh water for your children so that you are never tempted to take risks if stuck on a remote train or bus station at mealtime. Raisins, bread sticks, crisps, chocolate, glucose tablets or sweets will take the emergency out of a child's appetite.
- Always carry wet wipes and use them to clean your children's hands before allowing them to eat
- Avoid all high risk foods (see page 265) unless you can be absolutely certain that they have been hygienically prepared and thoroughly cooked from fresh. Reheated meats and steamed seafood are a likely cause of infection.
- Don't give in and allow your children to eat ice cream or have ice in their drinks
- Don't give your child local milk unless it has been boiled
- High prices and plush surroundings are not a guarantee of cleanliness. You can still fall ill after eating in the very best hotels. If your diarrhoea has cost a small fortune, you will feel even worse.
- Always ensure your crockery and dining utensils are clean and dry
- Don't let your child drink the bathwater. If they are likely to do so, pop a couple of sterilising tablets in the water before bathing.
- Drink only bottled or boiled water. Always check the bottle seal.
- Use bottled water for brushing teeth
- Don't let your child touch anything. Even in hotel or restaurant restrooms avoid touching the soap, flushing handle, the taps, toilet seat and even the door handles. All can spread illnesses. Make sure your child cleans their hands afterwards on a wet wipe.

- Be careful where your child swims. Can you smell chlorine in the pool? Is the sea clean?
- Keep your child's hands clean and out of their mouths as far as possible. Illnesses can be caught from playing in wet soil and sand or sucking thumbs after crawling around on dirty floors.
- In diarrhoea hot spots such as Egypt, Nepal, India and Peru, try to become a vegetarian for the week. Well-cooked vegetables are far less likely to transmit illness than similar dishes containing meat. Children often refuse to eat chick peas, lentils and tofu, but it is worth a try. Nuts are a good nutritious snack for older children who don't have any allergies.
- Rotavirus is more difficult to avoid as it can be passed on in a crowded street or theme park by coughing or sneezing. Discourage your child from playing with any children displaying symptoms of a runny nose or upper-respiratory illness. These are an early sign of infection and rotavirus is thought to be passed on at this stage.

Don't let your guard down but don't be paranoid. I have travelled all over India, South and Central America, Africa, China and South-East Asia without anything other than minor discomfort. I have fallen seriously ill on holiday three times – twice in America and once in Wales.

Treatment

Don't despair, most cases of diarrhoea will pass within forty-eight to seventy-two hours without any treatment at all. Vomiting usually passes even more quickly. Being sick is very unpleasant, but it is a natural defence against bacteria, toxins and poisons, getting them out of the body's system by their route of entry. Diarrhoea will then take over and flush them out of the other end.

In children, the combination of diarrhoea and vomiting for more than forty-eight hours can lead to severe dehydration, which is very dangerous. Small babies can deteriorate much more quickly and become very ill in a matter of hours.

- Your baby or child must be encouraged to drink plenty of clear fluids. Persuade them to drink slowly and continuously.
- Until vomiting subsides, encourage babies and children to take the breast or half-strength formula milk. Offer older children their favourite drink and persuade them to sip little and often. If they can't tolerate milk, a child must be encouraged to take in boiled water from a spoon or cup.
- Fizzy drinks are controversial, as many nurses and doctors abroad advise them, whereas UK doctors do not, but if children won't drink still water, try sparkling
- If your child is regularly taking in fluid, don't force them to drink more
- Water is absorbed more easily and efficiently in the presence of sugar. If your child can tolerate and keep down diluted sweet drinks they may help.
- If you suspect your child is becoming dehydrated, check with the list of symptoms below, and begin oral rehydration immediately (see page 276)
- Drugs may be needed to clear up the infection (see below), but medication can wait, fluid intake cannot.
- Local cures may be strange but effective, and specifically in line with the strain of bug you are most likely to be dealing with. I have come across such remedies as salted fresh mango juice, Coca Cola and fresh ginger, yoghurt, fresh pineapple and papaya. They all have logic.
- If your child feels like eating, let them. There is no benefit to withholding food if they are hungry.
- As their appetite begins to return, avoid fatty foods and try giving them dry toast, cereal or biscuit, then slowly introduce their favourites
- Viral diarrhoea, often caused by rotavirus, is characterised by an abrupt, watery onset, often preceded or accompanied by vomiting with a peak incidence at twelve to eighteen months. There may be a rise in temperature, but not necessarily. The incubation period is two to three days, and generally the disease lasts two to three days. Unfortunately, your children are likely to pass it on to

each other. If you suspect the infection is viral, you must not give your child antibiotics.

- Paracetamol will help ease headache, aching limbs and stomach and bring the temperature down
- Do not give children under four years anti-diarrhoeal drugs such as Lomotil and Imodium. These drugs paralyse the gut and prolong the time that pathogens linger. Toxin-producing bacteria have time to proliferate. Use of these drugs can only be recommended for children over four years old when travel on a long journey is necessary. Five millitres of syrup should be effective for six to eight hours. Dosage can been repeated three to four times in a day. Children over ten years may need 10ml.

Symptoms of Dehydration

- In children under eighteen months, you will be able to gauge whether or not your child is dehydrated by looking at the fontanelle (soft spot) on the crown of their head. If it is sunken you must start oral rehydration therapy immediately (see below), then seek medical help.
- For babies and children, check their tongue and the rest of the inside of their mouth. If it is dry, your child might be becoming dehydrated.
- Dark, infrequent passage of urine is a dangerous sign
- Headaches are also a symptom
- If your child takes on a sunken appearance around the eyes and if you are able to detect a looseness of the pinched skin, your child needs hospital treatment and will probably require urgent intravenous fluid replacement

Oral Rehydration Therapy

This is not a drug or medicine but is a calculated balance of salt and sugar which, when mixed with water as per instructions on the packet, will help combat severe dehydration.

Oral replacement salt sachets or effervescent tablets are available commercially as Rehydrat or Dioralyte. These can be found on the shelves of virtually every chemist in the UK in a whole range of flavours. Less-expensive alternatives are obtainable, but in fewer pharmacies.

If you haven't packed any you may be able to buy some locally. If not, you can make up a substitute yourself that is just as effective. In scientific terms, the ratio of salt to sugar is 1:8. That is, measure one litre of boiled water and add one level teaspoon of salt, plus eight level teaspoons of sugar. Fluid replacement is often sufficient when dehydration occurs, but salt and sugars need to be replaced, too. Persuade your child to drink slowly and continuously.

Remember that even life-threatening fluid loss caused by cholera, which would otherwise need intravenous fluid replacement, can be successfully treated with oral rehydration if begun soon enough.

Getting Medical Help

If illness does not abate, get medical treatment if possible. Describe to the doctor how the illness started, anything your child might have eaten that may be the source of infection, and the stools' characteristics. If they contain blood you must mention it. All details will help the doctor judge what treatment to prescribe. If the doctor prescribes an antibiotic, you must complete the full prescribed course unless the symptoms worsen or your child suffers side effects.

Antibiotic Treatment: The Double-edged Sword

If you visit a doctor and describe the symptoms of the diarrhoea, they will prescribe an antibiotic on a best-guess policy. Only by taking a sample of faeces and culturing it will they know for sure that the antibiotic they prescribe will be effective.

- If antibiotics are administered and the cause is viral, the antibiotics will be useless
- Many antibiotics cause diarrhoea in their own right and may worsen the situation

- If antibiotics are prescribed on a best-guess principle, the wrong antibiotic may be given. If the problem bacteria is not sensitive to the prescribed antibiotic, it will continue to flourish while all the good bacteria in our gut will be wiped out. Without competition the bad bugs will continue to proliferate and the situation will be made even worse.
- Using antibiotics incorrectly for minor illnesses contributes to worldwide bacterial resistance, which can be passed on between bacterial species
- In many cases, patients given antibiotic treatment do not recover any more quickly than those given placebo.

One of the few antibiotics specifically indicated for gastro-intestinal infection and recommended for children is nalidixic acid. This is available as Negram suspension or tablets in the UK. The drug should not be given to children under three months old.

Co-trimoxazole is effective against a wide range of pathogens, including many that infect the gut.

Diarrhoeal Illnesses Requiring Specific Drug Treatment

Blood and mucous in the stools (dysentery) should be treated to avoid complications.

Bacterial dysentery is characterised by an explosive onset with high temperature and abdominal pain. Amoxycillin and Co-trimoxazole are both effective treatments.

Amoebic dysentery (Amoebiasis) is caused by cysts that, once ingested, hatch, live and multiply in the gut. Some of the parasites penetrate the cells of the gut causing ulceration and necrosis, leading to blood loss and mucous in the faeces. Carriers may never have any symptoms, but need to be treated because they may pass on the infection. Metronidazole is the drug of choice when amoebiasis is confirmed.

Giardiasis is caused by a protozoa and is more common in children than in adults. If the diarrhoea is low grade and persistent, with foul-smelling, bulky stools, it is likely to be giardiasis. Anorexia, nausea and flatulence are common symptoms. Metronidazole is the drug of choice. Treatment may need to be prolonged or at least require a second course of antibiotics.

If You Are Outside the Reaches of Medical Help...

Concentrate on oral rehydation therapy.
    Antibiotics should only be used blindly if:

a) The illness has been prolonged (more than three days in children; five days in adults)
b) There is no sign of the illness abating
c) There is a high fever with blood and mucous in the stools
d) The symptoms are so severe you suspect cholera or typhoid

CHAPTER 13

Nature's Adversaries and the Diseases They Can Cause

When travelling, it is important to recognise that your most danger-ous enemy is the mosquito. These tiny creatures are the curse of mankind. They transmit many tropical diseases and are the cause of millions of deaths worldwide each year.

It is estimated that two million people die from malaria every year. Yellow fever, encephalitis, dengue-fever and various other para-sitic illnesses are also transmitted by the female as she descends on her victim to drink the blood she needs to enable her to make her eggs.

All other creatures, including sharks, snakes and spiders, cause an insignificant number of deaths by comparison.

Mosquitoes

Malaria

Malaria is the most common tropical disease. Those most at risk are pregnant women and children under five years old.

The parasite enters the bloodstream and attacks red blood cells, eventually causing them to burst. As the parasite multiplies in the bloodstream, more than half the red blood cells can be infected and destroyed. The host will become anaemic and suffer from a pattern of symptoms that parents should be able to recognise.

Symptoms

The first signs can be non-specific and include headache, vomiting, general malaise, intermittent fever, joint pain, backache and diarrhoea. Often this may be confused with other infections including flu and food poisoning. A child may seem quiet, uninterested, dejected and miserable.

If the early signs go unheeded, after approximately one week, the cycle of typical malarial attacks will occur every forty-eight hours. They comprise:

a) A cold stage with rigors and violent shivering. The patient will feel as if they are being plunged into cold, icy water.
b) A hot stage with high temperature and severe headache
c) Profuse sweats as temperature falls
d) The abdomen becomes distended over the liver and spleen as the body tries to cope and get rid of all the burst blood cells. Complications include cerebral malaria with fits and coma.

Prevention

Avoiding malaria is a combination of drug prophylaxis and avoiding being bitten. For details on drug treatment see page 283.

To avoid being bitten:

- The malaria-carrying Anopheles mosquito only bites between dusk and dawn and is most active after dark. Take precautions during this time.
- As evening falls, change your child into long trousers and long sleeves and ensure they wear shoes and socks. Mosquito bites are often clustered around the ankles and feet, where the mosquitoes know there will be least chance of detection.
- Spray insecticide containing diethyltoluamide on to the exposed areas of skin and the outside of clothes, especially around the socks and wrists. I have been bitten through tight clothing and over the sockline under loose trousers.
- Wearing arm and ankle bands soaked in diethyltoluamide means less will have to be applied to the skin. This is an advantage for

children because there have been reports of toxicity after excessive use of repellents.

- If walking out at night with a baby, cover the pram with a fitted net
- Fitted nets are now also available to buy for car carrying seats
- Don't use soaps and perfume at night, as they attract mosquitoes
- The contrast of light clothes in the darkness is possibly an attraction
- Take spray repellent out with you at night and spray away persistent mosquitoes. Reapply after a few hours.
- Sleep in a screened room, preferably under a mosquito net
- Kits for impregnating nets are available. This adds further efficiency to the nets, which should be tucked under the mattress all the way round the bed to prevent anything finding a way underneath.
- Use a knock-down insecticide spray each evening in the rooms, one hour before bedtime. Even aerosol fly spray will help.
- Don't leave a light on early in the room you all intend to sleep in
- Use a plug-in vapouriser. Change the tablet each morning and each night to protect from any stray insects during the day. Mosquito coils are useful if electricity is unreliable or if there is no socket near the sleeping area.
- If likely to kick off their covers, ensure children sleep in socks and pyjamas. Dress babies in a cotton sleepsuit.
- Air-conditioning may slightly decrease the risk
- Don't assume that if your child is not showing any allergic reaction (red lumps) to bites, they are not being bitten. Some people react more than others.

Treatment

If you are out of reach of medical help for longer than one to two weeks, you should consider carrying quinine and Fansidar. Treatment should begin within eight hours of the symptoms developing. A full course should be completed while continuing preventative methods.

Figure 5: Doses of Fansidar for curative treatment of malaria in children

Age	Weight	Dosage
Children under 4 years	5–10kg	½ tablet
Children 4–6 years	11–20kg	1 tablet
Children 7–9 years	21–30kg	1½ tablets
Children 10–14 years	31–45kg	2 tablets
Adults		2-3 tablets

Weight is the most important gauge of dosage. An underweight child should be treated as a younger child.

In severe cases quinine must be given too, preferably as an injection, when medical treatment is available. Quinine injections are available in most hospitals and clinics throughout the tropics and subtropics.

Returning Home

Malaria might develop several months after leaving an endemic malarial region.

Do not forget: A fever that presents itself when you return home could be malaria. If your doctor does not know you have recently travelled to a malarial region, he might mistake the symptoms for flu. This is particularly important after travelling to tropical Africa. Months later, it has been known for children to rapidly deteriorate and die without prompt diagnosis and treatment.

Dengue fever

Dengue fever occurs throughout the tropics and subtropics. It is endemic in regions you may not associate with tropical disease, such as the Caribbean and north-eastern Australia. Dengue is also common in South-East Asia, the Pacific Islands, West Africa, Central and South America.

Sporadic outbreaks occur in many other countries of the world, occasionally in south-eastern USA and even in southern Europe. The disease is transmitted by infected mosquitoes but classic dengue fever, although unpleasant, does not pose a grave risk to the travelling family.

Symptoms

In adults and older children, the illness begins with the sudden onset of fever, headache, pain behind the eyes, chilliness and generalised pains in the muscle joints. Between days three and five of the illness, a rash usually appears on the trunk and later spreads to the face and extremities.

In young children dengue fever may never be suspected, as the main symptoms are similar to a respiratory infection.

After ten days the patient will usually be completely recovered, although a few may feel weak for some time afterwards.

Prevention

There are no prophylactic vaccines against the disease, and the only real defence against dengue fever is to prevent mosquito bites (see page 281).

Treatment

There is no specific treatment other than paracetamol to relieve the pain and control the temperature. Therefore Disprol or Calpol will make your child feel much better while their bodies fight off the infection.

Dengue Haemorrhagic Fever

Dengue haemorrhagic fever is a much more serious illness and is often fatal. However, the syndrome is almost entirely confined to indigenous children, often orientals. It is exceptionally rare in children from travelling families or even expatriate children.

It is considered to be the result of a previous attack by the virus. The immunity built up during prior exposure appears to be damaging when a child is assaulted by the dengue virus again.

Sandflies

Sandflies inflict nasty bites and can spread leishmaniasis throughout the tropics and subtropics in every region except Australasia.

Leishmaniasis

Leishmaniasis – caught from the bite of a sandfly – can be contracted in Mediterranean countries as well as in the tropics and subtropics.

Symptoms
The symptoms of one form of the disease are skin nodules, often called tropical ulcers or yaws, which can develop in to ulcers that refuse to heal. A more severe form (Kala Azar) in tourist areas mainly affects infants and young children. Further symptoms are an enlarged spleen, fever and weight loss, all of which may present themselves up to two years after visiting an infected region.

Prevention
Prevention is by preventing sandfly bites with insect repellents and covering up with clothing.

Treatment
Specific and effective drug treatment is available – a course of the drug Pentostam will cure the majority of infections.

The TseTse Fly

Sleeping Sickness

Sleeping sickness (African trypanosomiasis) is caused by single-celled parasites and spread by the painful bite of the tsetse fly.

In the early to mid part of the twentieth century, epidemics of the disease caused hundreds of thousands of deaths in Africa. The incidence of sleeping sickness has progressively decreased so that now only a few thousand cases are reported each year, among which may be just a handful of tourists.

Symptoms

Approximately five days after being bitten by an infected tsetse fly, a boil-like swelling will appear at the site of the origin bite. Weeks or months after being bitten the patient develops a fever and general malaise.

The parasite then enters the central nervous system and the patient will undergo a personality change. The patient usually then begins to sleep excessively during the day. If the patient remains untreated they will continue to deteriorate and will eventually stop eating and die.

Prevention

The principal defence against sleeping sickness is first to recognise the tsetse fly and so to avoid its bite. It is approximately one to two times the size of the house fly, has a brightly coloured abdomen and folds its wings across its back in a characteristic overlapping manner. Any tour guide will be able to confirm your identification.

Tsetse in Eastern Africa are often found in game parks and are active during the day, which means that travellers on safari are potentially at risk. The flies are more attracted to the buses, and other larger moving objects that they may judge to be prey, than they are to humans on foot. However, once they get inside the tour bus they need to be sprayed or squashed.

Insect repellents are highly advisable and, as with mosquitoes, avoid deodorants or perfumed soaps which will attract them. Tsetse are also drawn to dark colours, apparently particularly dark blue, therefore light clothes are a further defence.

Treatment

The illness is serious but responds well to rehabilitation and drug treatment. The diagnosis in the early stages may be difficult, especially with the likelihood that your family doctor will probably never have seen a case of sleeping sickness. It is unlikely to cross his mind unless you point out that you have been bitten by tsetse in tropical Africa.

Because the drug treatment is potentially toxic to use, diagnosis should be confirmed before it is given. Reassuringly, it is very effective and although relapses of the disease may occur, most patients will be completely cured under a doctor's supervision.

Cone-nosed Bugs (Assassin Bugs)

Chagas' Disease

Chagas' disease is also known as American trypanosomiasis. It is a disease of Central and South America and is caused by a single-celled parasite called Trypanosoma cruzi (similar to the African trypanosomiasis responsible for sleeping sickness), which lives in the host's blood and immune system.

It is spread by the bite of cone-nosed bugs in infested houses. The bugs live in the cracks in the walls close to beds and come out at night to feed. They will bite, then sit and feast on their blood meal until they swell and fill. The parasite is carried in the beetle's faeces. Revoltingly, humans are infected when the beetle defecates and deposits it next to the fresh bite. The bugs are often known locally as assassin bugs, and you may be warned by guides or even in hotels if the insects are common in the region.

In poor areas of South America, from Brazil to Chile, the disease occurs most often in children under ten years old. But unless you intend to stay in low-standard, rural mud housing with the local population, the risk to your own children is extremely low.

Symptoms
The bite is unlikely to go unnoticed. A hard inflamed swelling develops at the site of infection. There may then be swelling of the lymph glands and a high fever. Death may occur in a small proportion of patients a few months after infection due to heart failure or

meningo-encephalitis; many others develop no symptoms at all and live normal lives infected by the parasite without symptoms.

Long-term complications can occur and involve various organs. In particular, the heart may fail ten years after the initial infection. The intestines are also commonly affected.

Prevention

The surest way of contracting the disease is to sleep next to a mud wall, under a thatched roof and with well-used, unwashed blankets. The cone-nosed bug feeds at night in infested houses.

To avoid being bitten by the bugs, avoid sleeping in mud houses and if you do not have a mosquito net with you the chances are that you are better sleeping outside. Interestingly, Chagas' disease is almost unknown in the Amazon Basin, where the local houses have no walls.

If you do sleep in a mud hut, you should cover yourself, your children and your mosquito net with insect repellent and make sure that it is tucked in underneath the mattress all around you. If possible pull the bed into the middle of the room and away from the walls where the bugs hide during the day.

Treatment

Treatment is easiest in the early stages of the disease. Once it has had time to develop it is much more difficult to cure.

If you suspect you or your children have contracted the disease you should be tested and treated by a doctor as soon as possible. The side effects of the drugs used to treat the disease can be serious, so should only be given under medical supervision.

Fleas

Murine (endemic) typhus and bubonic plague are both carried by rat fleas, the bite of which infects humans.

In Africa and tropical America the female jigger (sand flea) burrows into the skin on the sole of the foot. She must be removed because prolonged infestation can lead to amputation of the toes.

Typhus

The traveller is more at risk from typhus carried by ticks (see page 290).

Bubonic Plague

Who can imagine anything more fear-provoking than fighting an invisible, deathly assailant that you have no protection against as you have no understanding of how, when or where it will creep up on you?

The plague has wiped out entire communities throughout the world since ancient times. It hit Western Europe with recurring epidemics between 1347 and 1722 with huge death tolls, when bodies were piled up in the streets with no one left to bury them. Some countries lost two-thirds of their population to the disease. Millions and millions died and the plague came as close to wiping out the human race as any disease ever has. Every race and religion was struck. We now know that it is caused by the bacillus *Yersina pestis*, which is transmitted by the bite of fleas from infected rats or from patients who have developed a secondary plague pneumonia. These patients will pass on the bacteria by coughing. This airborne form of the disease is nearly always fatal. It is still present in some countries of the world but is very rare and, thankfully, is now curable.

Symptoms
The earliest symptom is a swelling in the groin or armpit that is usually between the size of an egg and a clenched fist. The incubation period of the disease is short and it may be just four days after an infected flea bite that a large swelling develops. High fever, excruciating headache and delirium follow within ten days, and without treatment 60 per cent of the victims will have died.

Pneumonic plague, caught from the breath of a patient, has a much more aggressive onset and, once caught, can be fatal in three days. The victim shows signs of respiratory distress with a high temperature, dusky face and shallow breathing.

Prevention

A vaccine is available but the chance of a traveller being infected is so very rare, even if visiting areas of epidemics, that it is not recommended.

The best means of prevention are avoiding flea bites by using insect repellent and ensuring that children do not go near rats or any other rodents including sweet little chipmunks, squirrels and rabbits.

Treatment

Treatment with antibiotics is very effective. Medical help should be sought, but if this is not available streptomycin is the best option.

Ciproxin is very effective but not indicated in children, although the benefits of giving it to your child would outweigh the risk if bubonic plague is suspected. Early treatment is essential, before complications such as the pneumonic form of the disease have a chance to develop.

Lice

The human body and head louse can transmit typhus (see page 291).

Mites

Mites are tiny arachnids, some of which are parasitic to man. Some burrow under the skin, causing scabies. Chiggers, which are the larvae of harvest mites, stick to the skin and cause severe itching.

Ticks

The principal reason to avoid ticks is that they are wholly unpleasant little characters. They sit in wait for a passing dog, human or other mammal who is walking by unsuspecting and enjoying the landscape. They will then attach themselves as sneakily as they can in hair, in a crevice or just inside any available orifice, where they sit and drink blood until they swell from a tiny speck to a huge, red, engorged creature the size and appearance of a red kidney bean. The size increase can be alarming.

They are easily removed and the careful grooming of a child at the end of each day will limit the time the tick has to feed. This in turn will limit the chance of developing one of the plethora of diseases passed on by ticks.

Small children are unlikely to notice the tick by themselves and will need your scrutiny. Most of the time a tick bite will be nothing more than repulsive. In the remaining 1-2 per cent of cases, the bite may lead to an infection which, without treatment, has the potential to be fatal.

If you do find a tick on yourself or a child carefully remove it (instructions below). The longer the tick has to feed, the longer it has to pass on disease.

Some, such as Lyme disease, take eighteen-hour feeding sessions to be transmitted. Don't worry, but be practical and, if there are any signs of fever, headache, rash or redness and swelling following a bite, you should seek medical advice. A tick bite can transmit typhus, encephalitis, Lyme disease, Q fever and tick paralysis.

Typhus

Typhus has several forms and can be transmitted by tick, lice, mites or fleas. Epidemic typhus is transmitted worldwide by the human body louse. The disease strikes in times of cold, famine, war and human misery, and in history has been one of the most-feared human diseases.

The modern-day traveller is at little risk from epidemic typhus, but other forms transmitted by ticks or mites can be caught when walking throughout the world.

Often referred to locally around the world as tick fever, or tick flu, typhus is an illness caused by a parasite called a *Rickettsia*, which is neither a bacteria nor a virus, but is something between the two.

Figure 6: Forms of typhus, their habitat and modes of transmission

Associated diseases	Habitat	Mode of transmission
Epidemic typhus	Man Rats and mice	Body louse Rat fleas
Rocky mountain spotted fever	Man, dog and rabbit	Ticks
Scrub typhus	Rodents	Mites
Rickettsial fever in Queensland	Man and animals	Tick
Trench fever	Man	Body and head lice
Q fever	Mammals	Tick and by contact

Symptoms

All types of typhus cause fever, chills, muscle pain, severe headache and a rash. There is usually a painful sore and spreading redness at the site of the bite. The illness is likely to last a number of weeks if left untreated.

Prevention

Prevention centres around avoiding louse, flea, mite and tick bites. This may be done by applying repellents such as diethyltoluamide and dimethylphthalate to the skin and clothing. Repellent-impregnated, snug-fitting hats provide a weak defence against the ticks hiding in hair, although you should still inspect the hairline.

Wear light-coloured clothes out on walks, which will help show up the ticks by contrast – though ticks do tend to aim for darker objects.

With children, it is advisable to avoid straying into areas that are heavily infested with the offending ticks. The locals will always be able to advise you where these areas are, or anything else you should know – for example, how to remove them, or any symptoms to look out for following bites.

Rambling through scrub, veldt or tropical bush crawling with waiting hungry ticks is where you will pick up trespassers. When out walking in these areas be meticulous with the application of repellent and dress accordingly, in long trousers well tucked into long socks. Long sleeves with snug wristbands and hats are added protection.

If you need to wade through waist-high grass, pop the kids on your shoulders so then at least the ticks will get you instead.

Your second line of defence against disease is to remove the tick as soon as possible and give it less time to pass on an infection. When you get home or even before, you must scour your children for ticks from top to toe. Comb, groom and search through their hair then look in deep nooks such as their groins and their orifices.

Tick Removal

Care should be taken when removing ticks. It can done by smothering the offender in Vaseline and waiting until it drops off voluntarily, although this can take a few hours. Otherwise, touch the tick with strong alcohol or any oil to encourage it to let go 'cleanly', although there is some debate as to whether this may 'shock' the tick and make it vomit into the bite, passing on any infection it is harbouring.

Do not squeeze or squash the tick. If you do, you will effectively transfer any parasites not already transmitted into your system via the bite. If you leave in the mouth parts, the bite will take much longer to heal and can become infected, so avoid this at all costs.

Removing ticks with your fingers or tweezers is tricky and needs patience. When I visited South Africa ten years ago, I was told that under no circumstances should I attempt to forcibly remove the tick, as if I did it would certainly pass on the fever in retaliation. Vaseline was the recommended line of defence. Vaseline suffocates the tick and forces it to let go of its own accord. However, it now seems to be generally recommended that you carefully remove the tick yourself. This, of course, has the benefit of being quick.

The guidelines are to grip the tick firmly between finger and thumb, or with tweezers, at the head end and as close to the skin as possible. Then pull steadily away in a perpendicular direction (at right angles, not downwards or upwards against the skin). The mouth parts will be well embedded and you may need to rock the tick gently from side to side to free its grip.

Personally I would go for the Vaseline every time. A squirming child and an inexperienced tick remover are a hazardous combination but, if you (unlike me) have a steady hand and the patience, do try and extricate it yourself.

As always, local knowledge is the best, and the alternative is to ask a native what they would do. It is likely that your tour guide or the elderly lady in the local store is far better equipped for the job. Even if no one around speaks your language, simply show them your problem and doubtless it will be resolved and your child will be tick and disease free within seconds.

Once the tick is removed flood the bite with the strongest alcohol available, be it tequila or rum. This will help disinfect the puncture.

Treatment
Typhus responds well to antibiotics.

Lyme Disease

Lyme disease is yet another pathological condition resulting from the bite of an infected tick. The infection is caused by a bacteria that is passed on when the tick feeds between deer and man. The species of tick responsible for carrying the infection is found in park and woodland in temperate climates such as that of the US and Europe, including the UK.

If the disease is left untreated, complications will arise including heart disease, nerve problems and arthritis.

Symptoms
The tick responsible is small and its bites may often go unnoticed. However, the useful warning sign in Lyme disease is an expanding red skin rash accompanied by a headache, muscle and joint ache, and a slight fever.

Prevention
As with other diseases transmitted by ticks, the best way of preventing the illness is by avoiding the tick bite. (See prevention of typhus, page 292.)

Treatment

Antibiotics are effective against Lyme disease. The drugs of choice would be tetracycline or Amoxycillin. In children Amoxycillin would be the better choice.

Tick Paralysis

Ticks picked up either in the countryside or from domestic animals can produce saliva that contains a neurotoxin passed on by the bites. The poisoning neurotoxicity that results is rarely fatal to adults, but can cause fatalities in children. The most common site of tick paralysis is in northern US.

A tick needs to be attached for a number of days to be a real danger, so checking for ticks is an important care regime. Your child may have been irritable, 'out of sorts' and even have collapsed after getting out of bed in the morning.

The scalp is the most common place of attachment, although orifices are regular sites.

Treatment

The tick must be detached without being squeezed. Smothered with Vaseline the tick drops off. Following detachment, a child will usually recover. An anti-venom is available.(See above for tick removal.)

Tick-Borne Encephalitis

Tick-borne encephalitis occurs throughout central Europe, from Scandinavia, the former USSR, the Czech Republic and Germany through to Austria.

It is caused by a virus related to dengue and yellow fever. The parasite involved is very different from the organism that causes typhus, and does not respond to antibiotic treatment.

Symptoms

There may be an area of redness or inflammation at the site of the bite. Fever and encephalitis will follow.

Prevention

Your children would be most at risk from a camping holiday in central Europe. It is important to advise them that they should keep to woodland paths and not walk through tall grass or foliage with bare legs or skin, even at the edge of the campsite. They should also be protected with insect repellent sprayed on to clothes and uncovered regions of skin.

Check above for advice on important grooming and the removal of ticks.

Treatment

If a victim becomes ill after a tick bite in central Europe, it may be advisable to have an injection. This must be given within four days of the bite.

Stinging Insects

Bees', wasps' and hornets' stings are usually more painful than dangerous. The problem arises if your child is allergic to the sting and develops anaphylactic shock.

If your child is allergic to stings discuss the possibility of carrying a prefilled syringe of adrenaline with you for emergency treatment, and learn how to use it.

Treatment

Stings should always be scraped off with a knife or fingernail and never removed with tweezers, as this is more likely to squeeze more venom into the skin.

Soothe with local anaesthetic. Oral antihistamine can ease the allergic reaction to stings. Antihistamine creams are not as effective and can cause sensitivity. Paracetamol will ease pain quickly.

For a sting in the mouth, give ice to suck to try to decrease swelling.

Spiders

Spider bites, even in Mediterranean countries, can be dangerous. Wherever you are in the world – including the US – you should teach your child to respect spiders. Empty shoes before putting them on and be careful in outside toilets and outhouses where flies are attracted. Spiders often make these their homes and a number of species have been known to hide under toilet seats. The Australian red-backed spider does this and can be fatal, but an anti-venom is available.

Treatment

You must get your child to hospital as soon as possible for anti-venom treatment. Try to minimise the spread of venom by keeping your child calm, immobilising the limb and keeping the site of the bite below the level of the heart (see snake bites, page 303).

Scorpions

Dangerous species exist in Africa, Asia, Trinidad and throughout the Americas, including the North. Mexico is home to a number of dangerous species.

Mortality is approximately 15–25 per cent higher in small children than in adults.

Avoiding Stings

Scorpions are nocturnal and feed at night, especially after rain storms. In the day they find somewhere snug and dark, such as a training shoe. Empty your shoes before putting them on.

Insecticides deter scorpions, so good hotels which spray for cockroaches etc. should not be plagued.

Teach your child to be very wary when lifting logs or boulders and never to poke fingers or sticks into holes or borrows.

Treatment

If you suspect the scorpion could have been poisonous, you should get your child to hospital as soon as possible for intravenous anti-venom. Try to minimise the spread of venom by keeping your child calm, immobilising the limb and keeping the site of the bite below the level of the heart. Most scorpion stings are painful rather than dangerous. Give paracetamol for the pain. Cold compresses and oral antihistamines can limit the reaction.

Millipedes and Centipedes

Children are particularly at risk when they try to handle or even eat these fascinating, huge arthropods.

Millipedes can squirt venom into the eye. If this happens, flush the eye with plenty of water to minimise irritation and prevent infection.

Centipedes can bite and no anti-venom is available. Giant centipedes are found in places you would least expect, such as Barbados. Make sure your child knows how dangerous it is to play with them.

Leeches

Land leeches infest the floor and lower vegetation of rainforests. They should be removed by alcohol, salt, Vaseline, a lighted match or a cigarette burn. Water leeches are common in rivers all over the world, including the UK.

Leeches do not pass on disease, but wounds can become infected and need to be cleaned and sterilised with an antiseptic.

Wearing long socks, long trousers and sturdy shoes, all liberally coated with repellents such as diethyltoluamide, helps deter them from attaching to the skin.

Worms

An entire plethora of worms can infect man and a whole host of symptoms can result, the most common being enteritis, abdominal distension, change in appetite and weight loss.

Roundworm, tapeworm, threadworm and whipworm have a worldwide distribution, so are not just a blight of the traveller. However, they are more common in tropical areas with poor sanitation.

None will cause a medical emergency while you are away, but care should be taken to avoid picking them up.

If you suspect that your child may have been infected you should seek medical treatment. All worms can be eradicated by specific drug treatment once they have been diagnosed.

Avoiding infection

Most species of worm are transmitted by eating undercooked food contaminated with cysts. Flukes are transmitted by eating raw fish or snails. Undercooked meat conveys tapeworm infection. Even watercress and water chestnuts can harbour parasitic worms.

Threadworms are highly infectious and commonly infect school children in the UK. They can be passed by food, water, air or contact. They cause intense itching around the anus, especially at night. A child will scratch and get eggs under the finger nails. These can be easily passed on to other members of the family.

The dragon or guinea worm is transmitted by swallowing or drinking water containing the immediate host. It causes swelling of the skin that can develop into an ulcer. The worm is removed by winding it around a stick, although care must be taken to avoid allergic reactions which occur if the worm is broken. Infected mosquitoes pass on elephantiasis. Blackfly bites transmit river blindness.

Other worms of the tropics and subtropics can actually penetrate the intact skin. Bilharziasis is caught (see below) while swimming, wading, bathing or even showering in contaminated water. Certain species of roundworm and hookworm contaminate soil and penetrate the skin, usually through the soles of the feet.

To avoid infection, children and adults should take the usual precautions against consuming undercooked food or drinking unpurified water. Mosquito and blackfly bites should be prevented with insecticides etc. (See page 281.)

Children should always wear light footwear to prevent penetration by worm larvae.

Bilharziasis (Schistosomiasis)

Bilharziasis is a chronic infection caused by minute worms whose life cycle revolves around fresh water. The disease occurs throughout the tropics and subtropics in approximately one third of the world's countries. It chronically infects more than 200 million people worldwide. It is particularly common throughout Africa, from the Nile delta to Lake Victoria, in Brazil, parts of the Middle East and China. Island paradises from Mauritius to Antigua are also hosts to the disease.

The parasite spends its early life developing in fresh water snails until it swims free. Once it comes across a person bathing or wading, it will burrow through the skin and migrate into the veins of the intestines or the bladder in the new-found host. Left untreated, it will remain there for up to fifteen years, continually producing eggs. Many of these eggs are not excreted but remain in the host where they cause an inflammatory reaction. Some of the eggs are excreted in the urine or faeces, and will contaminate rivers, streams and lakes.

Symptoms

The first symptoms may be tingling and/or a light rash around the area where it penetrated the bloodstream. Some weeks later a high fever might develop and so may be confused with malaria or typhoid. The patient will feel unwell with abdominal pain and possibly blood present in the urine.

If untreated, the long-term effects of the parasite include kidney and liver damage.

Prevention

Visitors to areas where bilharziasis is present should avoid swimming, bathing and wading in streams, rivers and lakes. Even showering in fresh water stores should be avoided.

If, for any reason, you or your children fall into fresh water of any depth, you must ensure that you quickly remove any clothing and vigorously towel-dry the skin. Do not put the clothes back on until they are fully dry. The larvae die quickly once they leave the water, so need to penetrate quickly. It is a race against time to brush them off.

Salt and chlorinated water are safe. However, if you can't smell chlorine in the pool there may be a fault in the system or the chlorine may have run out, leaving it unsafe to swim in.

Keep showers in remote, rural areas short and, again, towel off vigorously.

On a number of occasions in western India I was offered a shower and was led into a room with a bucket of fresh boiled water. This may not be perfect for a family but is not as bad as it sounds. If you are staying in good-standard accommodation, the water will be treated and although unsafe to drink it is very unlikely to be contaminated by bilharzias and will be safe to wash in.

If you have any suspicions about any member of the family having either been exposed to or contracted the disease, you should contact your doctor when you return home and arrange for a test. The presence of eggs can be detected in the urine or the faeces, but not until forty days after infection, so any tests before this may give a false negative result.

Treatment

The drug treatment should not be started without first confirming that the infection is present and eggs have been found in the faeces or urine.

At present, Praziquantel is the drug of choice. It is highly effective and only needs to be given as a single dose.

Mammals

Bites and scratches are dangerous because they can cause infections such as tetanus and rabies – even a lick from an infected animal can transfer rabies. Prophylactic injections should be given (see pages 184 and 187).

If wounds are severe, or if the bite is on the face, your child should be treated with oral antibiotics to protect against infection (penicillin, aminoglycoside and metronidazole combination).

A child should be taught to respect all animals and be wary of their unpredictability. All animals are potentially dangerous, even if they do not appear aggressive.

Just because animals gather around tourist spots does not mean they are tame. The cute little coatimundis all around the ruins and major tourist spots of Central and South America will readily, and suddenly, attack a baby to steal a bottle of milk. The monkeys which gather around the temples in Asia can carry rabies and you must not show them that you have food with you. Baboons from Gibraltar to Capetown will come to be fed, but will attack you for what you are eating if it is not offered.

Most bears are dangerous and the polar bear is one of the only mammals to actively seek humans out as food. Bears in North America and Canada are unlikely to judge you as a meal, but they will come looking for your scraps and you should lock all your food, waste and even toothpaste in the boot of your car or suspend it high on a small branch in a tree. Don't keep anything edible in the tent.

Beasts of burden can trample a child or easily knock them down a mountain side. Always pass animals on the higher side of the mountain track.

Rabbits and chipmunks carry the bubonic plague. Bats, raccoons, foxes and domestic animals carry rabies. Most other mammals can carry fleas, ticks or parasites. Even wild boar are highly dangerous and attacks can be fatal.

Treatment
1. Clean the wound thoroughly as soon as possible with soap/detergent and water (preferably running)
2. Pour alcohol over the wound that is a minimum of 40 per cent by volume. Gin, whisky, vodka etc. are all usually 40 per cent alcohol. Local rum is often stronger and so better.
3. Apply an antiseptic such as iodine
4. Seek medical attention as soon as possible. Your child could need antibiotics and immunisation against tetanus and rabies. Even if your child has already been vaccinated against rabies, he will need additional post-exposure protection if bitten by an animal that could possibly be rabid.

Snakes

After a snake bite, panic is the greatest enemy. Keeping calm and still will stop the venom spreading.

If the snake remains attached, apply a flame to the underside of the jaw to make it release its grip.

The pain will be immediate and severe at the site of the bite, but reassure your child, sit him down and try to keep him still. Flush the wound with water. Keep the bitten limb below the level of the heart and immobilise it with a splint or sling, as this will help contain the venom locally.

Take a note of the snake's appearance and get your child to medical treatment and hospital as soon as possible. Anti-venom is a life-saver.

DO NOT cut and suck the wound. Local incision and suction by an unskilled person is likely to cause further trauma that can lead to extensive bleeding and introduce infection.

Tourniquets may seem a logical approach but are often not advised and are not necessary if the journey to hospital is thirty minutes or less. If you are a long way from medical help, a local is likely to be more skilled than you at applying a tourniquet. Ask for help. It must not be so tight that it turns the extremities cold and blue. It must also be loosened every thirty minutes for fifteen minutes to allow oxygen to reach the limbs – if not, the limb may become gangrenous. A firmly (not tightly) tied bandage or your own tightly gripped hand around your child's limb above the wound would be less likely to cause lasting damage.

During transfer to the hospital, lie your child on his side to stop the inhalation of vomit. If you feel it may help, give paracetamol for the pain.

Avoiding Snake Bites

Boots, socks and long trousers should be worn for walking through the undergrowth and deep sand in places where snakes are common. Even if a snake appears dead, do not touch it as the venom is often still effective. Snakes will make every effort to avoid you, so to keep safe let them know that you are coming.

Carry a light at night, tread heavily and beat the undergrowth in front of you with a stick.

Tell children not to poke sticks into crevices, lift logs or boulders, swim in murky water matted with vegetation or climb trees and rocks with dense foliage.

Some snakes can eject venom in a fine stream in an attempt to distract their victims. If the venom gets into the eye it can cause intense conjunctivitis with a risk of further infection. Damage is minimised by flushing the eye with plenty of water and seeking medical attention.

Lizards

The Gila lizard, indigenous to southern US and to Mexico, is the only lizard with a venomous bite, although the Komodo dragon from Indonesia is said to bite its victims and leave them to die from the putrefying wound that results.

Sea Creatures

In many areas of the world you will be invited to swim with stingrays, barracuda, moray eels and sharks. All are potential killers and you should respect them. However, where there are scores of tourist boats coming to attract and feed them, you need not fear. Just ensure that your children do not tease, chase or corner anything underwater.

The most painful wounds are often caused by venomous creatures that are stepped on. The stingray is designed so that if you step on them, their tails will flick up and inject a painful sting as a defence. However, they are naturally gentle creatures and around most dive sites in the Caribbean the worst you can fear is a love bite from a young ray who confuses you with food.

Ensure that your children wear something on their feet, such as old pumps, jellies or rubber-soled diving shoes that are now available from the high street, even in baby sizes. Also advise them to shuffle clumsily into the water. This will warn any fish to move. Weeverfish bury themselves in the sand in shallow waters all around Britain, the European Atlantic and the Mediterranean, and can inflict a very painful wound. Stonefish are found in tropical regions, and if you were to step on one it could be fatal.

Many other species of fish in tropical waters can sting, including lionfish, catfish and dogfish. Starfish and sea urchins also possess venomous spines that can break off in the foot and cause prolonged discomfort and risks of infection.

The Treatment of Marine Puncture Wounds

Place the afflicted limb in water as hot as the victim can stand. Keep the limb immersed and the water as hot as you can, by topping up for thirty minutes.

If spines are stuck in the foot, they must be removed. You can do this yourself by softening the skin with an antiseptic/anaesthetic cream (for example, salicylic acid or magnesium sulphate) then removing with tweezers. Be wary of the spines breaking up and so urge your child to keep still and be patient.

I once went swimming with my dad off the coast of Jamaica. We were quite a way off shore and sharing a mask and snorkel between us. He swam around while I waited my turn. He then urged me to follow him as there was a huge rock rising from the seabed that I could stand on even though we were a long way off shore. I trusted him to guide my foot to the rock. Somehow he neglected to notice a resident sea urchin and guided my toes straight on to its spines. I was more amazed at my dad's imbecility than the pain and, back on shore, was relieved to find out that the spines came out easily.

Jellyfish, Portuguese Man-of-War, Sea Anemones and Corals

All these creatures possess stinging cells that can cause extreme pain. The sting of the box jellyfish, which is common at certain times of the year off northern Australia, is said to cause death due to excruciating pain. Fortunately it does not inhabit the Great Barrier Reef, but beaches on the mainland may be closed in the seasons when the box jellyfish is swept inshore.

The Portuguese Man-of-War looks like a pretty, blue bubble, but gives a nasty sting. Even jellyfish swept on to the beach can still sting if your child picks one up.

Coral stings are irritating rather than acutely painful, but coral cuts are very slow to heal as a result of the venom injected when you step on to the coral. Even non-stinging coral is very sharp and can inflict painful gashes that can become infected. Children should not be allowed to walk on or collect coral, as much for the sake of the dwindling reefs as for their own safety.

Treatment of Stings

The best antidote is vinegar poured over the stinging cells. This stops more cells firing and limits the damage. If you can then get hold of some talcum powder, dusting it over the area will make the remaining stinging cells clump together, enabling them to be brushed off safely. A rather crude alternative to vinegar is urine. Alcohol poured over the wound will not help.

Molluscs – Including Sea Snails, Cones and Octopuses

These creatures can be venomous. Blue-ringed octopuses bite with their beaks and have toxic saliva that has been known to cause fatalities.

Be aware that the bite from sea cones can cause respiratory paralysis. There is no specific treatment, only management of the developing symptoms:

1. Monitor the casualty's consciousness, breathing and heart rate and resuscitate if necessary
2. Lie in the recovery position
3. Seek medical help

NB: Sea snakes can also be venomous.

In Summary

Don't allow your children to pick up anything off the seabed or reefs, including corals, anemones, sea urchins and starfish.

Ensure that they adopt a shuffling gait when entering water, that they don't step on coral reefs and do not chase or tease any sea creatures.

If a dive leader offers a sea cucumber to hold or urges you to touch a giant clam and watch it close gently, then OK, but children should always be taught the importance of 'taking only memories and leaving only footprints'.

CHAPTER 14

Coping with Illness

Common Complaints

Ear infections

Ear infections are particularly common on holiday when children are swimming in the sea or pools where they can pick up infections in the water. Middle-ear infections may be the result of a throat or other upper respiratory tract infection that has spread the short distance up into the ears behind the drum. Your children are particularly susceptible while jumping in deep water and diving, especially if they get cold.

Symptoms
Hearing loss, severe earache and fever. There is also inflammation and redness inside the ear that will be obvious to any doctor on examination. Young children might tug at their ears with discomfort.

Treatment
Pain with discharge from the ear is usually a sign of infection in the outer ear, and this can be alleviated with antibiotic treatment. Eardrops will not be effective and your child will be more ill generally, probably having suffered from an upper respiratory infection.

Prevention

If your child has chronic tonsillitis, or suffers from ear infections on a regular basis, you should talk to your doctor before you leave, and ask about the possibility of him prescribing an antibiotic for you to take on holiday to use if your child presents with symptoms.

Insects in the Ear

Lay the child on its side. Pour tepid water or olive oil into the ear. The insect should float out.

Nose, Throat and Sinus Infections

If your child is unwell, paracetamol syrup will alleviate pain, discomfort and fever.

Infections on holiday that are prolonged and causing a lot of discomfort should be treated with an antibiotic. The cause may be viral, but the antibiotic will prevent any secondary bacterial chest or ear infections developing that are likely to occur if your child is in and out of the water.

Chest Infections

Chest infections can develop from an infection in the throat, ear or nose and, in young children, are serious because they hamper breathing. Your child is likely to have a cough, producing phlegm tinged green with pus. This is commonly a sign of bacterial infection that needs to be treated with an antibiotic. Your child will feel unwell, with laboured breathing. Paracetamol will keep the temperature down and make him feel better. Do not use cough medicines as the phlegm needs to be cleared from the chest.

Eye Infections

If eyes are bloodshot, swollen and weeping there is likely to be an infection present.

Infective conjunctivitis is highly contagious and will be spread from one eye to another just by rubbing. It can be caused by a virus or bacteria and can be picked up while swimming.

Your child will need eye drops, preferably containing an antibiotic. If none are available, rinse the eye with salt water, morning and night. If you have packed a syringe in your medical kit, use this (without the needle) to flush the eye clear from pus and crusting.

If there is no relief and the child continuously rubs at the eye, there could be a foreign body in it and you will need medical attention.

Cuts, Grazes and Skin Infections

Cuts heal very slowly in the tropics. Wounds do not dry out and scab over in the humidity, and wet wounds can readily become infected. Even small cuts can be problematic. Great care needs to be taken to keep any wounds clean and dry.

Treatment

- Run cuts and grazes under cold water and wash the wounded area with soap
- Dry by patting with clean tissue. Apply antiseptic spray or powder. Betadine or Savlon (povidine iodine) dry powder sprays are very effective.
- Cover with a sterile dressing
- If the cut is deep, hold together wound edges with skin closure tape or crude stitches. If deep and dirty, leave the cut open and flush with sterilising solution, Savlon solution, iodine or alcohol. Consider whether your child's tetanus boosters are up to date.
- Change dressings daily and watch for signs of infection, including:
  - Redness and swelling around the wound
  - Increasing pain and tenderness
  - The area around the wound feeling hot
  - More obvious symptoms such as the wound weeping with pus and failing to show any signs of healing

- If a skin infection occurs, antibiotic powder or spray would be the better option in the humidity of the tropics. If the infection is in the middle third of the face or if it is extensive, you should administer oral antibiotics too, as a precaution. If you are in a less humid environment, antibiotic cream should clear up the infection perfectly.

Bites, Allergic or Infected

Insect bites will only usually become infected if they are picked or incessantly scratched. If your child is suffering from a large number of bites, an oral antihistamine will ease the swelling and suffering. On the surface, calamine lotion will relieve the itching and is a better choice than tropical antihistamine 'bite' cream in humid conditions. Paracetamol syrup will ease the pain and discomfort.

If a bite does become infected, treat as you would an infected cut (see above).

Mammalian bites need more intensive treatment. You must seek medical help and consider the likelihood of infection as severe as rabies (see page 184).

Fungal Infections: Thrush, Athlete's Foot, Ringworm

These are more uncomfortable than serious and will not endanger your child on a short holiday. Fungi flourish in warm, moist conditions. Thrush, athlete's foot and ringworm are the most common blights.

If you are breast-feeding you may find that thrush infects your nipples and transfers to the baby's mouth. You must both be treated or re-infection will occur.

Thrush in the nappy region should be kept dry by keeping the nappy off and the bottom exposed for as much of the time as possible.

Anti-fungal medication is available as creams and powders, and treatments usually prescribed for women's thrush are safe to use in children, e.g. Canestan. Nystan suspension is also an effective alternative.

If you are unable to obtain any medication try plain yoghurt on the affected area.

Allergies

Existing allergies should be prepared for, and if these are serious, and there is a danger of anaphylactic shock, you could discuss with your doctor the possibility of carrying an adrenaline pre-filled syringe with you. Allergies to bites, plants, different food or even sunlight which are discovered on holiday should be treated by avoiding their sensitiser and, if the reaction is severe, by administering oral antihistamines such as Phenergan.

Sunburn

Superficial burns are readily acquired in a moment on fresh white skin and often take even the most careful parent by surprise.

On the first day of a holiday a young skin can burn within three minutes. Every effort must be taken to avoid this.

Blistering takes relatively long exposure and is more common in sunbathers who fall asleep in the summer sun.

Avoiding sunburn is relatively straightforward, but does require disciplined application of high-factor sun protection creams. Don't forget the tops of the children's ears.

Superficial burns following short exposure to the sun can be treated with after-sun or calamine lotion – both cool and soothe. Cool baths and damp towels may also provide some relief. Paracetamol syrup will ease the pain and swelling.

If the burns are severe, steroid creams might be recommended by a doctor.

Teething Pain and Mouth Ulcers

In my pre-teens I always seemed to get ulcers on holiday and I still have no idea why. Soothing gels and tablets were useless, and I even tried pouring on neat salt which was agony, but the pain afterwards seemed dull by comparison. Ambersol was brought out some years ago and it brought me great relief. It is a local anaesthetic which, when applied directly on to an ulcer, brings about total pain relief. It is effective for teething, too.

Urinary Tract Infection

Severe back pain, fever, blood in the urine or pain on urination suggest an infection of the urinary tract. Your child may have suffered from a sore throat a few weeks before.

You will need oral antibiotics. Nalidixic acid is useful against many urinary tract infections.

Stomach or Abdominal Pain

In the tropics, this could be caused by a whole host of organisms that often cause associated diarrhoea and vomiting.

If your child complains of a severe, sharp pain in the lower right-hand side of their abdomen, you should suspect appendicitis. They will also have a slight temperature, will refuse food and might vomit.

Nappy Rash

Good disposable nappies have limited the amount our babies suffer from nappy rash, but you may find that your baby will develop a rash in hot, damp, tropical conditions. It may be heat rash, which will improve if you leave the nappy off as often as possible and don't use plastic pants.

Nappies may need to be changed more regularly than normal, and if the rash lingers it could be thrush, which will need treatment with an anti-fungal cream or oral preparation, such as Nystan suspension.

Fever without Obvious Cause

- Very high fever with headache could be malaria, even if prophylaxis has been taken

- Fever with jaundice could be hepatitis or malaria
- High fever with severe headache, vomiting, neck sickness and aversion to light could be meningitis

Getting Medical Treatment Abroad

If your child needs anything other than a medical check up and an antibiotic and/or Calpol, you must consider asking your insurance company for help in getting good local treatment, and if necessary help getting home.

- Contact your insurance company as soon as you can. The emergency number should be stated on your policy. This then speeds up repatriation or, if your child is critically ill, they may decide to send a doctor out to travel home with you. The sooner you contact them, the sooner the wheels can be set in motion.
- Don't delay your decision unnecessarily. Travel home sooner rather than later.
- If you have to visit a hospital, take your passport, insurance certificate or valid E111 form and any vaccination certificates. If you have packed a medical kit, take it with you.
- If you do not have medical insurance, it is useful to know that many countries that have a reciprocal health care arrangement with the UK will only provide free, or reduced-cost treatment in hospital (see page 218). In this case you would be better to attend the hospital A&E department rather than a doctor's surgery.
- For minor illnesses, your hotel or accommodation reception would most likely be able to recommend an English-speaking doctor. If you cannot get any help don't be afraid to go into the best hotel in town and ask if they could recommend a good doctor for you.
- If your hotel is not comfortable and lacks air-conditioning, ask your insurance company if it would be prepared to fund moving to another hotel. Make sure that you stress you are worried about high fever and the danger of convulsing.

- **You must keep all proof of payment for treatment and medicines**
- If the doctors suggests an injection, check that the needle and syringe have not already been used
- Ask the doctor to explain any treatment and medication to you. Keep any x-rays, bottles of medication and notes in English to show the doctors at home. They can then decide the course of follow-up treatment.
- Unfortunately, NHS Direct are not able to help callers outside the UK, but your family may be able to get generic guidelines and advice about medication (the number is 0845 4647). Your own GP may be prepared to take your call and try to help. You may need to give the following details:
  - Your child's age and approximate weight
  - The symptoms of the illness
  - The name and prescribed dosage of medication recommended

Buying and Giving Medicines Abroad

You will often find that drugs, including antibiotics, are available over the counter.

Be wary, medicines abroad may be substandard:

- Check drugs have not expired
- Medicines in liquid form may need to be refrigerated, so check if this is necessary
- If the medicine is a suspension (liquid) check that it has not been mixed with local water
- Complete any course of medication prescribed. It may be hard work forcing antibiotics on to a struggling toddler four times a day, but if you neglect to give the course, the bacteria may develop resistance to an antibiotic and then it will be much harder to treat and eradicate.

Blood Transfusions

Many countries of the world cannot afford the expense of blood screening. The risk of contracting HIV, hepatitis or other infections from blood products is very real. Blood transfusions outside Western Europe, North America, Japan and Australasia should be consented to only in a medical emergency.

Most major cities will have a source of screened blood. Contact the embassy to find where this would be held or ask your insurance company to find out from the World Health Organisation. Do whatever you can to get screened blood. The best thing would be for you or your partner to give blood for your child. If you know your blood groups this will help the doctor decide who would be the best donor – it may even be a sibling.

CHAPTER 15

Coping with Accidents

How you act on the spot could make the difference between whether or not your child survives or has a long-term disability. Your action at the scene should take priority over calling an ambulance.

Choking Babies

If a baby begins to choke on an inhaled toy or piece of food, you must act quickly:

1. Lay your baby face down and upside down against your bended knee (see illustration page 318)
2. Give your baby five sharp slaps on the back
3. Check inside their mouth with one finger and remove any object that has become dislodged

If your baby is still in distress:

4. Turn them over on to their back and place two fingertips on the lower side of the baby's breastbone in the centre, just underneath the nipples. Give five sharp thrusts into the chest. When you make the thrusts be firm but also aware that you could easily damage the baby's internal organs or crack their ribs.
5. Again check inside the baby's mouth

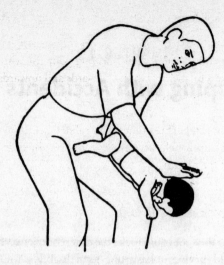

Figure 7: How to position a choking baby

Repeat the steps up to three times and, if the baby remains in distress, call for medical help and continue to try to dislodge the object until you are successful or help arrives.

Choking Children

If a child is choking on a piece of food or a small toy, ask the child to cough and give five sharp back slaps between the shoulder blades with one hand. This will hopefully dislodge the object and free the airways. Check inside his mouth and hook out any obvious obstruction.

If the object remains lodged you must:

1. Grab your child from behind
2. Make a fist and hold it against the underside of the breastbone
3. Grasp the fist with your other hand and thrust into the child's chest up to five times
4. Check inside his mouth

If the object is still lodged:

5. Again make the fist and place it below the breastbone but above the tummy button and, after grasping your fist with the other hand, make a further five thrusts inwards and upwards.
6. Again check inside the mouth

Repeat the above steps three times then call for help. You must continue the steps until help arrives or until the object is freed and retrieved from the mouth.

Fishbone Stuck in the Throat

Many Asian people will advise you to eat rice if a fishbone lodges itself in the throat, and this remedy does often work.

On most occasions, although the fishbone feels as if it is embedded, it will merely have scratched the membrane of the throat's lining and moved on. If a fish bone were lodged, the child would feel progressively worse over time and medical advice must be sought to remove the bone and to ensure that local inflammation of the throat does not interfere with swallowing or even breathing.

Swallowing an Object

Most small objects, once swallowed, pass directly into the stomach and will do no harm. It is the risk of choking when something 'goes down the wrong way' and is inhaled into the airways that is the concern. If there is no episode of choking you can afford to take things much more calmly.

I recall looking on in dismay as my seven-month-old son suddenly scurried across the bedroom floor and descended on a fallen earring. I made a dash to grab it out of his hand, but within a second it went from inside his fist, to mouth, to stomach. The earring was sharply hooked and I was frantic.

I telephoned the local hospital and every relative available. However, I calmed down as I was reassured by tales of my sister swallowing a penny when she was a baby and my husband swallowing a strapless watch at around ten months old. Accident and emergency assured me over the telephone that unless the object swallowed were exceptionally sharp, for example a needle, all I could do was wait.

The earring reappeared that same evening in a nappy.

If the same thing happens to you and the item isn't extremely sharp, your child will not be in terrible danger.

If there are any severe stomach pains or abdominal distension following the incident, your child will need very urgent medical attention. Otherwise, check for the item in the faeces and if it has not reappeared by the time you leave, then take your child for an x-ray when you get home. It is more than likely that the x-ray will be clear and you will simply have not checked thoroughly enough.

Convulsions (Fits)

A convulsion is likely to be an intense episode which, although dramatic, is very unlikely to do any lasting damage.

Typically, all the voluntary muscles of the body will contract violently. There will then be a period of relaxation followed by smaller, uncontrollable, jerky contractions. Lesser seizures vary from tingling in the arms and legs with lack of concentration to attacks during which a child may lie completely still yet rigid, displaying rapid repeated blinking, and be unrousable.

Such attacks are due to irregularities in the brain's 'waves' (electrical impulses), and may be the result of one of a number of obvious causes including a head injury (past or present) or poisoning. Alternatively, there may be no apparent reason at all and a convulsion may occur as an isolated incident. The diagnosis will rarely be epilepsy.

Convulsions in children are not unusual, and the most common cause is a high temperature associated with some infective illness – perhaps an ear or throat infection. The feverish attack would then be termed a 'febrile convulsion'. Any parent is likely to be extremely concerned, as their child may well act in a strange, unfamiliar manner. But provided the situation is coped with calmly and correctly, there is only a remote chance that any complications or problems will be lasting once the fit passes.

What to do:

1. Undress the child and cool them
2. Ensure that the child is protected from injuring themselves and cannot fall off a bed or settee and bang their head – a carpet or blanket on the floor is safest. Remain by your child's side but do not attempt to intervene or put anything in their mouth.
3. Sponge them down from top to toe with warm water to help cooling. Fan with an electric fan or even by hand with a book.
4. Lay your child on their side and blow cool air on to the upper back and the nape of the neck
5. Put your child into the recovery position (see page 337) and call for medical help, particularly if this is the first time it has happened, or if the child is running a high fever. A high fever indicates illness and could possibly be a symptom of cerebral malaria, meningitis or another serious condition that will need urgent treatment. But don't panic, this is the least likely cause.
6. Try to judge the severity and length of convulsions and in which part of the body (if any) the contractions are, as this will help the doctor to diagnose the course of action
7. Your child will want to rest after a convulsion, but while they sleep, monitor their breathing and gently nudge them occasionally to check that they stir

Head Injuries

Head injuries can be notoriously dangerous and, following a bad bump to the head, you must watch your child carefully for twenty-four hours. Your child might feel nauseous, drowsy, have visual disturbances and complain of a headache. The real danger signs following a head injury are neck stiffness, photophobia (aversion to light) and vomiting. Any changes in personality are also a huge cause for concern.

Relatively harmless bumps to the head can be dramatic. A scalp wound often bleeds profusely, far overdramatising the real extent of the injury, and a small knock can rise into a pulsating 'Brazil nut' in seconds. Rarely will these have serious consequences.

The bleeding usually stops when compressed with a dressing, and the bumps go down as quickly as they come up. The body is swift to defend the brain and any impact rapidly provokes a defensive cushion of bruising which quickly subsides.

If your child suffers concussion and loses consciousness for a few minutes, place them in the recovery position (see page 337) and monitor their breathing. Confusingly, concussion can occur several hours after the head injury, but should only last a short time, and your child will then recover completely. There may be some memory loss and dizziness with nausea. A straw-coloured liquid leaking from the nose or ears following a head injury could possibly be a skull fracture, which is serious. However, a standard bash on the nose can bring about the same alarming symptoms without the same degree of emergency.

In Summary

Healthy bleeding and big bruises are OK. Fear of light and vomiting are not (unless your child suffers from migraine).

You will need to explain or illustrate to your doctor that your child has suffered a blow or sharp knock to the head, and describe the severity of the symptoms.

Burns and Scalds

When assessing burns, one of the first rules is, 'the more they scream, the less the damage'.

The skin has many layers and the more severe the burn the deeper the wound goes, but the less the sensation of pain as nerve endings will be obliterated.

In treating you should:

1. Stop the burning by flooding the injured part with cool water for at least ten minutes. This will stop the burning, relieve the pain and prevent further tissue damage. If cold water is not available, any cold, harmless liquid will do including canned drinks, juice or even milk.

2. Carefully remove the clothing *unless it is sticking to the burn*. Remove watches or jewellery from the burnt area before it starts to swell.

3. Minimise the risk of infection by covering the area, ideally with a sterile, non-porous dressing or a clean, non-fluffy material. The large area of skin damage often involved in burns is extremely susceptible to infection. A freshly laundered cotton sheet, a clean plastic bag or cling film make good temporary shields until the wound can be dressed properly.

4. If possible, take your child to a hospital to have the wound cleaned and dressed properly. If you are unsure about changing the dressing ask for advice. If medical advice is unavailable (see page 314), keep the injury sterile and dressed as you would with other skin injuries.

5. Give your child plenty of fluids. The best relief from pain and swelling is paracetamol syrup (Disprol/Calpol).

DO NOT:

1. Break blisters. If you do, you will invite infection.

2. Apply ointments or creams, even those marketed and sold as 'burn creams'. They are rarely effective and often damaging. The fats or oils in the ointments hold the heat into the skin and so exacerbate the damaging process.

Paris' Scalding

Simon was on the telephone and I was in the kitchen. In between us darted our forever-busy little Paris. Suddenly, howls of surprise, then pain caused Simon to drop the phone and me to scream. Paris was gripping an upside-down empty mug that he could barely have reached. His body was bright pink and still steaming as the coffee slid down off him. His eyes, cheeks, chest and tummy were burned.

He was wearing a nappy when he grabbed my coffee off the kitchen table and poured it down himself. It had channelled directly into his nappy and bathed his groin in scalding fluid. As a result his 'beep beep' (as Paris called it) was scorched too. Paris was howling in agony.

I applied 'burn' cream but immediately realised that it was not going to limit the damage. Instead, Simon and I raced up to the shower and began to douse Paris in cold water.

Despite his protests, instincts told us that this was the best way. It was worth it. He had two blisters and no scars. The pain is, of course, forgotten.

Electric Shocks

Low standards of health and safety in many parts of the world result in unsafe electrics. Loose wires, frayed flex and absent fuses can lead to electric shock. Children should be taught as soon as possible that electricity and water are a fatal combination.

In mild cases, the patient can suffer mild burns but, in severe cases, a child might lose consciousness and his heart may stop.

What to Do

The most important point is to separate your child from the source of electricity before touching them. If not, you may be shocked too, and thereby unable to help.

If possible, unplug the source or separate your child from the electricity supply using wood (branch, broom etc.), plastic or news-paper, or anything non-conductive that will protect you. If you have no choice, grab a child by its clothing and drag him away. Once the contact has been broken, check for burns. Limit burn damage with cold water and sterile dressing. If a child is suffering from shock you may need to resuscitate them. If a child is breathing but unconscious, place them in the recovery position (see page 337).

Bleeding and Trauma

Abrasions, grazes and minor cuts are rarely serious, provided that nothing remains embedded in the skin and your child is up to date with his tetanus vaccinations. Even pin pricks can spread tetanus.

All mammalian animal bites and scratches that draw blood should be taken very seriously. Even if the wound is superficial, rabies could have been transmitted and so thorough cleaning and hospital treatment is necessary (see page 186).

Deeper cuts and lacerations, especially those to the scalp, often appear worse than they are, but don't panic, and act quickly to limit the bleeding.

Treatment of Severe External Bleeding

1. Apply pressure to the wound. Use a pad if possible, otherwise use your bare hands. If there is something stuck in the wound, such as a piece of glass, do not attempt to remove it. This may cause more damage and make the bleeding worse. Instead apply pressure to either side of the wound.
2. Elevate the injury above the level of the heart to stem the flow of blood to the area. This may be made easier by laying the child down on the floor.
3. Apply a pad or bandage. Alternatively, continue to grip the wound and apply pressure to the wound with your hands.
4. If bleeding is severe you may need to treat your child for shock (see page 327)
5. Call for medical help

Internal Bleeding

Your child may present with the following symptoms after a trauma or accidental ingestion:

- Pallor
- Cold, clammy skin
- Fast, weak pulse

- Pain
- Thirst
- Restlessness and confusion
- Bleeding from orifices

If you suspect internal bleeding:

1. Lie the child down and, if possible, raise the legs
2. Call for an ambulance or medical assistance
3. Insulate from the cold
4. Loosen constricting clothing
5. Check and, if possible, record pulse, respiration, and levels of response every ten minutes
6. Treat for shock (see below)

Shock

Shock occurs if the blood pressure drops or if there is a reduction in the amount of circulatory body fluid as a result of severe bleeding, leakage of fluid from burns and vomiting with diarrhoea.

Symptoms

Initial signs are a rapid pulse and pale, cold, clammy skin. Further signs include:

- Weakness and dizziness
- Nausea, possibly with vomiting
- Thirst
- Rapid, shallow breathing
- A fast, irregular pulse

As the oxygen supply to the brain dwindles, the child will become restless and anxious, and may yawn or gasp for air, eventually becoming unconscious.

Treatment

1. First remove or treat the cause
2. Lie the child down, keeping his head down
3. Raise the legs
4. Loosen tight clothing
5. Insulate from the cold
6. Check and record breathing, pulse and response levels

- DO NOT allow the child to move
- DO NOT allow the child to eat or drink
- Reassure them constantly and stay by their side

If bleeding is under control and there is no danger of shock developing, you must then concentrate on minimising the risk of infection (see page 186).

Fractures

Not all fractures are immediately obvious. Some, known as greenstick fractures, which are common in children, are splits in young bone and can be missed by a doctor even on an x-ray.

The extent of the pain and the difficulty in moving a part of the body indicate that a fracture may have occurred.

The pain will not abate and your child may cry ceaselessly for hours if untreated. They will refuse to let you touch the limb.

There may be signs of shock if a thigh, rib or pelvis is fractured.

Treatment

1. Urge your child to keep still
2. Steady and support the injured limb
3. Immobilise the site of the fracture by splintage or with your hands. Use anything for a splint that is available, such as a branch, a thick rolled-up newspaper or adjacent leg.

4. Use a bandage, if available, or strips of cloth to bind the fracture, but check that it is not so tight as to interfere with circulation
5. Treat for shock (see above)
6. If possible, raise the injured limb and check the circulation beyond the bandaging every ten minutes

If the fracture is open and bleeding, there is a great risk of infection in the bone, which can fester long after the fracture has healed and is notoriously difficult to clear up. You need to ensure that your child is treated with high doses of fairly aggressive antibiotics, and be absolutely religious about administering them.

Eye Injuries

If a foreign body or chemical gets into the eye, lie your child down and try to stop them rubbing it. A foreign body may scratch the surface of the eyeball and cause intense pain and/or infection later.

Hold the eye open and flush it with plenty of water. If a chemical has got into the eye you will need to flush the eye for as long as you can, preferably under a running tap. Unless there is something embedded in the eyeball you should be able to flush the foreign body into the corner of the eye, then remove it with the corner of a tissue. Objects embedded in the eye should not be touched and it is imperative that the child is prevented from rubbing. Medical attention is needed.

If your child's eye still feels gritty and painful once the object has been removed, there could be some superficial damage to the surface of the eye that might lead to infection. Place a sterile pad over the eye and keep in place until the eye settles. Keep a check on it, and if it becomes red and weepy your child will need antibiotics. If you do not have any antibiotic eye ointments or drops, oral antibiotics will work but are not as direct, so it may take a little bit longer to heal. Occasionally, sensitivity to antibiotics applied directly to the eye will cause swelling, which will necessitate discontinuation of their use. After trauma or injury the eye may be cut or bloodshot. Cuts to the eye need protection with a sterile pad and medical attention. A bloodshot eye often looks worse than it is and will slowly heal completely.

Poisoning

Despite the assumption that most poisons have a specific antidote, most do not. Treatment after acute poisoning involves a basic set of rules which help the patient recover. These include:

1. Monitoring the casualty's consciousness, breathing and heart rate, and resuscitating if necessary
2. Placing them in the recovery position (see page 337)
3. Seeking medical help
4. Trying to identify the causative agent, which could help the doctor to decide whether to pump the stomach, induce vomiting or administer an oral absorbent/neutraliser – for example, activated charcoal

- DO NOT induce vomiting yourself. You might cause further harm if the substance injested was caustic. In addition, vomiting may cause some of the substances to be transferred to the lungs, resulting in further serious complications and inflammation. (The exception would be drug poisoning – see below.)
- DO NOT give a concentrated salt solution to induce vomiting. It can be toxic on its own.

If, once you reach medical help, the doctor decides that your child should be made to vomit, they are most likely to administer a drug called Ipecacuana, which is safe and effective.

Poisonous Plants

In the UK there are a few poisonous plants and you will doubtless recognise them through instruction you had as a child.

In tropical countries, plants containing poisonous substances are more common, and so is the incidence of toxicity. The greatest risks are always to children, who need lower amounts of toxin to be fatal and are more likely to be inquisitive.

Even plants normally eaten by the locals can be toxic if collected and prepared by the inexperienced tourist. Cassava, plantain, ackee, yam and cycads are all potentially lethal.

Treatment
See page 329, steps one to four.

Household Poisons

These are very dangerous, but it is relatively rare for children to drink them in any quantity. Many are more dangerous due to the corrosive effects on the mouth, oesophagus and stomach than they are if absorbed into the blood stream. You should never make a child vomit as that could do more damage, especially if the substance gets on to the lungs. If your child will not stay in the recovery position, hold them on their side or face down so that they will not inhale if they do vomit.

The burning caused by oil-based fuels and corrosive substances such as paraffin/kerosene, petrol, bleach, weed killers and disinfectants can be eased by drinking milk or water. Pesticides and herbicides need careful and specific management. You must seek hospital treatment and take the bottle of substance with you to aid the diagnosis.

Drug Poisoning

Some of the drugs you might be carrying are highly poisonous. Paracetamol is very dangerous. If you are more than four hours away from medical help, your child is more likely to survive if they vomit. Never use salt water; use the gag reflex – a normal reflex elicited by touching the soft palate in the back of the throat, which induces retching and vomiting. This reflex is best evoked very basically, by putting your fingers into your child's mouth and touching the back of the throat until they vomit.

Alcohol Poisoning

Alcohol is very dangerous to children. Inhalation on vomiting can be fatal. Hypothermia is a possible complication. There can also be dehydration, with a dangerous lowering of blood-sugar levels. Position your child so that they will not inhale their vomit, wrap them up and give them plenty of sweet drinks.

Drowning

If, having been under water, your child is unconscious but still breathing, place them in the recovery position (see page 337) and continuously check on their breathing.

Replace wet clothing and protect your child from the cold. Submersion in cold water can cause hypothermia. If necessary, give resuscitation and don't give up, especially if the child has been under cold water. The cold slows down the metabolic rate and children can be revived after over thirty minutes under water.

CHAPTER 16

First Aid Treatment

The aim of first aid is to limit the damage of a condition, aid recovery and preserve life.

Action in an Emergency: Artificial Respiration

1. Assess the situation. In an emergency you will first need to carefully assess the situation and ensure that there is no further danger to your child or yourself. Don't panic. If you remain calm and logical and act quickly, you will be able to help and could save your child's life.
2. Carry your child to a safe place, depending on the type of emergency. Act appropriately (see above) to limit the damage and minimise the risk of infection.
3. Assess the casualty. Shake the child by the shoulders, ask a question and establish whether the child is:
   a) **Responding and fully conscious**
      Action:
      - treat the injury, calm the child, then lie them down in the recovery position

b) Unconscious but breathing, with pulse present

Action:

- Treat any life-threatening injury
- Check that there are no obstructions to the airway. If necessary, tilt the child's head well back to open the airway. (see figure 8).
- Place in recovery position and call for help

Figure 8: How to position the head of a baby or young child when opening the airway

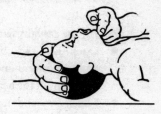

c) Not breathing but has a pulse

Look, listen and feel for breathing for five seconds before judging that breathing has stopped. Look for chest movement. Listen for breathing sounds and feel for breath against your cheek.

Action required for aiding babies and young children:
You must help babies and children under seven years old to breath by giving artificial ventilation for one minute:

- Lay the baby or child flat on his back
- Open the airway by placing one hand on his forehead and two fingers of your other hand under the point of the chin (place just one finger under a baby's chin), lift the jaw and then tilt the head back gently (see figure 8).
- Check for, and remove, any obvious obstructions to breathing by sweeping one finger around inside the mouth
- Seal your lips tightly around the nose and mouth of a baby. In small children, pinch the nose firmly to prevent air escaping and seal your lips over their mouth. Keep your fingers positioned under the jaw and the head tilted back.
- Breathe into the lungs until the chest rises. Repeat this five times.

- Check the pulse and look for signs of recovery. If the pulse is absent begin cardio-pulmonary resuscitation (see below).
- If the pulse is present continue artificial ventilation for one minute
- Get medical assistance

Action required for aiding children over eight years old and adults:
- Lay the casualty flat on his back
- Open the airway by placing one hand on the forehead and two fingers under the point of the chin, lift the jaw and then tilt the head well back gently (see figure 9)
- Check for, and remove, any obvious obstructions to breathing by sweeping one finger around inside the casualty's mouth
- Using your thumb and index finger, pinch the casualty's nose firmly so that the nostrils are closed. This will prevent the air that you breathe into the airways from escaping.
- Take a deep breath then seal your mouth firmly over the casualty's
- Blow until the chest rises and continue to blow for a couple of seconds to ensure that the lungs are fully inflated
- Keep your hands in position but remove your lips and allow the lungs time to deflate fully by noting the fall of the chest
- Repeat mouth-to-mouth resuscitation. Give ten breaths of artificial respiration, call for medical assistance, then continue artificial respiration at a rate of ten per minute. Check for a pulse every ten breaths and watch for signs of recovery until help arrives.
- If breathing begins again, place the casualty in the recovery position (see page 337)

If breathing has stopped, you will need to begin artificial respiration immediately. Any delay will starve the brain of oxygen and after eight minutes your child will be unlikely to

Figure 9: Failure to maintain a proper airway, as indicated in the left-hand picture, is a common cause of avoidable death in unconcious patients. The right-hand picture shows how the airway becomes unblocked once the head is tilted back

make a full recovery. Artificial respiration will keep a supply of oxygenated blood flowing to the brain, and will ensure that your child should be able to regain consciousness and recover completely.

d) Not breathing and pulse is absent

- Continue to check for a pulse for five seconds before deciding that it is absent. This is best done in babies by using two of your fingers to feel for a pulse in the groin. In children and adults, check for a pulse in the neck. Slide your fingers between the Adam's apple and the large muscle along the side.
- Call for medical assistance then begin cardio-pulmonary resuscitation by alternate chest compressions and mouth-to-mouth ventilation
- Chest compressions massage the heart so that it is able to pump a supply of blood around the body and should be carried out as follows:

In babies:

- Place your index and middle fingers one finger's width beneath the nipple line and press down to approximately one third the depth of the chest
- Do this five times in about three seconds
- Give one breath of ventilation then repeat the five chest compressions

- Alternate one breath to five compressions until help arrives. Constantly check for signs of recovery.

In children between the ages of one to seven years:
- Position the heel of one hand over the lower portion of the breastbone and press down sharply to approximately one third the depth of the chest.
- Do this five times in about three seconds then give one breath of ventilation
- Repeatedly alternate one breath to five compressions until help arrives
- Check constantly for signs of recovery

In children over eight years old and adults:
- Interlock the fingers of each of your hands over the casualty's breastbone and use the heels of your hands to compress the chest
- Lean well over the casualty with your arms straight. Press down vertically to depress the breastbone by approximately two inches/five centimetres.
- Do this fifteen times in approximately nine seconds then give two breaths of ventilation
- Repeatedly alternate fifteen compressions to two ventilations until help arrives or there are signs of recovery

NB: It is important that you are firm and put your weight behind heart massage. Most beginners are likely to be too gentle. Remember you have to push the breastbone down to squash blood out of the heart underneath to keep the brain alive.

Summary

After assessing the casualty, remember 'ABC':

A = Airways: open the airway by tilting the head back

B = Breathing: check the breathing

C = Circulation: check the pulse

Recovery Position

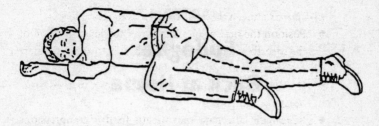

For babies under one:
- Cradle your baby on his side, in your arms
- Keep the head tilted downwards to prevent the inhalation of vomit or choking on the tongue

For all children aged one year old and above, and adults:
- Lie the casualty on his back and extend the limbs
- Open the airway by placing two fingers under the point of the chin and one hand on the forehead, lifting the jaw and tilting the head well back
- Position the arm nearest to yourself flat on the floor and bend at right angles to the body
- Reach across the casualty and bring their furthest arm across their chest, placing the back of the hand against their cheek. At the same time bend the casualty's far leg.
- Roll the child towards you on to the hand against his cheek and on to his side
- Ensure that the airway is open
- Bend the casualty's knee so that it is at right angles to the body
- Call for medical assistance if it is available
- Monitor and, if possible, record the breathing and pulse every ten minutes

NB: If you suspect that the neck may be injured, make sure you support it as the casualty is turned on their side and placed in the recovery position.

CHAPTER 17

Epilogue:
Back at Home

It is absolutely imperative that the whole family finish taking their malaria tablets after returning home. It is so easy to forget and miss tablets when you get back into your normal routine, but it is crucial not to risk your children's health by neglecting the importance of continuing to take the full dosage for another four weeks.

Any other persistent signs of illness should be discussed with your doctor. You must explain where you travelled to and which illnesses you may have been exposed to.

Diseases such as leishmaniasis are commonly misdiagnosed as leukaemia. When the correct treatment is so simple for tropical illnesses, such as leishmaniasis, it would be devastating to have a child go through chemotherapy and intensive treatment because a parent neglected to mention they had been badly bitten by sandflies in Greece three months before.

However, on balance from the millions of trips abroad each year, only a few patients will present with tropical diseases. Minor coughs, colds and ear infections are more of a problem but easily treated.

Fever and malaria

Malaria is considered to be the most commonly misdiagnosed illness in the UK. When high fever presents up to a year after travel to a malarial region, malaria is a possible cause and should be tested for. There are two thousand cases of malaria diagnosed in the UK each year by the malaria reference laboratory of the London School of

Hygiene and Tropical Medicine. From this it could be estimated that approximately three thousand new cases of malaria enter the UK each year.

Most UK doctors will never have seen a case of malaria, and if you neglect to mention to your doctor that you have been abroad they could diagnose the symptoms as flu. The disease is a good mimic of many other illnesses in its early stages and it is urgent that your children undergo a blood test to exclude it as the cause of any high temperature following their return from a malarial region, even if the full course of recommended anti-malarial drugs has been completed.

Pneumonia (including Legionnaire's disease and other atypical pneumonias), hepatitis and schistosomiasis may otherwise be the cause.

Diarrhoea

Diarrhoea associated with travel usually occurs while away or shortly after returning home. Most will be bacterial or viral and short lived. Persistent diarrhoea after tropical travel is most likely to be amoebic dysentery, giardiasis or cyclospora. Intestinal worms should also be considered.

Diseases such as amoebiasis are so rare in the UK that doctors are unlikely to diagnose persistent diarrhoea as a tropical disease unless you mention to your doctor that your child might have been exposed to infection. Discuss where you have been, the exact symptoms and the duration of the diarrhoea to help your doctor, who may then suggest that a stool sample is tested for parasites.

If you neglect to mention that your child may have picked up the infection abroad, your doctor will look for other explanations.

If you have been to a malarial region mention it. Malaria can disguise itself as a diarrhoeal illness.

Hepatitis

The incubation period for hepatitis is three to five weeks, so symptoms are likely to develop after returning from your trip abroad (see page 170). If you have travelled into a region where your child could have been exposed to hepatitis A without having been immunised, you must mention this to your doctor who will be able to screen for and treat the disease more quickly.

Rabies

Rabies can take a few years to develop. If your child has been bitten abroad you should have travelled home immediately to receive treatment or been treated there and then. However, in the unlikely event of your child presenting with any of the symptoms of rabies in the future (see page 185), always mention this to your doctor.

Schistosomiasis

Schistosomiasis symptoms can develop weeks or months after exposure. Even if your children are symptom free but have been at risk of exposure at any time during their trip abroad, you should visit your doctor on your return home and request a blood test. The timing of the blood test is important, as it may not be positive until three months after the initial infection.

Those at most risk of having picked up the infection are those who have been wading or swimming in African lakes, rivers, or in other areas where the disease is common (see page 300).

Tropical disease can be picked up and, although a carrier can remain symptomless for years, there may be an impact on health in future life. If you have any concerns or suspect that your child may have picked up any illnesses, or if your child fell ill abroad and appeared perfectly healthy by the time you returned home, it is still important to discuss it with your doctor. Most are happy to act on your concerns and screen for anything that is worrying you.

One week after we returned home from the Seychelles with Paris he developed a rash. While abroad we had been in casualty with him following an accident where he had gashed his wrist deeply and needed stitches. The casualty department had been crammed full with sick children, and although we were rushed straight through into a treatment room and rushed Paris straight out into the fresh air after he had been treated, I am certain this is where he picked something up.

The rash was initially quite faint, but seemed worse after a crying fit. I called the doctor out, but by the time he arrived the rash didn't looks so red and he was clearly deeply irritated. Two days later the rash re-erupted and we took Paris to hospital. The hospital treated the information very seriously and we were put into isolation immediately. Although Paris was pink and miserable rather than gravely ill, we were kept in for observation and he was monitored throughout the night.

The next morning Paris was bright as a button although the rash was still in evidence. We were sent home with the diagnosis of measles (despite the fact he had been given his MMR) or a similar virus.

The best doctors listen to the parent's instincts and should never make you feel paranoid. A doctor should always talk things through with you, even if you then decide between you that everything is fine and no screening is necessary.

Be reassured that the only virtually untreatable diseases of the world are sexually transmitted, so pose no risk to children.

I also believe that the immunity a child gets as a result of the exposure to different environments will protect them in all walks of life. You may wrap your child in cotton wool, but they might then catch meningitis from a child who has visited Mecca. An untravelled, cosseted child is likely to be more severely effected by an illness than a well-travelled child who may have been in contact with some form of the disease in life before. Travel is one of life's richest experiences, so to deny yourself and your family this in a time when travel is so accessible, affordable and pleasurable would be a real shame.

The memories and experiences

When you return home, keep your child's mind alive with the memories of your holiday. When the photos come back, set time aside to talk about them and, if you took one, set a special evening aside to watch the holiday video. You'll be surprised at your children's incredible capacity to remember intricate details of the holiday.

They may forget a lot and even be unprepared to discuss it all on cue, but Paris is now seven years old and recalls trips, days, food, people, children and places that slip my memory until he brings them up. Often the photographs become an important reminder. Paris has his own photograph album which he has been thrilled to put together and add to since the age of five.

Paris' school teachers now tell me how broad his general knowledge is, and I believe it is mainly through our travels and I hope Luca will be the same.

I believe the times we have spent together abroad, when I am not under the daily rigours and pressures from work and running a house, are priceless. I passionately believe that children who enjoysclose family holidays will always have a broader sense of fun and aspire to spread their wings. Going off the beaten track with a child will give them a taste for adventure and hopefully inspire them to be independent and confident in the future.

A child's formative years are incredibly crucial for their future contentment, trust and ambition. To be scientific, a child's brain is mapping, and neural connections are growing rapidly in children under seven years old, so stimulate them as much as you can and they will hopefully become healthy, happy adults. Experiencing different cultures and ways of life will help develop a child's spirit, and emotional development is certainly stimulated by all the experiences, too.

For my family nothing is more important than our time together when I am relaxed, too, and all the best memories I have are of our time on foreign soil. I haven't spent a fortune, and at times have flown with air miles and stayed in budget hotels, but every single day of it was precious and I wouldn't swap it for anything. Sometimes the budget holidays are the most fun, so even travel on a shoestring is a must, as children won't care if they are with happy parents.

So just do it. Take the opportunities and make the family holiday one of the highlights of the calendar, to be remembered, cherished and talked about all the year round.

Index